NETSCAPE NAVIGATOR

Surfing the Web and
Exploring the Internet

Macintosh® Version

NETSCAPE NAVIGATOR

Surfing the Web and Exploring the Internet

Macintosh® Version

Bryan Pfaffenberger

University of Virginia
Charlottesville, Virginia

AP PROFESSIONAL

Boston   San Diego   New York
London   Sydney   Tokyo   Toronto

AP PROFESSIONAL
1300 Boylston Street, Chestnut Hill, MA 02167

An imprint of ACADEMIC PRESS, INC.
A Division of HARCOURT BRACE & COMPANY

United Kingdom Edition published by
ACADEMIC PRESS LIMITED
24–28 Oval Road, London NW1 7DX

Library of Congress Cataloging-in-Publication Data
Pfaffenberger, Bryan, 1949–
    Netscape navigator : surfing the web and exploring the Internet /
Bryan Pfaffenberger.
        p.   cm.
    Includes bibliographical references and index.
    ISBN 0-12-553130-3.   --ISBN 0-12-553131-1 (CD-ROM)
    1. Netscape 2. World Wide Web (Information retrieval system)
I. Title.
TK5105.882.P43   1995a
025.04--dc20   95-24180
                                                    CIP

Printed in the United States of America
95 96 97 98   IP   9 8 7 6 5 4 3 2 1

Contents

Introduction   **xiii**
    What Is Netscape Navigator?   xiv
    Why Do You Need This Book?   xiv
    What's on the CD-ROM Disc?   xv
    How This Book Is Organized   xvi
    How to Read This Book   xix
    Acknowledgments   xix
    From Here   xx

Part I   **NETSCAPE QUICK START**   **1**

Chapter 1   **Getting Started with Netscape Navigator**   **3**
    Starting Netscape Navigator   5
    What's on the Screen?   5
    Basic Window Calisthenics   11
    Quitting Netscape Navigator   12
    From Here   13

Chapter 2   The Gentle Art of Web Surfing   15

Starting Netscape   17
Typing a URL Directly   17
The Subtle Mysteries and Finer Points of Hyperlinks   22
I'm Lost! (Navigation Fundamentals)   23
Help Me, Helper Applications!   27
I Want to See You Again, or, Setting Bookmarks   28
Excuse Me, Where's the Subject Catalog? (Subject Trees and
       Search Engines)   29
From Here   33

**Part II   NETSCAPE INSTALLATION AND
              CONFIGURATION   35**

Chapter 3   Connecting to the Internet   37

How the Internet Works (A Little Knowledge...)   38
Why You Need a Direct Internet Connection   41
What Is MacTCP?   41
Network Access Is Great—If You Can Get It   42
What Are SLIP and PPP?   42
Shopping for a Service Provider   44
From Here   45

Chapter 4   Obtaining and Installing Netscape Navigator   47

Downloading Netscape 1.1 with Fetch   48
Running the Netscape Installer   51
From Here   53

Chapter 5   Configuring Helper Programs   55

What's on the CD-ROM Disc?   56
Understanding MIME Types   58
Configuring Helper Programs: An Overview   59
Configuring Sound Players   60
Configuring Video Players   61
Configuring Decompression Software   61
Configuring File Viewing Software   61
Configuring the Telnet Helpers   61
A Note on Sound and Video Formats   62

Testing Your Viewers   65
Creating a Download Directory   66
From Here   66

Part III   SURFING THE WEB   67

Chapter 6   Change That Home Page!   69
What *Is* a "Home Page"?   71
Have We Got a Home Page For You!   72
Changing Your Home Page   75
Using Personal Home Pages   77
Using a Trailblazer Page as a Home Page   79
From Here   82

Chapter 7   Perfecting Your Navigation Skills   83
Stop! *Please* Stop!   84
This Document's Too Slow! (Too Many Images)   86
Selectively Loading In-Line Images   87
There's a History to This (The History List)   88
When—and How—to Open a New Window   90
Managing Multiple Windows   91
Reloading Documents   92
From Here   92

Chapter 8   Creating and Using Bookmarks   93
Adding a Bookmark   94
Choosing a Bookmark   96
Using the Bookmark List Dialog Box   96
Editing a Bookmark   99
Deleting a Bookmark   99
The Little Bookmark List That Grew   100
Finding a Bookmark   100
Reorganizing Your Bookmark List   102
Choosing the Menu to Display   109
Adding New Bookmarks to a Submenu   109
Exporting Bookmarks   110
Importing Bookmarks   111
From Here   113

Chapter 9   Using Trailblazer Pages   **115**
   Introducing Trailblazer Pages   116
   Starting Points Pages   117
   Trailblazer Pages   124
   What's Popular   126
   Best of the Web   126
   Cool Links   127
   Worst of the Web   127
   Weird Links   128
   What's New Pages   129
   From Here   129

Chapter 10   Using Subject Trees and Search Engines   **131**
   Understanding Search Techniques   133
   A Guide to the Web's Subject Trees   134
   Search Engines   147
   The Best of Both Worlds: EINet Galaxy   155
   From Here   159

Chapter 11   Managing Documents   **161**
   Finding Text in a Document   162
   Saving Documents   163
   Printing Documents   167
   Understanding Netscape's Disk Cache   168
   From Here   172

Chapter 12   Hypermedia Time!   **173**
   Listening to Sounds   174
   Viewing Videos and Animations   176
   Viewing Adobe Acrobat Documents   177
   From Here   182

Chapter 13   Customizing Netscape   **183**
   Fonts!   184
   Colors!   187
   Options Galore!   190
   From Here   192

Chapter 14   When the Surf Gets Rough   **193**
   I Clicked the Hyperlink—and Nothing Happened!   194
   It Says the DNS Lookup Failed!   195
   It Says "404 Not Found"!   196
   Wow! "Forbidden"!   196
   Connection Refused!   198
   It Says "This Site Has Moved"!   198
   They're Demanding a Password!   199
   It Says "The Information You Have Submitted Is Not Secure"! 199
   From Here   200

Part IV   EXPLORING THE INTERNET   **201**

Chapter 15   Digging Around in Gopher   **203**
   Accessing Gopher Sites   204
   Understanding Gopher Menus   205
   Gopher Jewels   206
   Searching Gopher: Veronica   206
   From Here   212

Chapter 16   Ransacking FTP File Archives   **213**
   Accessing Anonymous FTP File Archives   214
   Navigating FTP Directories   215
   What's in the Files?   216
   Finding FTP Resources: Archie   216
   Looking for Shareware with the Virtual Shareware Library   218
   From Here   223

Chapter 17   Searching WAIS Databases   **225**
   Understanding WAIS   226
   About the Directory of Servers   227
   Searching a WAIS Database   230
   Advanced WAIS Searching   231
   From Here   232

Chapter 18   Ranting and Raving in USENET Newsgroups   **233**

Introducing USENET Newsgroups   236
What's in a Newsgroup?   237
Reading USENET   238
Configuring Netscape to Access USENET   238
Subscribing to Newsgroups   241
Reading the News   243
Posting Your Own Messages   248
Replying by e-mail   251
Posting a Follow-up Message   252
Searching Today's USENET Postings   252
Searching USENET FAQs   252
What's Missing?   253
From Here   253

Chapter 19   Surviving Telnet and 3270 Sessions   **255**

Using NCSA Telnet   256
Using TN3270 (3270 Telnet Sessions)   258
Searching for Telnet Resources with HyTelnet   260
From Here   260

Part V   THE NETSCAPE MARKETPLACE   261

Chapter 20   Understanding Secure Transactions   **263**

What Is "Security"?   264
The Need for Encryption   265
Introducing the Secure Socket Layer Security Protocol   266
What about Standards?   267
Accessing a Secure Server   268
Is My Credit Card Information Really Safe?   268
From Here   269

Chapter 21   Let's Go Shopping!   **271**

Capital One   272
software.net   273
Internet Shopping Network   275
Virtual Vineyards   277

marketplaceMCI   278
DAMARK   280
From Here   281

Part VI   APPENDICES   283

Appendix A   Netscape Quick Reference   285
File Menu   285
Edit Menu   287
View Menu   289
Go Menu   290
Bookmarks Menu   291
Options Menu   293
Directory Menu   297
Help Menu   299

Appendix B   Installing the CD-ROM Software   301
What's Included   301
Installing the Software   302

Index   303

Introduction

I t's the fastest growing communication system in human history. It's loaded with useful information. And, it's fun. It's the World Wide Web. Academics, in their professorial way, call it a global hypermedia system. For you and me, it's an incredibly fun way that you can jump from one Internet computer to the next, just by clicking an underlined word or phrase called a *hyperlink*. After clicking the hyperlink, the Web goes to work accessing the information you requested—which might be a document, a sound, an animation, or a movie clip. And who knows where you'll wind up? You might find yourself browsing multimedia resources on a computer across the street—or halfway around the world.

The Web is entertaining, useful, fun, and—increasingly—just about indispensable. Many people, myself included, think that the World Wide Web is the opening salvo in the development of a global "information superhighway," knowledge of which will be required of any educated person. The time to start is now. And the perfect tool is Netscape Navigator.

WHAT IS NETSCAPE NAVIGATOR?

To access the World Wide Web, you need an Internet connection and a program called a *browser*. A browser decodes the hidden symbols in Web documents, turning them into richly formatted documents replete with fonts and graphics. In addition, browsers also originate messages that locate and retrieve documents every time you click a hyperlink. Many people believe that Netscape Navigator is the best Web browser available—and I concur.

WHY DO YOU NEED THIS BOOK?

You've probably heard that Netscape is easy to use. It is, up to a point. But Netscape is a tool for accessing the World Wide Web (and indeed, the whole Internet). When you learn Netscape, you learn the Web, and you learn the Internet. That's a lot to learn, and you'll need some help. You've come to the right place.

This isn't just a book about learning Netscape, although we somewhat immodestly feel that it does a pretty good job in that department. It's about mastering Netscape *and* surfing the Web *and* exploring the Internet. It's three books in one—and you need all three. Web surfing is more complicated than it appears on the surface, and the going gets rough when you're trying to use the Web to retrieve needed information. Moreover, Netscape provides the tools you need to access *all* of the Internet's riches, including Gopher menus, FTP file archives (free software!), WAIS databases, USENET newsgroups, and Telnet resources, including bulletin board systems and freenets.

So this book teaches *three* essential skills:

1. Becoming an absolute, flat-out master of Netscape, using the tricks and techniques known only to those who grow pale from all-night Netscape sessions;

2. Surfing the Web with an unerring aim, locating the cool, the informative, the useful, the wacky, and the irreverent; *and*

3. Using Netscape to harvest the incredible information and entertainment resources of the *entire Internet*, including Gopher, FTP, WAIS, USENET, and Telnet.

No matter whether you're a beginner with Netscape or a seasoned vet of all-night surf sessions, you'll find that this book is packed with knowledge, strategies, techniques, and cunning tricks. It presents a comprehensive strategy for total mastery of the Internet!

WHAT'S ON THE CD-ROM DISC?

While we're on the sales pitch here—you *are* reading this in the bookstore, aren't you?—let me mention this book's CD-ROM disc. Even if this book were full of patent nonsense (which it isn't, I hasten to add), it would *still* be worth buying just for this disc alone.

You may not realize this just yet, but Netscape needs help if you want to access all the Web's riches. It needs *helper programs*. In fact, you need to choose, obtain, install, and configure at least a half dozen helper programs to bring Netscape to its full potential.

To obtain all of these programs from the Internet, you'd need to spend hours—even days—researching the best helper program options, finding them on the Internet, and downloading them in a tedious, byte-by-byte process.

But not with this book! We've packed the CD-ROM disc with the best helper programs available for use with Netscape. You'll find programs for listening to sounds of every conceivable kind, software for viewing movies and animations (including MPEG movies), a fully functional version of Adobe's Acrobat Reader for viewing richly formatted documents, StuffIt Expander software for decompressing all that neat software you're going to download, and more.

Netscape's the ideal tool for surfing the Web and exploring the Internet. This book makes this tool come to life, putting you in touch with the fun, the knowledge, the resources, and—yes—the wonderful zaniness of the World Wide Web.

HOW THIS BOOK IS ORGANIZED

This book is designed for a fast start with Netscape. As the need arises, you can use the additional chapters to round out your knowledge of this fantastic program, the Web, and the Internet.

Part I: Netscape Quick Start

Already got Netscape installed and running? Check out the first two chapters for all the Netscape fundamentals.

In Chapter 1, "Getting Started with Netscape Navigator," you'll learn the parts of Netscape's screen, including what all those buttons do. It's worth a skim, even if you've already played with the program a bit.

Chapter 2, "The Gentle Art of Web Surfing," provides an introduction for much of the rest of the book. You'll learn all the fundamentals of Web navigation the Netscape way. In addition, this chapter shows you some of the advanced functions of Netscape, which is a very powerful tool for accessing all kinds of Internet resources.

Part II: Netscape Installation and Configuration

If you haven't gotton your Internet connection yet, be sure to read Chapter 3. You'll find a clear, nontechnical explanation of the various Internet connectivity options, and you'll learn exactly what you need in order to run Netscape.

Once you're connected to the Internet, check out Chapter 4. You'll learn how to access Netscape's FTP server and obtain the latest version of Netscape. This chapter also shows you how to install Netscape on your Macintosh or Power Macintosh system.

Chapter 5, "Configuring Helper Programs," shows you how to set up Netscape to access the many helper programs included on this book's CD-ROM disc. What could be an ordeal lasting hours or days—obtaining these programs from the Web and configuring them without documentation—becomes an easy, 20-minute task. When you're done, the multimedia riches of the Web will lie at your fingertips.

Part III: Surfing the Web

Hopping around from Web site to Web site is lots of fun. To make the Web useful as well as entertaining, you'll need an informed, structured approach—and that's just what you'll find in Part III.

Chapter 6, "Change That Home Page!," gets you started the right way, namely, with a default home page that's much more useful than the one Netscape accesses automatically. You'll find this home page on this book's CD-ROM disc, and it's jammed with useful tools for navigating the Web.

Chapter 7, "Perfecting Your Navigation Skills," shows you how to gain confidence as you move around the Web. You'll understand what the history list does, for example, and why it sometimes seems to lose track of Web sites you've visited. This is essential knowledge that can save time and reduce frustration.

Chapter 8, "Creating and Using Bookmarks," fully explores Netscape's Bookmarks menu, which enables you to save location information about Web sites you've visited. You'll learn how to organize your Bookmarks menu so that it becomes a treasure-trove of Web information that *you* find useful.

Chapter 9, "Using Trailblazer Pages," shows you how to locate Web documents stuffed with topic-specific information, in just about every conceivable field of human knowledge.

In Chapter 10, "Using Subject Trees and Search Engines," you'll learn how to make full, intelligent use of the subject classification and topic-searching tools that have been developed for Web users. Once you've learned a few simple tricks, you'll get far more from these tools than people who use them casually.

Chapter 11, "Managing Documents," unveils the secrets of Netscape's cache system, which stores copies of documents on your computer so that they do not have to be re-accessed from the network. You'll learn how to control the cache for maximum retrieval speed. This chapter also covers saving and printing techniques.

Chapter 12, "Hypermedia Time!," fully documents the helper programs included with this book. You'll learn how to listen to sounds, view movies and animations, view Adobe Acrobat documents, navigate Telnet sessions, and more.

Chapter 13, "Customizing Netscape," shows you how to put your personal touch on this great piece of software. You'll learn about options that can simplify Netscape's interface and speed its operation.

In Chapter 14, "When the Surf Gets Rough," you'll learn what to do when you encounter roadblocks on the Web, such as "Access denied" messages—and much more.

Part IV: Exploring the Internet

Netscape unlocks the wider Internet as well as the Web—and this section fully explores the Netscape approach to the Internet's riches.

Chapter 15, "Digging Around in Gopher," shows you how to use Netscape to find and access the rich resources of Gopher, a menu-based Internet information system. You'll learn how to search with Veronica and how to find Gopher Jewels.

Chapter 16, "Ransacking FTP File Archives," shows you how to navigate the file systems of distant computers, finding and retrieving useful files and software. Special emphasis is placed on the Virtual Shareware Library, your key to more than 90,000 shareware programs.

In Chapter 17, "Searching WAIS Databases," you'll learn how to use Netscape to access the information stored in publicly accessible databases. You'll learn how to use the WAIS directory of servers, how to shape successful WAIS searches, and how to make sense of WAIS retrieval lists.

Chapter 18, "Ranting and Raving in USENET Newsgroups," fully covers the wonderful Netscape approach to USENET. You'll learn how to post your own messages as well as read those placed by others.

Chapter 19, "Surviving Telnet and 3270 Sessions," shows you how to use Netscape to access the information stored in text-based computers, such as mainframe computers and bulletin board systems. With Telnet, another door opens to a huge variety of information that you can access with Netscape.

Part V: The Netscape Marketplace

Netscape isn't just a great Web browser and a tool for accessing Internet information, it's also the pathway to an amazing new world of Internet commerce, all based on secure, encrypted transmissions made possible by Netscape's Secure Sockets Layer (SSL) technology. In Chapter 20, you'll find a nontechnical, easy-to-understand introduction to this technology and why it's needed.

In Chapter 21, you'll find an introduction to some of the first commercial sites on the Web—sites that enable you to use your credit card to order on-line. Let's go shopping!

Part VI: The Appendices

This book includes two useful appendices, which will help you round out your knowledge and enjoyment of Netscape. Appendix A presents a quick reference guide to Netscape's menu commands, while Appendix B fully covers the installation of all those great helper programs on this book's CD-ROM disc.

HOW TO READ THIS BOOK

With Netscape Navigator close by, naturally. Also, I recommend Mountain Dew for those all-night sessions (yawn). Check out the "From Here" section at the end of this introduction, and at the end of every chapter of this book, for pathways to follow.

In addition, keep your eye out for icons. They provide cues and clues that help you find your way through this book. Here's a quick overview of this book's icons:

 Look for the Navigation icon for tips on a chapter's contents. Is it essential, or can you skim it? Is it for every Netscape user, or just some readers? You'll find out here.

 Here you'll find tips, shortcuts, suggestions, insights, and other helpful information about Netscape. The dinosaur, incidentally, is named Mozilla, and he's Netscape's unofficial mascot. Cute little thing, isn't he? Or is it she?

 We've tried to anticipate the problems you'll run into—this icon shows where to look for solutions.

 Terms, terms, terms—unfortunately, you'll have to learn some. Look here for definitions!

 The Treasure Trove icon marks a cool Internet resource of some kind. Check it out!

ACKNOWLEDGMENTS

Thanks to everyone who contributed to this book, including Jenifer Niles (Sponsoring Editor), Jacqui Young (Editorial Assistant), and Cindy Kogut (Production Editor).

Thanks also to Netscape Communications for permission to use the reproductions of the program icon and other graphics and of Netscape's mascot, Mozilla. Not much in evidence these days at Netscape's Web site, Mozilla lives on, as attested by the Prototypical Mozilla Icon,

> http://home.netscape.com/home/demo/I.I.bI./mozilla/doc.html

Mozilla fans will want to visit the Mozilla Museum,

> http://www.snafu.de/%Etilman/mozilla/

for evidence of the reptile's past glory. But take heart: Mozilla Will Return.

FROM HERE

- A total beginner with the Web and the Internet? Skim Chapter 2, "The Gentle Art of Web Surfing," to find out what the Web is like.

- Not yet connected to the Internet? Check out Chapter 3, "Connecting to the Internet," to find out what you need in order to use Netscape.

- Connected to the Internet, but don't have Netscape yet? Fire up the FTP program included on this book's CD-ROM disc, and check out Chapter 4, "Obtaining and Installing Netscape Navigator."

- Installed Netscape, but haven't used it yet (much)? Turn to Chapter 1, "Getting Started with Netscape Navigator."

- Done some browsing and know the basics? Go directly to Chapter 6, "Change That Home Page!"

Part I

NETSCAPE
QUICK START

Chapter

1

Getting Started with Netscape Navigator

On-screen, Netscape Navigator looks like most other Macintosh applications—with a few strange twists. What's the big "N," and why is the Earth being attacked by giant comets from outer space? And what's that funny broken key thing?

Whether or not you've already started surfing with Netscape (I'll bet you have), sooner or later you will want answers to such questions. You'll find them here, arranged for quick look-up. And if you're really busy, just scan the section entitled "For the Time-Challenged," at the beginning of the chapter, which hits the high points succinctly.

 Are you a seasoned Macintosh user? You'll find lots of important stuff in this chapter about the features that differentiate Netscape from other Macintosh applications, such as the Toolbar's navigation buttons, the directory buttons, the broken key, and the hyperlinks. You can skim this chapter to get the information you need.

♦ Netscape is preset to display the Netscape welcome page as its default home page. (You can change this if you want, as explained in Chapter 6.)

♦ Don't spend too much time trying to learn all the options on the menu bar. You won't use them frequently. With the exception of Bookmarks, the options you'll frequently use are available on the Toolbar.

♦ The Netsite box displays the URL (the Web address) of the document you are currently viewing. (The name of this box changes to "Location" if you're accessing a server other than those offered by Netscape Communications.)

♦ The doorkey icon tells you whether you're accessing a secure server (if it's broken, you're not).

♦ Hyperlinks, shown in color and underlining on color monitors, enable you to access another Web document. Just move the pointer to the hyperlink, and click the mouse button *once*.

♦ The big "N" (the status indicator) displays a cute animation while Netscape is downloading a document you've requested. At the bottom of the screen, the status bar tells you what you're downloading, and the progress bar tells you how much of the job is finished.

♦ Netscape doesn't save your window-sizing and positioning options until you choose Save Options from the Options menu.

Are you a beginning Macintosh user? Read on. You'll find an introduction to Netscape that's designed for all readers, including beginners.

This chapter has the following sections:

• **What's on the Screen?**   A quick guide to the features you see in Netscape's window. Get a quick, visual overview!

• **Basic Window Calisthenics**   Minimize, maximize, stretch, shrink— until you get it just right.

• **Quitting Netscape Navigator**   Mommy, Daddy stayed up all night again!

Starting Netscape Navigator

Assuming you've already installed Netscape Navigator (see Chapter 4), you're ready to surf the Web. Open the Netscape folder, and double-click the Netscape icon.

What's on the Screen?

 When Netscape Navigator starts, you'll see the program's window on-screen. The program icon (the big "N") shows a comet storm, informing you that Netscape is downloading information. In about a minute (or less, if you have a fast connection), you'll see the *default home page*, the welcome page. Appearing within Netscape's application workspace, this page (Figure 1.1) is coming to you from Netscape Communications Corporation's headquarters in sunny California. In Netscape, as in any graphical Web browser, the default home page is the Web document that the program is preset to display when started.

 My screen doesn't have this stuff! Don't see the buttons, the Netsite box, or some of the other stuff shown in Figure 1.1? Somebody has messed with your Options menu, baby. On the menu bar, pull down the Options menu. Below the first separator bar, look for options that don't have a check mark. These have been turned off. To turn them on, just choose the option. Continue doing this until all the options have been turned on. Then open the Options menu one more time and choose Save Options.

Menu Bar

At the top of the screen is the menu bar. On the menu bar, you'll find the titles of Netscape's menus, from which you can choose additional options. Frankly, you won't use the menu bar very often—most of Netscape's most useful tools are available on the Toolbar (see below). Here's a very quick overview of what's on these menus:

- **File**   This menu enables access to a grab bag of display, storage, and printing options. You'll use it most frequently to open local files.

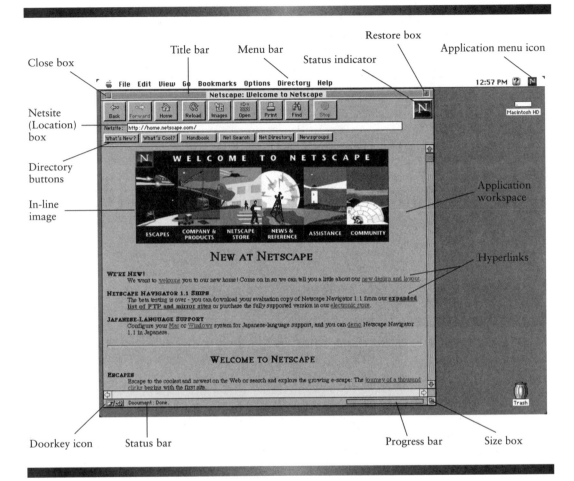

Figure 1.1   Netscape on-screen

- **Edit**   This menu contains the standard Macintosh editing options, including Undo, Cut, Copy, Paste, and Find. The keyboard shortcuts are faster and easier. In Chapter 11, "Managing Documents," you'll learn how to use these options and the keyboard shortcuts.

- **View**   From this menu, you can choose options controlling the way Netscape obtains documents, but most of them can be chosen more quickly by using the Toolbar (discussed below).

- **Go**   Like the View menu, this menu contains several commands that are more easily accessed by clicking buttons on the Toolbar. But there's one gem: At the bottom of the menu, you'll see a list of the documents you've accessed recently. To go back to any of them, you just choose the document's name from the menu.

- **Bookmarks** This is probably the most useful menu of all. From it, you can choose options that enable you to create *bookmarks*. A bookmark is a saved document address that enables you to return to this document quickly, just by choosing it from the Bookmarks menu. You'll learn more about bookmarks in Chapter 8.

- **Options** This menu enables you to choose the way Netscape appears on-screen. Netscape is preset to display all of its optional screen features, such as the Toolbar, and that's the way I recommend that you use the program.

- **Directory** This menu enables you to go directly to valuable Web resources, including search services. It duplicates the Directory buttons and gives a few additional options.

- **Help** This menu offers access to Netscape Navigator's on-line help directory—but hey, you've got this book. Much of the rest of this menu is a rather thinly disguised marketing tool.

Title Bar

At the top of Netscape's window is the title bar, a standard Macintosh feature. Here, Netscape displays its own name. In addition, you see the title of the document you are currently viewing.

Toolbar

The toolbar contains buttons, or tools, that enable easy access to frequently used Netscape commands. Here's a very quick once-over-lightly (you'll learn how to use these buttons in this chapter and the next):

 Back Go back to the document you just viewed.

 Forward Return to the document you went back from. This button isn't available unless you've displayed a document and then clicked the Back tool.

	Home	Redisplay the default home page.
	Reload	Retrieve the currently displayed document again
	Images	Turn off the automatic downloading of in-line images.
	Open	Type a URL (Web address) directly.
	Print	Print the document that Netscape is currently displaying.
	Find	Finds text in the current document.
	Stop	Stop downloading the current document.

Netsite Box

The Netsite box indicates the URL (Web address) of the document you are currently viewing. If you're accessing a Web server that doesn't use Netscape's server software, this box is entitled Location.

What's in a URL?   A URL has three parts. The first part (http://) indicates the type of resource you're viewing. If you're viewing an FTP file archive, the first part of the URL reads "ftp://", while a Gopher menu's URL reads "gopher://". The second part of the URL indicates the name of the computer you're accessing (such as home.netscape.com). The third part of the directory indicates the *path* that Netscape must take to locate the document, and it also includes the document name (/home/welcome.html). Sometimes the third part of a URL is missing, which tells Netscape to look for and obtain the default document. Do you really need to know all this? Not really, but sometimes you'll need to type URLs and it's important to do so correctly. For more information, check out Chapter 2.

Directory Buttons

The Directory buttons enable you to access Web resources quickly. All of these options are also available on the Directory menu.

What's New!	**What's New**	Displays a list of new and interesting Web sites.
What's Cool!	**What's Cool**	Here are some Web sites that Mozilla likes. See you in a couple of hours.
Handbook	**Handbook**	Frequently asked questions about Netscape Navigator and Netscape's secure servers.
Net Search	**Net Search**	Displays a great list of Web *search engines* (programs that search databases of Web documents). You'll learn more about searching the Web in Chapter 10.
Net Directory	**Net Directory**	Displays a page that provides access to the Yahoo *subject tree* (which is like a library subject catalog). Through Yahoo, you can access other equally useful Web subject trees. You'll learn more about subject trees in Chapter 10.
Newsgroups	**Newsgroups**	Accesses USENET. This works only after you've told Netscape where your USENET server is located, as explained in Chapter 18.

Application Workspace

Here, Netscape displays the document you're currently viewing. If the document is bigger than the available window space, the scroll bars activate. You can click the scroll arrows or drag the scroll bars to bring hidden portions of the document into view.

Doorkey Icon

This icon indicates whether you're accessing a secure server. If not, the key is broken. *Don't give your credit card number to any on-line vendor unless the connection is secure!* If you're accessing a secure site, the key is unbroken.

Status Bar and Progress Bar

Next to the doorkey icon, there's a panel called the *status bar*. Netscape uses the status bar to display messages about what the program is doing. Most of the time you can ignore these messages, unless you're curious.

Next to the status bar, you see a blank panel called the *progress bar*. When Netscape retrieves a document from the Internet, you'll see a graphical display indicating how much of the document has been obtained.

Hyperlinks

Note that some of the words and phrases you see are highlighted with colors and underlining (if you're using a monochrome monitor, you'll see only underlining.) These are *hyperlinks* (also called *anchors* or just *links*). When you click on a hyperlink, Netscape locates the Web document that is linked to this hyperlink, and initiates the transfer.

Try clicking one of the hyperlinks now:

1. Move the tip of the mouse pointer so that it's positioned over the hyperlink, and take a look at the *status bar* at the bottom of the screen. This displays the URL of the document to which this anchor is linked.

2. With the mouse button, click the link. Forget all that double-clicking stuff; you just click *once*.

Several things happen now:

- The big "N" comes to life. This tells you that Netscape is obtaining the document you requested, through a process called *downloading*. Incidentally, the official name for the big "N" is *status indicator*. (I like "Big 'N'" better.)

- The status bar indicates that Netscape is downloading a document.

- You see the document within Netscape's application workspace.

 What does "downloading" mean? When downloading occurs, Netscape transfers an entire document to your computer's memory, along with any associated graphics. This is called "downloading" because the information is coming *from* a distant computer *to* your computer. (As you might guess, the term "uploading" means sending information *from* your computer *to* a distant computer.) Once the document is in your computer's memory, you can scroll through it quickly. In addition, Netscape stores recently accessed documents in memory so that you can redisplay them quickly, should you wish to return to them.

Now try going back to the document you displayed previously. To do so, just click the Back button on the Toolbar. Take a look at the hyperlink you just clicked.

 If you're viewing Netscape on a color monitor, note that the hyperlink you just clicked has changed color. This is a *visited hyperlink*, a hyperlink to a document that you've already seen. You can still click the link to redisplay the visited document, but Netscape wants you to know that you've been down that road before.

BASIC WINDOW CALISTHENICS

Like the program window of any Macintosh application, Netscape's window can be adjusted until it suits your fancy. The following instructions quickly detail these procedures.

To move Netscape's window on the screen:

- Move the mouse pointer to the title bar, hold down the mouse button, and drag. You'll move the whole window. When you've moved the window to where you want it to appear, release the mouse button.

To size Netscape's window:

- Move the mouse pointer to the size box (lower right corner) and drag. When you've sized the window the way you want, release the mouse button.

To restore the previous size of the window:

- Click the Restore box (upper right corner of the window).

To hide Netscape's window:

- Click the Application menu icon (the one at the extreme right end of the menu bar), and choose Hide Netscape.

To view Netscape again:

- Click the Application menu icon, and choose Show Netscape.

 Using System 7.5? Here's a neat trick. To hide Netscape's document display window temporarily (so that you can do something underneath), just double-click the title bar. The window "rolls up" so that only the title bar is shown. To redisplay the window, double-click the title bar again.

QUITTING NETSCAPE NAVIGATOR

So, you're done. It's about 5 AM, isn't it? Hope you had fun.
    To quit Netscape Navigator:

- From the File menu, choose Quit

    or

- Press Command + Q

FROM HERE

- Surf's up! Explore the Web, and access Internet resources, in Chapter 2, "The Gentle Art of Web Surfing."

- Not connected to the Internet yet? Check out Chapter 3.

- Haven't obtained, installed, and configured Netscape Navigator yet? Flip to Chapter 4.

- Install those helper applications! See Appendix B to learn how to install them from the CD-ROM disc included with this book, and see Chapter 5 for information on configuring Netscape to use these applications.

Chapter
2

The Gentle Art of
Web Surfing

Wouldn't it be cool to learn how to surf the Web with the best of 'em, and in just an hour or two? If you agree, read this chapter. Sure, there's more to learn than this chapter covers. In this chapter, though, you'll learn 90% of what you need to know to have some *serious* fun with Netscape. Plus, this chapter serves as a guide to much of the rest of this book. Later chapters explore this chapter's topics in more detail. By reading this chapter, you can learn which subjects you'd like to explore more deeply.

Just what does *surfing the Web* mean? It means exploring, discovering, navigating—and above all, being swept away by a series of awesome hyperlinks that you can ride all over cyberspace.

Netscape's your surfboard. You start by finding a cool Web document, one that's loaded with hyperlinks, and then you begin exploring. As you navigate link after link, you'll connect with computers all over North America, Europe, Australia, and even more remote places. You can look forward to countless hours of discovery, fun, and even enchantment, with a bit of boredom thrown in (admittedly, not every Web site is worth accessing).

The surfing metaphor is highly appropriate: Sometimes you'll put your "board" on an amazing series of hyperlinks, and they'll carry you off to who-knows-where. And sometimes the hyperlinks you'll ride aren't very interesting, although (happily) some of them are so stupid that they are truly hilarious (see the following Treasure Trove). But there's gold in those links, as you'll surely agree. Have fun, and be sure to cancel tomorrow's appointments.

If you're curious to know what a really *dumb* Web site looks like, check out the wonderful Useless Pages site,

http://www.primus.com/staff/paulp/useless.html

Webmaster Paul Phillips created this site after discovering that somebody named Kenny Z had typed his entire CD collection in an HTML document and made it available on the Web. Paul reflects that this was the first Web document that, as he puts it, "overtly crossed the line from tolerably frivolous to truly inane." Paul has since collected dozens of useless pages—you just have to check this out. For some reason, one of Paul's finds, the National Texture Administration's home page

http://ftp.std.com/homepages/stevec/NTA/intro.html

just kills me. Maybe it's the link to "Man, the texturing animal." Read a treatise on fish and whale regurgitation, talk to Michael's cat, visit Edward's Scratch-n-Sniff Theater, read Dan's Dream Journal, and identify Ferret-Free Zones.

This chapter will benefit every reader of this book, and that's true even if you've already done some Web surfing with Netscape. In this chapter, you'll find a Web-savvy approach to Netscape, the approach that experienced Netscape mavens use every day. Working through this chapter, even the stuff that seems obvious, will reveal the Netscape secrets and strategies that make this program the Web browser of choice. Mozilla's got lots of tips for you, so look for his funny little face.

For the Time-Challenged

◆ To access a Web document that you've read or heard about, you can type its URL directly. From the File menu, choose Open Location, type the URL, and click OK.

◆ An in-line image surrounded by a border functions as a hyperlink; click it, and you'll see another document or a graphic.

◆ Use the Back button to return to previously viewed documents. Once you've gone Back you can go Forward to see more recently viewed documents. Click Home to return to the default home page.

◆ Within a *web* (a series of internally linked Web documents), look for internal navigation buttons. These are the best choice for navigating among the web's links.

◆ If you find a really cool Web page while surfing, add it to your bookmark list. With the page displayed, choose Add Bookmark from the Bookmarks menu, or press Command + D.

STARTING NETSCAPE

Assuming you've already installed Netscape and configured your Internet connection (see Chapters 3 and 4), you're ready to go. In the Finder, open the Netscape program folder and double-click the Netscape program icon. You'll see Netscape on-screen, and the program displays the default home page (see Figure 2.1).

TYPING A URL DIRECTLY

You've picked up your copy of *Netguide*, and you've read about this seriously cool Web site. The only problem is, there's no hyperlink to this site on Netscape's default home page. How do you get there? You can type the URL directly, and go straight to the site.

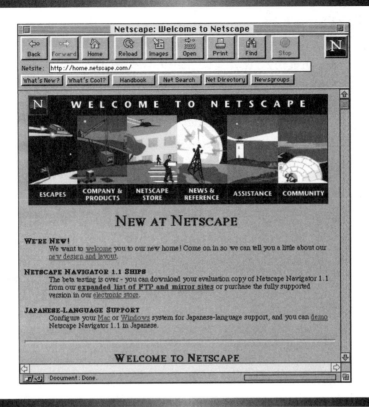

Figure 2.1   Netscape's default home page

 Don't waste time trying to find a site by clicking hyperlink after hyperlink. Chances are you'll never make it: At this writing, there are over 3 million Web documents in existence! If you know the site's URL (Uniform Resource Locator), you can type the URL in Netscape and access the site directly. A URL looks like this: http://dmf.culture.fr/files/imaginary_exhibition.html.

Try typing a URL now. Let's go to France! To type a URL directly:

1. From the File menu, choose Open Location, or use the Command + L keyboard shortcut.

 Solutions

Not Enough Memory to Launch Netscape!

Try quitting other application programs. If that doesn't work, choose Control Panels from the Apple menu, and choose Memory. In the Memory dialog box, turn on virtual memory, if it's not already enabled. (Virtual memory permits part of your computer's hard disk to be used as an extension of RAM memory. It's slower than RAM memory, but hey, at least you can start your programs. Virtual memory isn't available on 68000- and 68020-based Macs.) When you're finished in the Memory dialog box, click the close box.

You'll see the Open Location dialog box, shown in Figure 2.2. Type the following URL, exactly as it is shown here (don't use capital letters):

http://dmf.culture.fr/files/imaginary_exhibition.html

2. Check your typing carefully. Be sure to omit spaces. Between "imaginary" and "exhibition," there's an underline character (to type this, you must press the Shift key and then press the hyphen key). Don't forget the colon (:) and the two slash marks (//) after "http" or the URL won't work.

3. Click the Open button.

 Here's an even faster way to type a URL directly. In the Netsite box, select the existing text and start typing your URL. This will erase the existing URL. When you've finished typing your URL, check your typing carefully and press Enter.

If you typed the URL correctly, you'll see the welcome page of a cool online exhibit, called "The Age of Enlightenment in the Paintings of France's National Museums" (Figure 2.3). That's right, this page comes from France. What you're seeing on-screen snaked its way through the Internet to your computer screen, all the way from Paris. Uncork some Burgundy or Bordeaux, or heck, just grab a beer, and let's explore.

Figure 2.2   Open Location dialog box

This page has some *in-line graphics*. An in-line graphic is a picture that's mixed with text.

I don't see any darned art exhibit on my screen! Whoops. Well, there are several possible reasons. Here's a rundown:

- **You may have typed the URL wrong.**   Even a little tiny mistake, like putting a period at the end of the URL or adding a space, can mess things up. Remember, too, that URLs are *case-sensitive* (uppercase and lowercase letters are different). There are no capital letters in the URL you just typed. If you find a mistake, just edit and correct it within the Netsite box, and press Enter to try again.

- **The French Ministry of Culture may have pulled the plug on this site.**   That wasn't very nice of them, was it? They're probably still sore about that spy scandal. You'll know the site is dead for sure if you checked your typing carefully and still get the cheery "Error 404" message shown in Figure 2.4.

- **Too many people are trying to access the site.** Netscape is trying, trying, trying to access the site; the comets keep shooting, but nothing appears... minutes go by, fruitlessly. Give up, and click Stop. Try again later—like 2 AM. So many people are surfing the Web that it's sometimes hard to get through to popular sites during prime daytime hours (10 AM to 4 PM). If you can't access the Page of Enlightenment, check out the

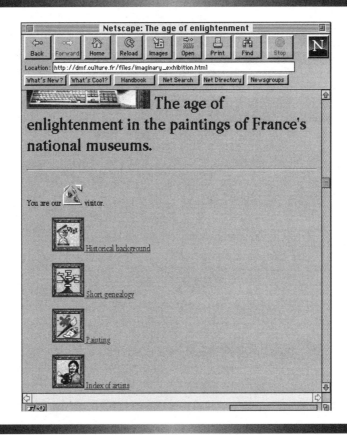

Figure 2.3 An on-line art exhibit (http://dmf.culture.fr/files/imaginary_exhibition.html)

following Treasure Trove icon, and see if the URLs mentioned there are working.

 Like to see more on-line art exhibits? Check out Margaret L. McLaughlin's interesting on-line essay on the subject: http://cwis.usc.edu/dept/annenberg/artfinal.html. Included are links to dozens of on-line exhibitions. Don't miss McLaughlin's fascinating analysis of the emergence of a Web exhibition culture and how it differs from museum exhibition cultures. For more information about art on-line, check out the Virtual Library's on-line art page (http://www.w3.org/hypertext/DataSources/bySubject/Literature/Overview.html). In the Virtual Library's URL, note that some of the letters must be capitalized.

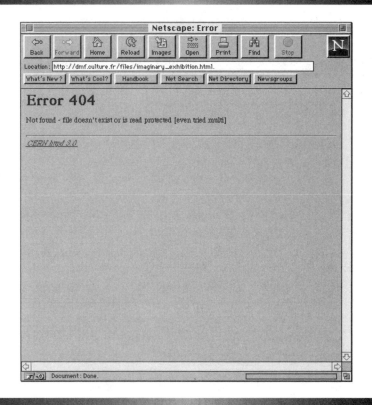

Figure 2.4   Bad news (black hole)

THE SUBTLE MYSTERIES AND FINER POINTS OF HYPERLINKS

You already know that hyperlinks appear in distinctive formatting (color and underlining, if you're using a color monitor), and *visited hyperlinks* (ones you've clicked before) appear in a distinctive color. Here are a couple of additional points you need to know about hyperlinks:

- To activate a hyperlink, you just move the pointer to it, and click. Yes, that's right—click *once*. Because many Macintosh and Windows functions are initiated by double-clicking something, you may have to unlearn the tendency to double-click. That second click may activate an unwanted hyperlink on the page that's about to be displayed, taking you to who-knows-where.

- Some in-line graphics are hyperlinks—you can click these links to display a Web document. Here's how to tell whether an in-line graphic is a hyperlink: Look for a border around the graphic. With most browsers, the border appears in blue.

You can access most of the hyperlinks shown in Figure 2.3 in two ways. You can click the text (such as "Painting"), or you can click the in-line graphic next to the text. You get the same results, no matter which you click.

Try clicking "Painting" now. (Click the word or the icon.) You'll see some text with hyperlinks. Look for "Boucher," and click it. Here's another document, containing in-line graphics that function as hyperlinks (see the border around the graphic?). Try clicking "Morning Coffee." You'll see a beautiful on-screen graphic (in GIF format) of one of Boucher's best paintings (one of the few that's G-rated, incidentally; Boucher had an inordinate fondness for the rumps of pinkish, plump, and scantily clad damsels).

 It's taking forever to download this GIF graphic!   This isn't the Information Superhighway—it's more like a two-lane road, jammed with trucks. Be patient.

 If you just clicked on a big graphic and then decide you really *don't* want to wait for the whole darned thing to download, just click Stop. Click the Back button to return to the document you were just viewing.

I'M LOST! (NAVIGATION FUNDAMENTALS)

Two exclamations are heard from beginning Web surfers: "Cool!" followed shortly by "Where am I!!?" Here's a very quick mini-course in Web navigation.

Going Back

At any time, you can go back to see the document you previously viewed. To go back, you click the Back button. If you just love toying with menus, you could choose Back from the Go menu, but mouse-haters are cheerfully invited to use the Command + [keyboard shortcut. ("[" is the right square bracket symbol, which you'll find to the right of the letter P on your keyboard.)

If you're viewing Boucher's *Morning Coffee*, try clicking Back now.

 You can keep clicking Back to return to previously viewed documents, but if you're going back more than two or three documents, there's a better way. See "There's a History to This," in Chapter 7.

Going Forward

Once you've gone back by clicking the Back button, the Forward button becomes available. Try it now (or press Command +]). You'll see Boucher's *Morning Coffee* again.

So what does the Forward button do? It lets you return to the document you just went Back from. Oh, heck, it's easier to do than to talk about.

 Notice how fast that GIF graphic redisplayed when you clicked Forward? That's because Netscape retrieved the document from its *cache* (pronounced "cash"). A cache is a part of your computer's memory that Netscape has set aside for storing recently accessed documents. Because these documents are retrieved from your computer's memory, they redisplay much faster than they would if Netscape had to retrieve them from the Internet.

Look for Internal Navigation Buttons!

Many Web sites offer more than just a page; they offer a *web*, and within this web each page has navigation buttons to help you find your way. A web (as opposed to *the* Web, the World Wide Web) is a collection of related Web documents, all stored on a single site; each document explores one facet of the topic at hand. The Page(s) of Enlightenment, stored on a French Ministry of Culture computer, provide an excellent example of a web within the Web.

A *navigation button* is an in-line graphic that's designed to enable you to find your way around the web. And our French web has quite a few of them, as you'll see. Figure 2.5 shows two navigation buttons, and here's what they do:

Figure 2.5 Navigation buttons within a web

 Click here to display the main Painting page.

 Click here to return to the welcome page, the one you see when you access the site.

If you click the Painting button, you see the Painting page—and lots more navigation buttons. Try clicking them to see where you wind up, and keep clicking around until you've figured out how to go to where you want and how to get back.

I don't know what this darned navigation button does!   Too many Web authors use button graphics that don't really suggest what's going to happen when you click on the navigation buttons—so don't feel bad, it's not you. Thoughtful Web authors include explanatory text along with the buttons, unless the buttons' meanings are so clear that it's obvious what they do.

 If the web you're browsing has internal navigation buttons, by all means use them! Internal navigation buttons always give you the best way of navigating within a multi-document web. That's because the web's author knows just how the web is structured. The navigation buttons have been designed to help you navigate the web logically. You can use Netscape's Back and Forward buttons to redisplay pages you just accessed, if you wish, but the navigation buttons are your best bet for internal web navigation.

Using Clickable Maps

Some Web sites offer *clickable maps* as a way of helping you navigate (see Figure 2.6). In a clickable map, portions of the map contain hidden hyperlinks. If you click one of these areas, Netscape displays the linked document. Incidentally, a clickable map needn't be an actual geographical map, though some are; the term "map" is meant to suggest that the graphic provides a visual key, one way or another, to the documents in the web. In Figure 2.6, the various parts of the graphic provide access to parts of the White House web. You can click First Family, for instance, to see a picture of Bill and Hillary.

How I Got Here, I Haven't a Clue (Go Home)

If you're *really* lost, you'll know it: *hyperdisorientation* sets in. (Hyperdisorientation is a well-documented malady of cyberspace, a recently discovered syndrome with distressing symptoms: Patients do not know how they got to where they are, haven't the foggiest idea how to retrace their steps, and babble incessantly about lost URLs.) Netscape provides a quick cure: Click the Home button. You'll see the Netscape welcome page again.

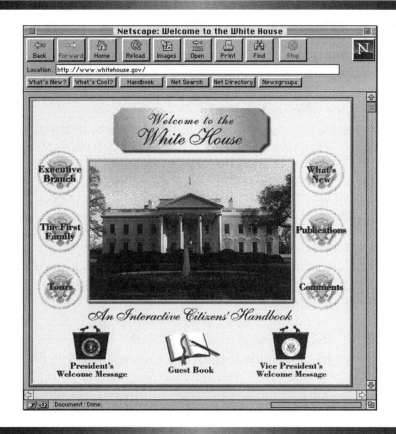

Figure 2.6 Clickable map (http://www.whitehouse.gov/)

HELP ME, HELPER APPLICATIONS!

Netscape can't do everything by itself, although it does a great job of displaying GIF and JPEG graphics. Sounds, movies, and animations are dinosaurs of a different color, though—the program needs *helper applications*, programs that start when they're needed in order to play a movie or sound. In Chapter 5, you'll learn how to configure these programs. The example to follow assumes you've installed SoundApp, one of the fine applications included on this book's CD-ROM disc.

```
┌─────────────────────────────────────────────┐
│                  Sound App                    │
├─────────────────────────────────────────────┤
│ File Name:  greato.aiff                       │
│                                               │
│ File Type:  AIFF @ 22254 Hz                   │
│ File Size:  884.0 K     Time: 0:40.7          │
│   Status:  Playing...                         │
│                                               │
│ Volume:  5         Memory:  240.1 K / 1134.0 K │
└─────────────────────────────────────────────┘
```

Figure 2.7   SoundApp

Try out your helper application now, and listen to a little Neil Young. To access the *Sleeps with Angels* page, type the following URL directly:

http://www.iuma.com/Warner/html/Young,_Neil.html

This is legit, incidentally; it's a 30-second excerpt from "Change Your Mind," one of the cuts from the album, and it's offered by Warner Brothers—for promotional purposes, obviously.

To hear the mono version of "Change Your Mind," click the Sun-AU (271K) option. Netscape downloads the sound (this takes a while), and then displays the SoundApp window (Figure 2.7). The sound starts playing automatically.

 It says that no application has been configured for this file!   To use sounds, videos, Adobe Acrobat documents, and other multimedia files, you must install your helper applications (as described in Appendix B) and configure them (as described in Chapter 5).

I WANT TO SEE YOU AGAIN, OR, SETTING BOOKMARKS

You've found a cool Web site, haven't you? And you want to know how to get back without having to click for six months, or type the URL, don't you? That's why Netscape lets you set bookmarks.

A *bookmark* is a URL that you've saved to a special list of ultra-cool Web sites, a list you have constructed yourself. Whenever you run across a Web site you like, just set a bookmark, as explained here.

To set a bookmark:

1. Display the Web page that you want to mark.
2. From the Bookmarks menu, choose Add Bookmark, or use the Command + D keyboard shortcut.

Netscape adds the name of the document you're displaying to the Bookmarks menu. To visit this document again, just open the Bookmarks menu and choose the document's name.

 I've added too many documents to my Bookmarks menu! This happens pretty fast, you'll find. Once you've added one or two dozen documents to your Bookmarks menu, it isn't very much fun to use anymore. Time to get organized! Netscape provides a cool way to create submenus, so that you can pack dozens and dozens of bookmarks in this menu without creating something overwhelming to the eye. Flip to Chapter 8 for the lowdown on organizing your Bookmarks menu.

EXCUSE ME, WHERE'S THE SUBJECT CATALOG? (SUBJECT TREES AND SEACH ENGINES)

Let's start with the bad news. It's really difficult to find information on the Web. Here's why. You've probably heard that the Internet is an experiment in controlled anarchy—there's no central headquarters of Internet, Inc. You don't have to get anyone's permission to hook up your computer or network to the Internet. So the Internet just grows and grows, hooking up an estimated 35 million people so far.

Because the Web uses the Internet for its communication base, the Web's just as gloriously disorganized—you don't have to ask anyone's permission to put documents on the Web. There's no single, central repository of records concerning Web documents.

With some 3 million Web documents now in existence (make that 6 by the time you read this), we're talking about an information-retrieval nightmare. There's stuff on the Web concerning the chardonnays of Western Australia, the role of community networks in improving health care delivery, or the history of punk rock in the funkier districts of London—but good luck finding it, unless you're lucky enough to stumble on a starting points document that summarizes all the relevant links. (A *starting points* document, discussed in Chapter 9, stems from some charitable individual's attempts to sum up a number of interesting links, often on a single subject area, such as gardening.)

Although there's no official, central database of Web documents, lots of clever computer people *have* been trying to solve the information-retrieval problem. They've taken two approachs, called *subject trees* and *search engines*.

A *subject tree* is a subject-oriented catalog of URLs, organized by topic (such as "Astrology," "Astronomy," "Astrophysics," etc.). The "tree" part of the name comes from the catalog's hierarchical organization; under "music," for instance, you find branches of the tree such as classical music, folk music, techno-rave music, etc. No subject tree is complete; it is a *really big pain* to keep one of these things updated. Most of the work is done by civic-minded volunteers, who have only so much time for such things. Out of some 3 million Web documents, for example, Yahoo—one of the best subject trees—indexes only about 40,000 (Figure 2.8). On the bright side, though, Yahoo contains 40,000 *good* URLs. There's a lot of junk out there, but it doesn't pass the subject tree's screening mechanisms.

A *search engine* provides key-word searching of a database that has been compiled by a *spider* or *worm* (a program that automatically "crawls" the Web, finding Web documents and recording information about them). A search engine enables you to type in one or more search words (such as "Neil" and "Young"). The search engine then tries to match these search terms against a database of URL names and topics. Search engines and spiders are helpful tools, but bear in mind that they retrieve the chaff as well as the wheat: A search for CDs, for instance, will retrieve Kenny Z's useless list of his CD collection along with some on-line compact disc vendors and an unbelievable assortment of other stuff.

Let's take a look at subject trees in more detail; Chapter 10 delves into the mysteries of search engines.

Yahoo

The name "Yahoo" stands for Yet Another Hierarchically Officious Oracle. On Yahoo's help page, you'll find a pull-down box that lets you choose words other than "Officious," if you like, including "Obstreperous" and "Odiferous." Self-effacing Yahoo may be, but you'll probably supply another "O" word: Outstanding. Actually, "Yahoo" means "a member of a race of brutes in Swift's *Gulliver's Travels* who have the form and all the vices of man"—but none of the virtues. Yahoo was created by David Filo and Jerry Yang, computer scientists extraordinaire at Stanford University.

To access Yahoo, use the following URL:

http://www.yahoo.com/

Exploring Yahoo

Now you'll see why Yahoo is called a subject tree. Click **Government**, and you'll see some the main Government "branches" (subheadings), as shown in Figure 2.9. And if you click one of these subheadings, you'll see a page like the one shown in Figure 2.10; note that there are more subheadings (followed by parentheses indicating the number of items), as well as document names.

Here's the cool part. These document names are living, breathing hyperlinks, which you can click just like any other hyperlink.

Have fun. There are over 30,000 hyperlinks in Yahoo!

Using Yahoo

Like all excellent webs, Yahoo offers a set of internal navigation buttons. Here's what the buttons do:

Yahoo	Displays the top-level Yahoo subject headings.
Up	If you've gone down into the subheadings, this button takes you back up one level.

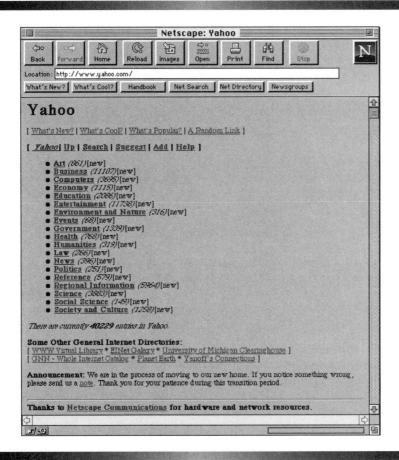

Figure 2.8   Yahoo's main subject tree

Help   Get help with Yahoo's features.

Search   Type one or more key words to see if there's a
                        match somewhere in Yahoo.

Yahoo explorers, look for an asterisk next to a document's
name. This indicates an especially good document of its type.

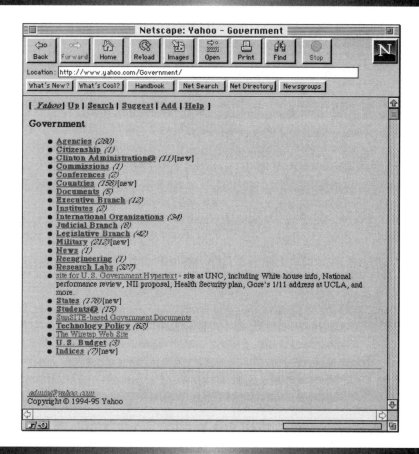

Figure 2.9 Subheadings under "Government"

FROM HERE

- Change the default home page. To do so, flip to Chapter 6.
- Run into some trouble navigating the Web? Check out Chapter 14.
- Deal with an unwieldy Bookmarks menu in Chapter 8.

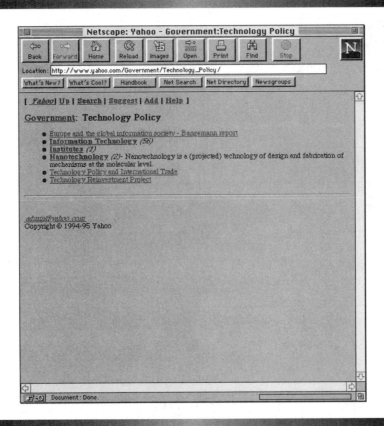

Figure 2.10 Subheadings under "Government: Technology Policy"

- Learn how to save and print the documents you display on the Web in Chapter 11.

- Learn more about starting points, subject trees, and search engines in Part III, "Surfing the Web."

Part II

NETSCAPE INSTALLATION AND CONFIGURATION

Chapter

3

Connecting to the Internet

T o run Netscape Navigator, you need a *direct* Internet connection. Unless you're lucky enough to be using an Internet-connected computer at work, that means you'll need a SLIP or PPP connection with a modem and phone line. You will also need an Apple utility program called MacTCP (included free with System 7.5). MacTCP enables your computer to communicate with other Internet-savvy computers.

 By far the easiest way to get connected to the Internet is to find an Internet service provider that's Macintosh-friendly. If you succeed in this, you'll receive all the information you need to configure MacTCP correctly. Plus, you'll receive a SLIP or PPP dialup program that's preconfigured to access the service provider's computer. If you're lucky enough to pull this off, you can skip the rest of this chapter, unless you'd really like to immerse yourself in painful, boring, technical details.

For the insatiably curious, this chapter explains how Internet connectivity works. Here's what's covered:

- **How the Internet Works**   It isn't difficult to learn a little about this subject, and it will help you understand your connection options.

- **Why You Need a Direct Internet Connection**   You can't run Netscape by dialing up to services such as bulletin board systems (BBSs) or America Online.

- **What is MacTCP?**   A clear, plain-English description of the software that enables your Macintosh computer to "talk" to the Internet.

- **Network Access Is Great—If You Can Get It**   If you use a networked computer at work or school, it might be connected to the Internet. Here's how to find out.

- **What Are SLIP and PPP?**   If you want to use Netscape by using a high-speed modem, you'll need to know the answers to these questions.

- **Shopping for a Service Provider**   Tips on getting the best Internet connectivity deal.

 This chapter is for readers who don't have an Internet connection yet. If you already have an Internet connection, lucky you—skip to the next chapter to find out how to obtain Netscape. And if you already have Netscape, skip to Chapter 5 to find out how to configure your helper programs.

HOW THE INTERNET WORKS (A LITTLE KNOWLEDGE . . .)

To understand why you need a direct Internet connection to run Netscape, you will find it helpful to know a little about how the Internet works. This isn't rocket science; once you get the basic idea, it's pretty simple.

For the Time-Challenged

♦ To run Netscape, you need a direct connection to the Internet. A connection to a bulletin board system, CompuServe, America Online, or other on-line services won't cut it.

♦ To connect your computer directly to the Internet, you need MacTCP, an Apple utility program that is included with System 7.5. MacTCP enables your computer to exchange data directly with any other computer on the Internet.

♦ Most readers of this book will need to obtain a SLIP or PPP dialup account with an Internet service provider. Look for a local telephone number, flat-rate billing, a software package with Internet utilities, and above all else, a preconfigured dialup program. To establish the SLIP or PPP connection, you need a high-speed modem (at least 14.4 Kbps).

You can thank Cold War paranoia for the idea underlying the Internet. Back in the 1960s, the Department of Defense was concerned that Soviet missile strikes might wipe out portions of its communications systems. They asked leading computer scientists to design a computer network that would still function, even though parts of it were not working at any given moment.

These computer scientists came up with the idea of a *packet-switching network*. Computer A in Langley, Virginia, sends a message to Computer B, in Santa Monica, California. Computer A breaks up the message into segments called *packets*, each containing a fixed number of characters (letters or numbers). Each packet has a *header*, or delivery section, which says, "Please give this to Computer B." Each packet's header also says something like, "This is part 9 of a 12-part message."

So Computer A sends all of its little packets out over the network. Along the way, there are machines called *routers* that examine each packet. The router looks at the packet and says to itself, in effect, "Oh, this one is for Computer B," and sends it along the wire that goes to Computer B. What if that wire isn't working? Well, there should be two or more different ways to get to Computer B, so the router looks up alternative routes, and if there is one, that's where the packet goes. Eventually, the packets start arriving at Computer B, although not necessarily in the order they were sent. Computer B reassembles the packets, putting them in the correct order. Computer B also checks to make sure that all the packets arrived safely. If one or more of them didn't make it, Computer B sends a message to Computer A, and says, "Hey, I didn't get Number 9." Computer A sends it again, and eventually, the whole message is present at Computer B.

The foregoing tells you just about everything you need to know about the Internet, from a technical angle. Basically, the Internet is a packet-switching network—or more accurately, a network of networks, each of which is connected to the larger network by means of routers.

Each time your computer sends out a message on the Internet, it's capable of reaching any of the millions of computers that are currently connected to this amazing network. Each of these networks has a distinct address, called an *IP address*. ("IP" stands for Internet Protocol, one of the fundamental standards underlying the Internet.)

In this sense, the Internet is somewhat like the telephone system, because any one computer can link to any other Internet-connected computer. In another sense, it's totally unlike the telephone system. The telephone system is a *circuit-switching* network: When you dial someone up, circuits are switched so that you have a direct connection to another telephone. But the Internet is a *connectionless* network. When your computer sends a message to another computer on the Internet, it has no way of knowing whether the destination computer is turned on and operating, or even whether it exists at all. It just sends out the packets. Along the way, the routers fling them along their path. If there really is a destination computer with the address you've used, your computer gets a response. If not, your computer doesn't get a response; it just waits and waits, fruitlessly.

After you've used Netscape for a while, you'll learn to recognize when the program is trying to access a URL that no longer exists: The big "N" shoots comets, but nothing happens. This indicates that, for one reason or another, the destination computer is not responding. Maybe it's down for the night; maybe its owner gave it to the Salvation Army; maybe it never existed in the first place. Whatever the reason, don't waste your time. If you don't get a response within a minute, click the Stop button, and try again later.

WHY YOU NEED A DIRECT INTERNET CONNECTION

When your computer is directly connected to the Internet, the little data packets discussed in the previous section flow to and from your very own computer. This is a seriously good thing.

To understand why, let's look at the alternative, called *dialup access*. In dialup access, you use a *communications program* such as ProComm Plus to access a remote computer: a bulletin board system, an Internet service provider's computer, or an on-line service such as America Online. The computer you're accessing is directly connected to the Internet, but your computer is not. With your communications program, you're running Internet-capable programs on the remote computer, not on yours. If you try to obtain any data from the Internet, it goes to the remote computer, not to yours, for temporary storage. Later, you'll have to download this data to your computer in a separate, tedious operation. Dialup access is fairly inexpensive, but you can't use Netscape. Netscape requires a direct Internet connection. You get stuck with whatever Web browsing software that the service's computer makes available, if any.

With a direct Internet connection, you have a ticket that admits your computer to the worldwide flow of Internet data packets. If you discover data on the Internet that you want to obtain, it comes directly to your computer. Plus, you can use any Web browser you like. Netscape is your choice, and it's a good one.

There are two kinds of direct Internet connections: *SLIP/PPP*, which permits direct Internet access using a modem and phone line (this is different from garden-variety dialup access), and *network connections*. Both are examined later in this chapter, but both require that you equip your computer with MacTCP software. So let's look at MacTCP more closely.

WHAT IS MACTCP?

Essentially, MacTCP is a Control Panel that enables your Macintosh to handle the Internet's data packets. In the previous section, you learned that an Internet-linked computer must break up a message into packets, assign each of these packets an address, and send it out over the Internet. The recipient computer must reassemble the packets into a recognizable message, and it must also ask for retransmission if some of the packets didn't arrive. For Macintosh computers, MacTCP does the trick.

 To use MacTCP, you will need to configure the program. This will require you to type in all kinds of strange numbers and words. Rather than spending six months figuring this out by yourself, *insist* that your service provider give you step-by-step information on configuring MacTCP. If a prospective service provider won't do this, find another service provider that does!

 But I don't have System 7.5!   You can obtain MacTCP separately from Apple, but it's a much better idea to upgrade to System 7.5—and get MacTCP thrown in for free.

NETWORK ACCESS IS GREAT — IF YOU CAN GET IT

If you use a computer at work that is connected to a *local area network (LAN)*, you may already have direct Internet access without knowing it. Ask your computer department's help desk whether your network is connected to the Internet. If so, ask to have a technician install and configure MacTCP for your network. Don't try to do this yourself; getting MacTCP to talk to LANs requires experience and detailed knowledge of the local LAN setup.

Network access is *fast*. Those big sound and picture files download at a very satisfying clip. But Netscape works pretty well with dialup connections, too.

WHAT ARE SLIP AND PPP?

SLIP and PPP are Internet standards (called *protocols*) that enable a computer to connect to the Internet directly by means of a high-speed modem and a telephone line. To use SLIP or PPP, you need the following:

- MacTCP.
- A high-speed modem. By "high speed," I mean *at least* 14.4 Kbps (14,400 bits per second). A 28.8 Kbps modem is even better, but

bear in mind that relatively few Internet service providers have upgraded to 28.8 Kbps access; if you have a 28.8 Kbps modem, chances are it will "fall back" to 14.4 Kbps after contacting the service provider's modem and negotiating a mutually agreeable speed.

- A telephone line that you don't mind tying up for inordinate lengths of time. I've got one that I use just for Internet access.

- A SLIP or PPP subscription from an Internet service provider. This costs a bit more than garden-variety dialup access, but it's worth it.

- SLIP or PPP access software. You should get this from your service provider.

What's the difference between SLIP and PPP? SLIP, short for Serial Line Internet Protocol, is the older of the two standards; it's fairly simple, and lacks things like sophisticated error correction. PPP, short for Point-to-Point Protocol, is more recent, and has fancier features.

 Modem hunters, beware—there are lots of modems on the market that won't cut the mustard for high-speed Internet access. Forget about anything slower than 14.4 Kbps. If you're looking for a 14.4 Kbps modem, look for one that conforms to the V.32*bis* and V.42*bis* standards. For 28.8 Kbps modems, look for V.34 compatibility—and don't settle for a "V.FC" modem. (The "V." numbers come from the ITU-TSS, an international standards body.) The "V.FC" or "V.Fast Class" standard isn't a recognized international standard at all, even though it *sounds* like one. It's a preliminary V.34 standard created by manufacturers impatient with the ITU-TSS's very slow progress in publishing the V.34 standard. But because V.34 is available now, V.FC and its imitators will be history—and if you buy a V.FC modem, you may be stuck with a modem that you can't upgrade and that can't talk to your service provider's modem.

Which is best, SLIP or PPP? Chances are you won't have much choice; your Internet service provider will most likely offer one, but not the other. Either one is fine. If you have a choice, though, there's a convincing argument that SLIP is the best choice. Today's modems have built-in error correction capabilities that are much better than anything PPP can offer, so PPP just needlessly duplicates a lot of processing that really isn't needed.

SHOPPING FOR A SERVICE PROVIDER

As the previous section emphasized, picking the right Internet service provider can make all the difference in the world for smooth installation and configuration of a SLIP/PPP connection. Here's what to look for:

- **Local Telephone Access**   You don't want to have to pay long-distance charges, if possible. Some service providers offer access by means of 800 numbers. This may be the best choice if you're trying to get connected from a rural location.

- **Flat-Rate Billing**   If you shop around, you should be able to get a SLIP or PPP connection for as little as $29 per month for unlimited or practically unlimited usage. It's an increasingly competitive market.

- **Low Up-Front Fees**   Watch out for high up-front fees. It's justified to some extent, though, if you get a really great Internet software package, such as Internet Chameleon or Internet in a Box.

- **Preconfigured Software**   Ideally, your service provider can supply you with software, a SLIP/PPP dialer program and additional Internet utilities, such as an FTP client and (probably) a Web browser. Make sure the dialer program has a preconfigured login script, so all you have to do is type the phone number, and go.

If you've a friend who already has Internet access and Netscape (or any other Web browser), check out Yahoo's directory of Internet service providers (http://www.yahoo.com/ Business/Corporations/Internet_Access_Providers/). At this writing, there were more than 550 listed. Are you in a metropolitan area? Chances are you can access Performance Systems International's InterRamp service, (http://www.psi.net/ indivservices/interramp/instaramp.html/) which offers free software and a seven-day trial period.

FROM HERE

- Now that you're connected, you can obtain Netscape! Flip to the next chapter.

- Once you've obtained Netscape, you can install all those cool helper programs. See Chapter 5 for the details.

Chapter

4

Obtaining and Installing Netscape Navigator

To obtain the latest version of Netscape Navigator, you use FTP—the File Transfer Protocol—to get the program directly from Netscape's computers in Menlo Park, California. In this chapter, you'll find all the instructions you need to obtain Netscape successfully. On the CD-ROM disc packaged with this book, you'll find a very nice FTP program that you can use for this purpose.

Flip to Appendix B for information on installing Fetch, which you'll need to download the Netscape archive.

For the Time-Challenged

♦ There are three versions of Netscape for Macintosh, one for 680x0 Macintoshes, one for Power Macintoshes, and a third (Fat binary) that runs on all Macintoshes.

♦ Before installing Netscape, create a folder called Netscape. That's where you'll store the Netscape software.

♦ Use the FTP client included with this book, Fetch, to download the Netscape software to your Netscape directory. You will be downloading a single file, the Netscape Installer.

♦ Run the Installer program to install Netscape on your system.

DOWNLOADING NETSCAPE 1.1 WITH FETCH

To obtain the latest version of Netscape Navigator, you will need an *FTP client*. An FTP client is a program that enables you to access *anonymous FTP* file archives, which are accessible to the public.

Included with this book is an excellent FTP client, Fetch. This program is a copyrighted product of Dartmouth College, and it's free for non-commercial or educational use. For use in a business or government office, a payment of $25 is required. For more information, write to fetch@dartmouth.edu.

Although you can access FTP file archives with Netscape, Fetch is better if you want to download more than one file. Fetch also does something that Netscape can't: It enables you to *upload* files to an FTP directory. Netscape's a good choice for casual browsing in FTP file archives, but Fetch is better if you've got some serious FTPing to do.

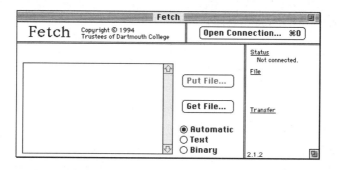

Figure 4.1   Fetch (FTP)

Obtaining Netscape with Fetch

The following instructions assume that you've installed Fetch, as described in Appendix B.

1. Double-click the Fetch icon to start the program. You'll see the Fetch window, shown in Figure 4.1.

2. Click the Open Connection box. You'll see the Open Connection dialog box, shown in Figure 4.2.

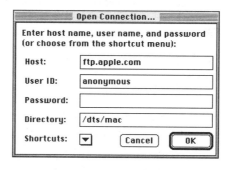

Figure 4.2   Open Connection dialog box

3. In the Host box, type **ftp.netscape.com**.

4. In the User ID box, type **anonymous**.

5. In the Password box, type your e-mail address.

6. In the Directory box, type **/netscape1.1/** (*Note:* Do not use capital letters).

7. Click OK. Fetch accesses Netscape's FTP server, and you see a dialog box like the one shown in Figure 4.3.

 I can't access this server! It's always busy! Lots of people are trying to download Netscape. But cheer up! There are plenty of additional FTP sites, called *mirror sites*, from which you can download the program. You'll find a complete list in Table 4.1.

8. Double-click the Mac folder to display the Macintosh files.

9. Double-click the file named **Netscape1.1N.hqx**. You'll see a dialog box asking you where you want to store the file after it is downloaded.

10. Select the Netscape folder, and click Save. Fetch downloads the file; this may take a few minutes. The pointer changes to a running dog, which indicates that the downloading is taking place.

11. When Fetch has finished downloading Netscape, click Close Connection.

12. From the File menu, choose Quit.

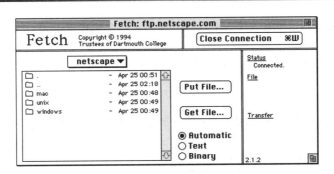

Figure 4.3   Netscape's FTP server (Fetch)

Table 4.1   Netscape FTP Mirror Sites*

Netscape Communications
ftp://ftp.netscape.com/netscape1.1/
ftp://ftp2.netscape.com/netscape1.1/

North America
ftp://wuarchive.wustl.edu/packages/www/
   Netscape/netscape1.1/
ftp://ftp.cps.cmich.edu/pub/netscape/
ftp://ftp.utdallas.edu/pub/netscape/netscape1.1/
ftp://ftp.micro.caltech.edu/pub/netscape/
ftp://unicron.unomaha.edu/pub/netscape/
   netscape1.1/
ftp://server.berkeley.edu/pub/netscape/
tp://SunSITE.unc.edu/pub/packages/infosystems/
   WWW/clients/Netscape/
ftp://ftp.orst.edu/pub/packages/netscape/
ftp://magic.umeche.maine.edu/pub/Mirrors/
   nscape/
ftp://consult.ocis.temple.edu/Big_Kahuna/Pub/
   MAC/Comm/ (Mac only)

South America
ftp://sunsite.dcc.uchile.cl/pub/WWW/netscape/
   netscape/

Europe
ftp://sunsite.doc.ic.ac.uk/computing/information-
   systems/www/Netscapes/
ftp://ftp.sunet.se/pub/www/Netscape/netscape1.1/
ftp://ftp.luth.se/pub/infosystems/www/netscape/
   netscape/

Africa
ftp://ftp.sun.ac.za/pub/archiving/www/mcom/
   netscape/

Asia
ftp://sunsite.ust.hk/pub/WWW/netscape/
ftp://SunSITE.sut.ac.jp/pub/archives/WWW/
   netscape/
gopher://SunSITE.sut.ac.jp:70/11/archives/
   WWW/netscape/
http://SunSITE.sut.ac.jp/arch/archives/WWW/
   netscape/
ftp://bash.cc.keio.ac.jp/pub/inet/netscape/
ftp://ftp.glocom.ac.jp/pub/net/netscape/
ftp://ftp.pu-toyama.ac.jp/pub/net/WWW/
   netscape/
ftp://ftp.cs.titech.ac.jp/pub/net/WWW/netscape/
   netscape1.1/
ftp://ftp.nc.nihon-u.ac.jp/pub/network/WWW/
   client/netscape/
ftp://ftp.elcom.nitech.ac.jp/pub/netscape/
ftp://ftp.leo.chubu.ac.jp/pub/WWW/netscape/
   netscape1.1

Australia
ftp://ftp.adelaide.edu.au/pub/WWW/Netscape/
ftp://ecto.curtin.edu.au/pub/internet/clients/
   netscape/

*Note: FTP file archives come and go, so not all of these may be operational—or contain Netscape—by the time you obtain this book. Note that some of these sites do not have the latest version of Netscape.

RUNNING THE NETSCAPE INSTALLER

To complete the installation of Netscape, you need to run the Netscape Installer program, which you'll find in the Netscape folder. This program automatically detects the type of Macintosh you're using (680x0 or Power Macintosh), and installs the correct version of the program.

To run the Netscape Installer program:

1. Open the Netscape folder.

2. Double-click the Netscape Installer icon.

3. Click Continue... to confirm the initial Installer screen. You'll see the Netscape 1.1 Installer window, shown in Figure 4.4.

4. In the Install Location area, click the Select Folder button. This button enables you to choose the folder for storing Netscape.

5. In the dialog box that appears, select the Netscape folder, and click Select.

6. Click Install to begin installing the program. This will take a minute or two.

7. When the installation is complete, you'll see a dialog box informing you that the installation was successful. Click Quit to exit the Installer.

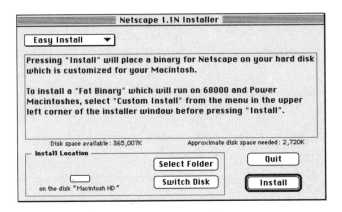

Figure 4.4   Netscape Installer window

FROM HERE

- Before browsing the Web with Netscape, install those helper programs. Check out Appendix B for information on installing the programs from the CD-ROM disc included with this book.

- Configure Netscape to use your armada of helper programs. For the lowdown, see the next chapter.

Chapter

5

Configuring Helper Programs

Netscape Navigator can display GIF and JPEG graphics without any assistance, but the program needs helper programs to play movies, animations, and sounds. In addition, it needs helper programs to decompress compressed files and to display formatted documents. Here's a quick rundown of what you need:

- **Sound Players**   Sounds are stored in a variety of file formats. When you click a hyperlink that accesses a sound, Netscape determines the format in which the sound file is stored, and starts the appropriate sound player. You'll need to install several sound players if you wish to hear all the sounds available on the Web.

- **Video Players**   Videos, animations, and movies are stored in several formats, including Motion Picture Expert's Group (MPEG) and Apple's QuickTime format. The nifty video player included with this book, Sparkle, can handle both movie formats.

- **File Decompression Software**   Many of the files you can obtain with Netscape have been compressed. You won't have much interest in files compressed with the PC/Windows compression format (*.zip), since most of these are Windows executable files that won't run on your Macintosh. For Macintosh software, the two most important compression formats are StuffIt and BinHex, both of which are automatically decoded by StuffIt Expander. You may also run into files compressed with common UNIX compression programs called Gzip (*.gz) and TAR.

- **File Viewing Software**   Netscape displays HTML documents beautifully, but many authors find that HTML does not meet their formatting needs. For this reason, they sometimes save their documents in formats that require special reading software. In increasing use among Web authors is Adobe Acrobat. On the CD-ROM disc included with this book, you will find the Adobe Acrobat Reader, which you can use to read Acrobat-encoded files.

- **Telnet Viewer**   To access Telnet sessions, you need special software that can communicate with large mainframe computers. Included with this book is the National Center for Supercomputing Application's NCSA Telnet, as well as a super viewer for TN3270 mainframe sessions.

 Where do I get all this stuff?   You've already got it. The CD-ROM disc packaged with this book contains all the helper software you need.

WHAT'S ON THE CD-ROM DISC?

The CD-ROM disc packaged with this book contains a suite of helper applications, ready for installation on your system (see Appendix B).

Flicks! Animation!

- **Sparkle** This program springs into action when Netscape downloads an MPEG movie. You can view the movie, rewind it, step the movie frame by frame, and play it in a continuous loop.

- **Quicktime** Included on the CD-ROM disc is the full version of Apple's superior QuickTime movie technology, which enables you to hear sound.

Sounds! Music!

- **SoundAPP** Plays just about any sound you can throw at it: Sound-Cap™ (including Huffman compressed), SoundEdit (including stereo), AIFF, AIFF-C, System 7 sound, QuickTime MooV (soundtracks only), Sun Audio AU and NeXT .snd (including μ-law, a-law, 8-bit linear, 16-bit linear, G.721 ADPCM, and G.723 ADPCM), Windows WAV (including MS ADPCM-compressed), Sound Blaster VOC, many varieties of MODs, Amiga IFF/8SVX (including compressed), Sound Designer II, PSION sound files, DVI ADPCM, Studio Session Instruments, and any 'snd' resource file. SoundApp can convert all of these formats to System 7 sound, sound suitcase, AIFF, WAVE, and NeXT formats.

- **MPEG/CD** Plays MPEG stereo sound files with CD quality— Internet Underground Music Archive, here I come!

Other Cool Stuff

- **NCSA Telnet** This program enables you to access the resources available at Telnet sites, which are widely accessible through the Web and through Gopher.

- **TN3270** Like NCSA Telnet, this application enables you to contact mainframe computers—here, those that require emulation of IBM 3270 terminals.

- **StuffIt Expander** This great little program enables you to decompress files that were compressed using a variety of Macintosh compression formats: AppleLink, Compact Pro, BinHex, and StuffIt.

- **Adobe Acrobat Reader** Using this program, you can display and print documents with rich formatting and graphics.

UNDERSTANDING MIME TYPES

To configure your helper programs for Netscape, you must associate each helper application with a given *MIME type*. MIME stands for Multipurpose Internet Multimedia Extensions. An Internet standard specifying how Internet applications should handle multimedia, this standard defines the connection between multimedia file extensions (the part of the file name that comes after the dot) and specific data type (such as a specific kind of sound file). For example, files named with the extension *.txt are associated with the data type called Text/plain. Such a connection is called a MIME type. Table 5.1 lists the MIME types you'll encounter frequently on the Web.

For more information on MIME—nay, the last word—see the MIME FAQ, available at http://www.cis.ohio-state.edu/text/faq/usenet/mail/mime-faq/top.html.

Table 5.1   MIME Types in Common Use on the World Wide Web

MIME Type	Explanation	Extension(s)
application/pdf	Adobe Acrobat file	pdf
application/postscript	PostScript file	ai, eps, ps
application/rtf	Rich Text Format file	rtf
application/x-compress	UNIX compressed file	Z
application/x-gzip	GNUzip compressed file	gz
application/x-tar	TAR file archive	tar
application/x-zip-compressed	PKZIP compressed file	zip
audio/basic	Sun/NeXT sound file	au, snd
audio/mp2	MPEG sound file	mp2
audio/x-aiff	Apple (AIFF) sound file	aif, aiff, aifc
audio/x-wav	Windows sound file	wav
image/gif	GIF graphic	gif
image/jpeg	JPEG graphic	jpeg, jpg, jpe
image/tiff	TIFF graphic	tiff, tif
text/html	HTML file	html
text/plain	Plain text file	txt
text/tab-separated-values	TSV graph	tsv
video/fli	Autodesk video	fli, flc
video/mpeg	MPEG video	mpeg, mpg, mpe
video/quicktime	QuickTime movie	qt, mov
video/x-msvideo	Windows movie	avi

CONFIGURING HELPER PROGRAMS: AN OVERVIEW

To configure Netscape to use helper programs, you must tell the program where to find the helper applications you have installed. You do so using the Helper Applications page of the Preferences dialog box.

If you have not already done so, please turn to Appendix B to learn how—and where—to install the helper applications.

To display the Helper Applications page, follow these instructions:

1. From the Options menu, choose Preferences.

2. In the list box, choose Helper Applications.

You'll see the Helper Applications page, shown in Figure 5.1. Take a moment to look at this dialog box. As you can see, for each MIME type you can define an action. You can choose from the following:

- **Use Netscape as Viewer**   This choice is appropriate only for those MIME types that Netscape can display directly. By default, these are already configured.

- **Save**   This option saves the file to disk.

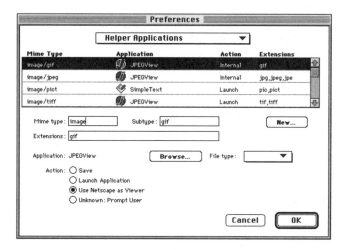

Figure 5.1   Helper Applications Page (Preferences)

- **Prompt User**   This is the default setting. It tells Netscape to display the Unknown File Type dialog box. From this dialog box, you can save the file to disk, cancel the transfer, or configure a helper program (viewer).

- **Launch Application**   This option tells Netscape to start the associated helper application.

Here's the basic procedure. To tell Netscape which application to launch when a multimedia file is encountered, you do the following:

1. Select the MIME type. For example, to tell Netscape which helper application to use for WAV audio files, select audio/x-wav.

2. Click the Launch Application button.

3. Click the Browse button, and use the directories list to locate and select the application.

4. Click OK to associate the application and the MIME type.

I can't find the MIME type in the list!   Netscape doesn't list all the MIME types in the world. If you want to install a helper application that isn't in the list, click the New button. You'll see the Configure Mime Type dialog box. In the MIME type box, type the MIME type you want to define. For example, to define the MPEG audio format, you type Audio. In the MIME Subtype box, type the second part of the MIME type (the part that comes after the slash mark). For example, to define the MPEG audio format, you type x-mpeg. Click OK to confirm your choice. Then follow the instructions just given to associate an application with this MIME type.

CONFIGURING SOUND PLAYERS

The following table lists the recommended associations for sound players. The audio/basic and audio/x-aiff types are associated by default with SoundApp.

MIME Type	Program
audio/basic	SoundApp
audio/x-mpeg	MPEG/CD
audio/x-aiff	SoundApp
audio/x-wav	SoundApp

CONFIGURING VIDEO PLAYERS

The following table lists the rcommended associations for video players.

MIME Type	Program
video/mpeg	Sparkle
video/quicktime	Sparkle

CONFIGURING DECOMPRESSION SOFTWARE

The StuffIt Expander software included with this book's CD-ROM disc can decompress virtually any compressed file you are likely to encounter. The following table shows the recommended configuration settings for compressed file MIME types.

MIME Type	Program
application/Mac-Binhex40	StuffIt Expander
application/x-StuffIt	StuffIt Expander

CONFIGURING FILE VIEWING SOFTWARE

Included with this book's CD-ROM disc is Adobe Acrobat Reader, which enables you to view and print documents richly formatted with Adobe Acrobat text and graphics. Adobe Acrobat is the successor to the popular PostScript file viewing format.

MIME Type	Program
application/pdf	Adobe Acrobat

CONFIGURING THE TELNET HELPERS

To configure Netscape to use your Telnet applications (NCSA Telnet and TN3270), you do not use the Helper Applications page of the Preferences menu. Instead, you use the Applications and Directories page, as explained in the following.

To configure your Telnet application, follow these instructions:

1. From the Options menu, choose Preferences.

2. In the list box, choose Applications and Directories. You'll see the Applications and Directories page, shown in Figure 5.2.

3. In the Telnet Application box, use the Browse button to locate NCSA Telnet.

4. Click OK.

A NOTE ON SOUND AND VIDEO FORMATS

You will encounter a profusion of sound and video formats on the Web. For the most part, you can simply ignore the differences; as long as you've got a helper application to play these files, you can use them. If you're curious to know how the sound files differ, here's a quick rundown:

- **Amiga (*.IFF) File**   This is a standard sound format for Amiga computers. Since the Amiga is no longer produced, this file format is becoming increasingly rare.

- **Apple IFF (*.AIFF) File**   This sound format was developed by Apple Computer and resembles the Amiga *.IFF format, but it isn't compatible with *.IFF files.

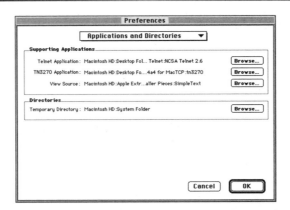

Figure 5.2   Applications and Directories (Preferences)

- **MPEG (*.mpg) Audio File**   This sophisticated sound format is the result of work by the Motion Picture Experts Group (MPEG), a joint committee of the International Standards Organization (ISO) and the International Electro-Technical Commission (IEC). There are two current MPEG standards for joint audio/video files, MPEG-1 and MPEG-2. MPEG audio files are highly compressed (at ratios of 4 to 1 or more), and yet—thanks to algorithms based on studies of human sound perception—there is little apparent degradation of quality. A plus: MPEG audio files can handle stereo.

- **SoundBlaster (*.VOC) File**   This is the format used by the popular SoundBlaster sound cards, but it isn't commonly encountered on the Web.

- **Sounder/Soundtools (*.SND) File**   This is a standard Macintosh sound format.

- **Sun/NeXT (*.AU) File**   This sound file format is the most common one to be found on the Web. It employs an advanced storage technique that gives the equivalent of 14-bit sound depth even though only 8 bits of data are used.

- **Windows (*.WAV) File**   This is the sound file format that is native to Microsoft Windows. SoundApp can play these sounds.

Here's a quick guide to the video formats you'll encounter:

- **FLI (Autodesk) Video File**   Employing 8-bit data storage, this format does not produce high-quality video, but it requires less storage space and transmission time than most other video formats. FLI videos are fairly rare.

- **MPEG Video File**   The MPEG video standard is defined by the Motion Picture Experts Group (MPEG). It incorporates a lossy compression technique that deletes some of the video information, but in a way that is not obvious to human viewers. It is capable of achieving a compression ratio of 26 to 1 without objectionable loss of image quality.

- **QuickTime**   This is the standard Macintosh format for computer movies. It supports a variety of compression techniques that can achieve compression ratios as high as 40 to 1. Quality is excellent, and QuickTime movies can include sound.

Understanding Stereo MPEG Sound

MPEG (Moving Pictures Expert Group) is an emerging video and audio compression standard that produces high-quality audio and video at low rates and allows professional-quality audio files to be easily distributed over the Internet. MPEG was formed in 1988 to establish a standard for the coded representation of moving pictures and associated audio stored on digital storage media. MPEG compressed audio provides CD-quality fidelity at a 10:1 compression rate or better, which means that a standard 600 megabyte audio CD compresses to 60 megabytes or less with little loss in audio fidelity.

The method by which MPEG achieves this level of compression is by playing with inaccuracies inherent in the human ear. In its simplest form, picture two adjacent keys on a piano keyboard that are struck simultaneously, but one is struck a bit harder than the other. The human ear masks the lighter struck key and primarily hears the louder key. If you hit the lighter struck key even yet lighter, the overall perception is still that of the heavier struck key. MPEG effectively removes or lessens adjacent tones and uses the digital bits it would have used to represent those tones for more critical tones within a musical piece. This is how the audio "loss" occurs— yet to most people the loss is imperceptible. Controversy abounds regarding this approach, similar to subjective discussions found when audiophiles talk about speaker systems. No one person is "right." One thing is certain: if compression of this nature didn't exist, high-quality audio on the Internet would not be possible.

MPEG audio decompression is CPU intensive, although recent advances in RISC-based computer architectures that include instructions to accelerate audio processing have made real-time audio decompression viable in software. Kauai Media of Del Mar, California creates software-only MPEG audio compression and decompression products for Macintosh and Power Mac computers. A version of Kauai's MPEG/CD shareware MPEG audio decompressor that performs real-time and non-real-time decompression for most Mac and all Power Mac computers is included on the CD accompanying this book. Configure the enclosed MPEG/CD as a Netscape helper application as described in the included instructions and begin listening to high-quality audio over the net.

Contact Kauai Media regarding information about their MPEG audio software compressor, MPEG/CDE, and streaming real-time audio player, MPEG/CDS. The former MPEG compresses your audio directly from a CD,

AIFF file, or PCM data file. MPEG/CDS allows true point-and-click audio on demand, eliminating the audio file download prior to play. Kauai Media is found at http://www.kauai.com/~bbal, or send e-mail directly to bbal@kauai.com.

 Two web sites serving MPEG audio that you shouldn't miss are the Internet Underground Music Archive (IUMA) out of Santa Cruz, California at http://www.iuma.com and iStation Online from the Intouch Group Inc. of San Francisco, California at http://istation.internet.net. The Intouch Group delivers 40,000 CDs to the net, including many well-known artists, while IUMA caters to aspiring lesser-known, but equally talented, artists.

TESTING YOUR VIEWERS

 Got your helper programs installed? Give 'em a try. A useful place to test them out is the WWW Viewer Test page, located at the following URL:

http://www-dsed.llnl.gov/documents/WWWtest.html

To access this URL with Netscape, open the File menu, choose Open Location, type this URL, and click OK. You don't have all the helper applications listed in this page—some of them are for esoteric scientific applications—but there are buttons for AU and AIFF sounds, QuickTime and MPEG videos, and Adobe Acrobat documents. Have fun!

 My helper application won't start! This is a very common problem. Are you sure you typed the helper application's name and disk location correctly? If so, make sure you have enough memory left for the helper application to run. Try closing all other applications save Netscape. If that doesn't work, restart your Macintosh, make your Internet connection, start Netscape, and try again—chances are that will solve the problem.

CREATING A DOWNLOAD DIRECTORY

When you access a sound, video, or formatted document, Netscape downloads the file and saves it to your hard disk. To do so, the program uses the temporary directory setting found in the Applications and Directories page of the Preferences menu. Even though this setting is called Temporary Directory, Netscape does not erase the files when you quit the program. You may wish to play them later, or you may wish to delete them so that they do not take up disk space.

So that you can keep track of your downloaded files, create a Temporary folder within Netscape's directory, and use the Browse button to identify this folder in the Temporary Directory box (Applications and Directories page).

FROM HERE

- You're all set to surf the Web! For a review of the basics, try going through Chapter 2 ("The Gentle Art of Web Surfing") again, this time trying everything out with Netscape.

- If you've learned the very basics and you're ready to begin mastering Netscape, flip to the next chapter.

- Can't wait to explore your multimedia helper applications? Check out Chapter 12.

Part III

SURFING

THE WEB

Chapter

6

Change That Home Page!

You start Netscape, and every time you do, you see Netscape's welcome page. Wouldn't you like to see something more useful, something more tailored to your Web-browsing needs? If so, you've come to the right place: This chapter shows you how to change your default home page, the page you'll see every time Netscape starts. (You also see this page when you click the Home button.)

What's the point of changing your home page? The improvement is more than cosmetic. A good home page gives you instant access to a huge variety of resources: starting points, subject trees, search engines, news, weather, sports, time-wasting diversions, humor, entertainment, and more.

You can choose any home page you like—this chapter shows you how to hunt down cool home pages and make them your own—or you can use the home page included on this book's disk, HOME.HTML. Either way, your enjoyment of Netscape and the Web will increase by leaps and bounds.

Every reader of this book should check out this chapter and change Netscape's default home page. It's easy, and you don't need to know any HTML. The home page that's included with this book will really increase your enjoyment of the Web.

This chapter begins by examining a thorny terminological issue, namely, just what *is* a home page? Check this out for some clear distinctions that will help you make sense of what's out there. The chapter continues by examining the virtues of changing one's default home page and describes HOME.HTML, the home page included with this book. You'll then learn how to change the default home page with the Preferences option. The chapter concludes with a discussion of additional home page resources, including some very nice personal home pages and the amazing Virtual Library, from which you can choose a page that Netscape will display every time you launch the program.

For the Time-Challenged

◆ A *home page* is what you see when you click the Home button. You should change the default home page (Netscape's welcome page), substituting something of more personal value to you.

◆ This book comes with a home page called HOME.HTML, and it's a good choice. It's packed with useful hyperlinks that enable you to search for information, obtain news and weather reports, check out movie and video reviews, and much more.

◆ To install HOME.HTML as your home page, flip to the section called "Changing Your Home Page," and follow the instructions carefully.

◆ You can use someone else's home page as your own. A great place to hunt for home pages is Who's Who on the Internet (http://web.city.ac.uk/citylive/pages.html). This is a good option for hobbyists and enthusiasts of all kinds.

◆ Another good home page option is to use one of the many subject-oriented metapages of the Virtual Library (http://info.cern.ch/hypertext/DataSources/bySubject/Overview.html). This is a good option for students, teachers, and professionals.

WHAT *IS* A "HOME PAGE"?

I'm convinced that most Web users don't have the vaguest idea of what they're talking about when they utter the words "home page." This can refer to everything from the page you see when you start your browser, to the Web-accessible home pages created by thousands of college students with too much time on their hands, and even the CIA "home page." (I am not making this up—try http://www.ic.gov/. Your access has been noted and a dossier has been generated.)

In an effort to introduce some precision into this book's vocabulary, at least, I'm using the following distinctions:

- **Home Page**   The page you see when you click the Home button on a graphical browser.

- **Default Home Page**   The page that a browser (such as Netscape) is preset to display by default every time you start the program or click Home.

- **Hotlist**   A list of interesting or useful Web documents, saved in a format that is proprietary to a given graphical browser. Some browsers can import other browser's hotlists, but don't count on it.

- **Web Site**   An Internet host that contains Web-accessible resources.

- **web** (small "w")   A series of hyperlinked documents that have been created with a consistent overall style and purpose, and organized in such a way that internal navigation is facilitated (for example, through the provision of internal navigation buttons, index pages, and a welcome page that summarizes the available resources).

- **Welcome Page**   The page that a web displays by default every time you access it. For example, if you use the URL http://www.virginia.edu/, you'll get the University of Virginia's welcome page. Confusingly, this is often called a home page, because the welcome page often is the top-level ("home") page of a web, with lots of additional, internally linked documents. I think it's clearer to call this a welcome page instead of a home page.

- **Personal Home Page**   A home page that you've created for yourself. To do this, you'll need to learn some HTML, the markup language used to create Web documents. It isn't very hard, but it's beyond the subject of this book (check out AP Professional's forthcoming *Publish*

It on the Web! (Macintosh Edition)). Your personal home page won't be accessible to others unless you set up a web server (a program that enables anyone to access your Web documents through the Internet).

- **Web-Accessible Personal Home Page**   Here I am. This is my personal home page. This is the stuff I like. As for me, I'm totally cool. Here's my picture! And I'm so sure that everyone else will like everything I like, that I've made my personal home page available on the Web for all the world to access. You can use it, too, or even make it your home page! And then you get to look at my picture every time you start your browser! Usually, it's not worth it.

- **Starting Points Page**   A page of URLs designed to help you get started with the World Wide Web. Included are links that introduce the Internet and the Web, as well as links to subject trees and search engines.

- **Trailblazer Page**   A page containing many interesting links on a well-focused subject, such as cartoons, juggling, Macintosh computers, or Jell-O recipes containing alcohol. The Virtual Library contains dozens of extremely cool trailblazer pages.

To sum all this up: After you've learned the basics of Netscape, you will want to change the program's default home page, which you can always access by clicking the Welcome button. A good choice is this book's HOME.HTML. By learning a little HTML, you could create your own personal home page. You could also use someone else's Web-accessible personal home page (there are some good ones) as your home page. Another strategy: You could find a trailblazer page that's relevant to your interests, and make it your home page. The following sections detail these three options.

HAVE WE GOT A HOME PAGE FOR YOU!

On this book's CD-ROM disc is one heck of a nice home page called (you guessed it) HOME (actually, HOME.HTML). Part of it is shown in Figure 6.1.
    At the top of this home page are four useful buttons:

- **Lycos**   Click here to access the Lycos search engine. For more information on Lycos, see Chapter 10.

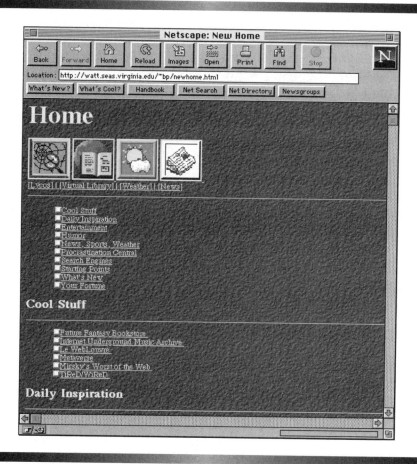

Figure 6.1 The home page that comes with this book (HOME.HTML)

- **Virtual Library** Click here to access the WWW Virtual Library, a subject tree with amazing information resources. For more information on the Virtual Library, see Chapter 10.

- **Weather** Click here to access an interactive weather map of the United States.

- **News** Click here to display the News Page, with links to several on-line newspapers.

Below the buttons, you'll find links to the main subheadings. In Figure 6.1, you can see the Cool Stuff items. Here's an overview of the rest of HOME.HTML:

- **Cool Stuff**   Some of the most impressive and popular Web pages. If you're curious about what the Web *should* be like, take a look at these sites.

- **Daily Inspiration**   Check out the Deep Thought of the day, the quotations of the day, and more—including the Shakespearean insult of the day. Lots of fun stuff, and it changes every day.

- **Entertainment**   The latest reviews of movies, videos, and music of all kinds.

- **Humor**   Search for lightbulb jokes, play MadLib, and find out what happened to the guy who tried to use a $2 bill at Taco Bell.

- **News, Sports, Weather**   Find out what's going on from sources such as CBS News, the *San Francisco Chronicle*, the *San Jose Mercury-News*, and more.

- **Procrastination Central**   You didn't really want to get any work done, did you? Mr. Potato Head and Tic Tac Toe will make sure that you don't.

- **Search Engines**   The best search engines, a click away.

- **Starting Points**   Some great starting points pages.

- **What's New**   All kinds of new Web sites to explore.

- **Your Fortune**   The Magic 8 Ball knows all, and if it doesn't, there's always the Fortune Cookie Server, an on-line Tarot reading, and the I Ching.

HOME.HTML doesn't contain thousands or even hundreds of hyperlinks; it contains just a few dozen. Apart from the hyperlinks in Cool Stuff, most of them share one element in common: They aren't boring, static pages that just show you the same text and graphics every time you access them. In Daily Inspiration, for example, you'll find lots of links that display something completely different at each access. Many other links connect you with fast-breaking news pages, which are updated frequently, and still others access databases that permit you to search for information.

HOME.HTML isn't perfect, since there's no way I could have anticipated all of your interests and hobbies. But it points the way. If you like, you can learn a little HTML and modify HOME.HTML for your own purposes.

I don't have a CD-ROM drive! You can still obtain HOME.HTML, and here's how. From the File menu, choose Open Location, and type the following URL into the text box:

http://watt.seas.virginia.edu/~bp/newhome.html

Click OK to access this page. Flip to Chapter 11 to learn how to save this document to your hard disk, replete with all the cool icons.

Note that the following instructions assume that you have installed the HOME.HTML file and the GIF graphics that it requires, as explained in Appendix B.

CHANGING YOUR HOME PAGE

To change your default home page to HOME.HTML, follow these instructions:

1. From the Options menu, choose Preferences. You'll see the Preferences dialog box, which probably displays lots of things that have nothing to do with the default home page.

2. In the list box at the top of the dialog box, choose Window and Link Styles. You'll see the Styles preferences, shown in Figure 6.2.

3. In the text box next to Home Page Location, select the existing URL.

4. Assuming that your hard disk is named Macintosh HD, and that you installed Netscape as Chapter 4 suggested, carefully type the following:

file:///Macintosh%20HD/Netscape/home.html

What's the "%20" for? You need this code if there's a space in any of the disk or folder names you type. For example, if your hard

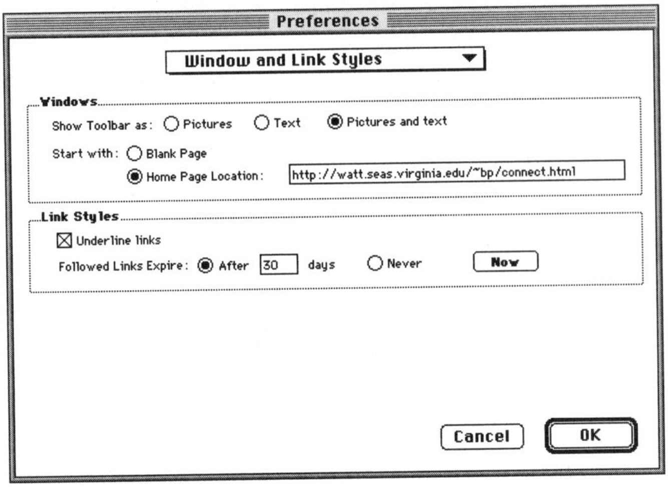

Figure 6.2   Change the default home page here

disk is named "Old Stinker," you have to type "Old%20Stinker." Aren't computers fun?

5. Click the Home Page Location option button, if necessary.

6. Click OK or just press Enter to confirm your choice and return to Netscape.

7. Click the Home button to test your new home page.

It doesn't work! If you see a message stating that Netscape cannot find the file, you probably typed the URL wrong. Here's a trick to make sure you get it right. From the File menu, choose Open File. In the dialog box, select HOME.HTML, and click OK. Netscape opens the document. In the Location box, select the URL, and press Command + C to copy the URL to the Clipboard. Then repeat steps 1 through 3 in the above instructions, ending with selecting the existing URL. Press Command + V to paste the correct URL into the dialog box. Then follow steps 5 through 7 to confirm and test your new home page.

USING PERSONAL HOME PAGES

Somewhere out there, there's somebody who shares a lot of your interests. And just possibly, this someone has created a publicly accessible home page—one of those "aren't-I-cool personal home pages for the masses" discussed above. You can make it *your* home page (that is, your default home page) easily enough; you just type the page's URL in the Preferences dialog box, as explained earlier in this chapter. The trick lies in finding a useful page. Here are some good bets:

- **John S. Makulowich's Awesome List** (http://www.clark.net/pub/ journalism/awesome.html)   An alphabetized list of useful Web sites, created by an Internet trainer.

- **Meng Weng Wong's Home Page** (http:///www.seas.upenn.edu/ ~mengwong/meng.html)   A very useful page, created by a brilliant University of Pennsylvania graduate student.

- **Lorrie Cranor's Home Page** (http://dworkin.wustl.edu/pub/lorracks/ home.html)   Lorrie's picks of the Web; a great page.

 How can you learn about additional personal home pages? Thanks to a very remarkable on-line resource, the task of finding home pages has just gotten a lot easier. Here it is, folks: Who's Who on the Internet (formerly the Complete Home Page Directory) at http://web.city.ac.uk/citylive/ pages.html (Figure 6.3). This web contains a list of hyperlinks to several thousand individuals' home pages, which you can access alphabetically, if you wish, by clicking the alphabet buttons.

The best way to search WWOTI is to use its search capabilities, which you can access from the site's welcome page. Unfortunately, WWOTI does not permit searches unless *your* site is registered (and it probably isn't). Paging through the alphabetical listings manually is time-consuming, but it's quite an interesting diversion, a classic Internet time-waster in itself. Here are a few jewels, including the description that the page authors themselves posted:

- **Anders Pages**   Big sections about Transhumanism and the roleplaying game Mage: The Ascension. Also information about General Weirdness, Magick, and Weird Science.

Figure 6.3 Who's Who on the Internet (WWOTI) (http://web.city.ac.uk/citylive/pages.html)

- **Arachnaut's Lair**   The Arachnaut's Lair is the home page of Jim Hurley. The focus of the page is on electronic music and aquariums. You'll also find an assortment of links cataloged there.

- **Billy Boy's Home**   Lots of goodies. This page is a gold mine of philosophy-related links: if you're interested in Aristotle, Kant, or any of the other biggies, you can download everything they wrote by following philosophy-related links from here. If physics is your bag, you can surf to all sorts of stuff on that topic from here. Also, you can download graphics of all sorts from my hard drive and link to graphics elsewhere.

- **Cliff Ecology Research Group** A page devoted to the study of cliff ecology and ancient cedars on cliffs [GIFS!].

- **Cynthia Marasco's Home Page** My personal page with lots of ways to waste time. It also includes tons of links to legal information.

- **Don't panic eat organic** An organic farmers home page. May be of help to others interested in organic farming. A way organic farmers can network.

- **Expecting Rain** Bob Dylan information: the Dylan Atlas, Dylan Who's Who, Dylan pictures, Dylan links, and other links.

- **Mike's ARMY Home Page** Contains info on the Army, including weapons facts pages and GIFs of actual training.

- **Steve Rapport Photography** Steve Rapport's virtual portfolio of original rock'n'roll photos: also stories, gossip, comedy (Young Ones, Monty Python, Simpsons), his kitties, West Ham United and Fortune's Always Hiding home pages, Counting Crows discography.

- **The Electronic Zoo** Vast collection of animal and veterinary Internet resources.

USING A TRAILBLAZER PAGE AS A HOME PAGE

A *trailblazer page* is a Web document that attempts to sum up the URLs pertaining to a particular subject, such as astronomy or wine. If you're a student, teacher, or professional working in such an area, you may wish to find a trailblazer page and make it your home page, so that all these links are instantly available to you.

An excellent source of trailblazer pages is the Virtual Library, maintained at CERN (the Swiss birthplace of the World Wide Web). The Virtual Library is described as a distributed information system, and rightly so: The only page stored at CERN is the overview document, which lists the trailblazer page topics. Each trailblazer page is maintained by a volunteer and stored at the volunteer's Web site. Of course, this doesn't mean anything to you in practice; you just click away, and where you are—and where you wind up—doesn't really matter.

To access the Virtual Library's table of contents, use http://info.cern.ch/ hypertext/DataSources/bySubject/Overview.html. Table 6.1 lists the subject headings current at this book's writing:

Table 6.1   Subject Headings in the Virtual Library

Aboriginal Studies	Environment
Aeronautics and Aeronautical Engineering	Finance
African Studies	Fish
Agriculture	Forestry
Animal Health, Well-being, and Rights	Fortune-telling
Anthropology	Furniture and Interior Design
Applied Linguistics	Games
Archaeology	Geography
Architecture	Geophysics
Art	German Subject Catalogue
Asian Studies	History
Astronomy and Astrophysics	Home Pages
Autos	Human Computer Interaction
Aviation	Human Factors
Beer and Brewing	Human Rights
Bio Sciences	International Affairs
Biotechnology	Italian General Subject Tree
Chemistry	Landscape Architecture
Climate Research	Languages
Cognitive Science	Latin American Studies
Collecting	Law
Commercial Services	Libraries
Communications	Linguistics
Community Networks	Literature
Computing	Mathematics
Conferences	Medicine
Cryptography, PGP, and Your Privacy	Medieval Studies
Crystallography	Meteorology
Culture	Middle East Studies
Dance	Movies
Demography and Population Studies	Museums
Design	Music
Earth Science	Oceanography
Education	Paranormal Phenomena
Electronic Journals	Philosophy
Encyclopedia	Physics
Energy	Political Science
Engineering	Politics and Economics

Table 6.1 *Continued*

Psychology	Statistics
Publishers	Sumeria
Recipes	Telecommunications
Recreation	Tibetan Studies
Reference	Treasure
Religion	U.S. Federal Government Agencies
Russian and East European Studies	U.S. Government Information Sources
Secular Issues	Unidentified Flying Objects (UFOs)
Social Sciences	United Nations and other International
Sociology	Organizations
Spirituality	Vision Science
Sport	Whale Watching Web
Standards and Standardization	Wine
Bodies	World Wide Web Development

Solutions

How to "Capture" a URL and Add It to Your Preferences Dialog Box

If one of the Virtual Library pages (or some other page you see) looks like a good candidate for your home page, you can copy its URL and paste it into the Preferences dialog box. Here's how:

1. Display the page you want to use as your home page.

2. In the Location box, select the URL. To make sure you've selected all of it, click at the left edge of the box and drag all the way right.

3. Press Command + C to copy the URL to the Clipboard.

4. From the Options menu, choose Preferences.

5. Select the Window and Links Styles preference option, if necessary.

6. Select the text that's currently in the Home Page Location box.

7. Press Command + V to paste the URL from the Clipboard. This action deletes the current URL and places the new one into the box.

8. Click OK to confirm.

9. Click the Home button to test your new home page.

FROM HERE

- Continue learning fundamental Netscape navigation skills in Chapter 7.

- Find a cool, interesting, or useful Web site? Save its location with a bookmark, as explained in Chapter 8.

Chapter

7

Perfecting Your Navigation Skills

Where Am I?

I n this chapter, you'll learn how to go beyond the average Netscape user's skill level—and in so doing, you'll increase your enjoyment of Netscape (and the Web) immensely.

It's a shame, but it's true: Too many Netscape users just don't know what to do when they inadvertently access a lengthy but unwanted document, or one that's loaded with in-line images that they don't need to see. They don't know how to get back to documents they've previously viewed, and they haven't the foggiest idea how the history list works. They don't know when, or even how, to take advantage of Netscape's ability to display multiple independent windows, and they couldn't tell you about the Reload option if their lives depended on it. Lacking this knowledge, they just take what the Web dishes out to them.

In this chapter and the next, you'll learn a *strategy* for Netscape navigation that makes full and intelligent use of all its time-saving, Web-taming capabilities. This chapter fully discusses the Stop button, selective downloading of in-line images, the history list and the mysterious way it works, multiple windows, and the Reload option. The next chapter, equally important, discusses bookmarks, which enable you to save a document title and URL so that you can return to the document easily.

This is an important chapter for every reader of this book. Although savvy Netscape users will have already discovered the virtues of stopping unwanted downloads and selectively loading in-line images, I'll bet that even those most familiar with Netscape don't understand how the history list works, why document titles mysteriously disappear from the history list, and how you can cure this problem by opening new windows at just the right time. So read on, read on.

STOP! *PLEASE* STOP!

You just clicked a hyperlink. It looked interesting. But now you can see that it's going to be a pain. There are at least 50 pictures of the Brady Bunch. And it's taking *forever* to download. Stop the madness! Here's how:

- Click the Stop button

  or

- Press Command + period (.)

  or

- From the Go menu, choose Stop Loading

After you stop downloading, you may see part of the document on-screen, but it may show signs of its brutal treatment (for example, in-line images that didn't download will be shown with placeholders, like the ones in Figure 7.1. Just click the Back button to abandon this battle scene. If you feel sorry for the document and would like to give it an opportunity to live once again, click the Reload button.

Image placeholder —

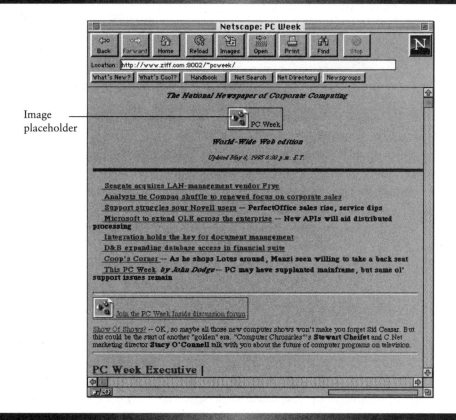

Figure 7.1   Image placeholders in stopped document

For the Time-Challenged

♦ If you've inadvertently clicked a hyperlink and Netscape begins download-ing a huge, unwanted file, click the Stop button.

♦ To speed document downloading considerably (a plus if you're using a slow SLIP/PPP connection), turn off the automatic display of in-line images. You can selectively display an individual graphic by holding down the mouse but-ton and choosing Load This Image from the pop-up menu.

♦ If you've redisplayed a previously accessed document and suspect that the original may have changed, click the Reload button.

THIS DOCUMENT'S TOO SLOW! (TOO MANY IMAGES)

If you're accessing the Web over a SLIP or PPP connection, documents stuffed with in-line images can take forever to download. That's OK if you're really interested in the pictures; after all, why else would you access Le WebLouvre, or, for that matter, the Playboy Home Page? (I *only* read the interviews.) Often, though, you're searching for some specific information, and the graphics—however pretty—serve only to delay your journey. For such Web ventures, you'd be wise to turn off the automatic downloading of in-line images. Here's how.

 In the Options menu, the Auto Load Images option is a *toggle command*. A toggle command has two states, on or off. When a toggle command is on, you see a check mark next to the command name. When a toggle command is off, there's no check mark. To change a toggle command, you choose the command. You can't really see what happens, because the menu disappears after you choose the command. If you open the menu again, though, you'll see that choosing the command did one of two things: It made the check mark appear (on), or it made the check mark disappear (off). It's simple, once you get the basic idea.

Let's assume that Netscape is automatically downloading in-line images, which is the default setting. That means there's a check mark next to Auto Load Images on the Options menu. You need to get rid of that check mark.

To turn off the automatic downloading of in-line images, do the following:

1. From the Options menu, choose Auto Load Images.

2. Just to make sure, choose Options again, and look at the menu; there should be no check mark next to the Auto Load Images option.

3. If you would like Netscape to save this option, open Options again, and choose Save Options.

You've turned off automatic image downloading. Great! Documents load quickly, but they aren't much visual fun anymore, are they? Well, read on.

SELECTIVELY LOADING IN-LINE IMAGES

After you've turned off automatic image downloading, you can view any *single* in-line graphic, just as you please. This is very cool. The technique makes use of the pop-up menu that appears when you hold down the mouse button.

To view an individual in-line graphic (when automatic image downloading has been turned off):

1. Point to the image's placeholder, and hold down the mouse button until you see the pop-up menu (Figure 7.2).

2. From the pop-up menu, choose Load This Image (to display the image within the current document) or View This Image (to view

Figure 7.2 Pop-up menu

the graphic in a new, separate document). Netscape will download the image you've clicked.

You can also download *all* the images in a given document:

- From the View menu, choose Load Images

  or

- Press Command + I

 I don't care how long it takes to download the pictures! I want images on by default!   No problem. From the Options menu, choose Auto Load Images again, so that the check mark reappears.

THERE'S A HISTORY TO THIS (THE HISTORY LIST)

After a good, long Web surf, you'll be wondering, "Where am I?" And after spending five hours in biancaTroll's house, you'll be thinking, "How do I get back to that *useful* page I saw half an hour ago?" You've surfed *so* many sites, you'd have to click the Back button six zillion times. But there's a better way, maybe.

 You *may* be able to use the *history list* to go back to previously accessed sites. Unbeknownst to you, Netscape has been keeping a record of your travels. The program *knows* where you've been. Fortunately, it doesn't know whether you've been naughty (you didn't fumble around in biancaTroll's bedside drawer, did you?). It just keeps a record of the URLs you've visited, with certain important limitations, which I'll explain in a minute. You'll find a list of recently visited sites on the bottom portion of the Go menu (Figure 7.3).

Go	
Back	⌘[
Forward	⌘]
Home	
Stop Loading	⌘.
View History...	⌘H
✓GIF image 235x85 pixels	⌘0
PC Week	⌘1
Welcome to Netscape	⌘2
USL Front Desk at the OAK Repository (oak.oakland)...	⌘3
Who's Who on the Internet	⌘4
TCC 402 - Pfaffenberger	⌘5
TCC Home Page	⌘6
contents.html	⌘7
Table of Contents	⌘8
New Home	⌘9
Index of /~bp/	
Download Compress-Translate/stuffit-lite-35.hqx	
Results of search in Virtual Shareware Library	
Virtual Shareware Library Search Form	
USL Front Desk at the OAK Repository (oak.oakland)...	
Virtual Shareware Library Front Desks	
USL Front Desk in Ljubljana, Slovenia	
Connections	

Figure 7.3   The Go menu

To go back to a document you've visited previously in the current Netscape session, do the following:

- From the Go menu, choose the title of the document to which you want to return.

You can also go back to a document by using the History dialog box, as explained in the following:

1. From the Go menu, choose View History, or use the Command + H keyboard shortcut. You'll see the History dialog box, shown in Figure 7.4.

2. Highlight the document to which you want to return, and click Go to (or just press Enter).

3. Click the close box.

Figure 7.4   History dialog box

WHEN — AND HOW — TO OPEN A NEW WINDOW

When you open a new window for Netscape, you see what appears to be a new, independent copy of the program—and as far as you are concerned, it is. In the new window, Netscape automatically displays the home page that you've chosen, just as if you were launching the program at the beginning of a new Netscape session. The new window's history list is blank, waiting for you to begin a new lineage. Your actions in this window will not affect the history list in other Netscape windows.

To open a new window:

- From the File menu, choose New Window

   or

- Press Command + N

Use this great trick to open a hyperlink in a new window. Point to the hyperlink, and hold down the mouse button until the pop-up menu appears. From the pop-up menu, choose New Window with This Link. Netscape opens a new window. Instead of displaying the home page, the program displays the document you've chosen.

How many Netscape windows can you open? As many as your Mac's memory can accommodate. By default, Netscape is set to open a maximum of four independent windows. See Chapter 13 for information on increasing this number, if you wish.

 Here's another good reason to open a new window. If you suspect that you'll have trouble accessing a hyperlink, perhaps because it's lengthy or the site is situated on a 56 Kbps network in Tasmania, use the pop-up menu to open the link in a new window. While the new window is stalled pending retrieval of the document, you can switch back to the original window and continue enjoying the Web.

Managing Multiple Windows

When more than one Netscape window is open, you can switch between them as you please. When you're done with a window, you can close it without quitting Netscape. The following instructions detail these procedures.

To switch from one Netscape window to another:

- Click on the window you want to activate.

To close a Netscape window:

- From the File menu, choose Close

   or

- Press Command + W

   or

- Click the window's close box

RELOADING DOCUMENTS

On the View menu, you'll find an option called Reload, and there's a Reload button on the toolbar. When you choose Reload, Netscape goes back to the network and retrieves a new, complete copy of the document you are currently viewing.

When should you Reload? As you will learn in Chapter 11 ("Managing Documents"), Netscape saves a copy of recently accessed documents in its memory *cache* (a special storage area designed for fast re-retrieval of documents). When you click a previously visited hyperlink, Netscape checks to see whether there's a copy of the document in the cache, and if there is, the program loads the cache's copy rather than retrieving the document from the network. In most cases, that's fine—the document appears much more quickly. But what happens if the original, network-based version of the document has changed? You wouldn't know this, because Netscape is showing you the old copy. If you suspect that the network version has changed, choose Reload from the View menu, or press Command + R, or just click the Reload button.

FROM HERE

- To complete your navigation skills, be sure to read Chapter 8, "Creating and Using Bookmarks."

- Learn how to find documents on the Web! Chapters 9 and 10 introduce trailblazer pages, subject trees, and search engines.

- Deal with documents—view them, print them, save them. You'll find all the information you need in Chapter 11.

Chapter

8

Creating and Using Bookmarks

Save That URL!

Y ou've just found *the most awesome* Web site. It holds the key to
your dreams—nay, your job. And then, following links, you surf off
in a zillion directions—only to find, to your dismay, that you've
started a new lineage, somehow, and the darned history list has erased that
awesome site's URL. (For the lowdown on lineages and history lists, see the
previous chapter.) No matter what you do, you can't find it again. You give
up in frustration, and late that night you sob softly into your pillow.

Don't let this happen to you: Set bookmarks.

  In Netscape, a *bookmark* is a document title that you've
added to the Bookmarks menu. In addition to the document
title, Netscape saves the URL. To return to the document,
you just choose the bookmark name from the Bookmarks

menu. *Note:* In other browsers, a bookmark is called a *hotlist item*, and the bookmark list is called a *hotlist*. Hotlist item, bookmark—same thing. The next time you run into some Mosaic user who says, "You ought to see my cool hotlist," you can sniff disdainfully and say, "We Netscape users call them *bookmarks*." Then run.

This chapter presents indispensable Netscape skills for all readers of this book. In particular, you'll learn what to do when your Bookmarks menu gets over-stuffed—a malady, you will find, that befalls every Netscape user, including you. A plus: This chapter's tutorials will prove invaluable in learning how to reorganize bookmarks, a crucial Netscape skill that's among the most difficult to learn. Another plus: You'll learn that there's an extremely nice hotlist, er, bookmarks file available on the CD-ROM that came with the book.

ADDING A BOOKMARK

You can add a bookmark in two ways—by pointing to the document's hyperlink and using the pop-up menu, or by displaying the document and using the Add Bookmark option.

Of the two methods for adding bookmarks, it's best to display the page and then use the Add Bookmark command (Bookmarks menu). This command places the page's title on the Bookmarks menu. If you hold down the mouse button while pointing to the page's hyperlink and use the pop-up menu, Netscape adds the URL to the Bookmarks menu. URLs are harder to read than document titles.

To add a bookmark using the pop-up menu (not recommended):

1. Point to the hyperlink you want to mark.

2. Hold down the mouse button. You see the pop-up menu shown in Figure 8.1.

3. Choose Add Bookmark for This Link.

For the Time-Challenged

♦ Add bookmarks by choosing Add Bookmark from the Bookmarks menu; return to one by choosing its name from the same menu.

♦ The Bookmark List dialog box (accessible by means of the Bookmarks menu's View Bookmarks command) permits you to restructure, edit, and find bookmarks, as well as to import and export bookmark files.

♦ In the Bookmark List dialog box, you can quickly change a bookmark's menu name by highlighting the bookmark and editing the text in the Name box.

♦ To delete an unwanted bookmark, highlight the bookmark's name and click Remove Item.

♦ To find a bookmark, click the bookmark at the top of the list. Then type the search text in the Find box, and click Find.

♦ To add a submenu to your bookmark list, click New Header in the Bookmark List dialog box, and type a name for the menu.

♦ To add a bookmark to your submenu, highlight a bookmark. Then use the Down or Up arrow buttons to position the bookmark so that it is beneath the submenu's header name, and also indented.

♦ To choose a submenu to display on the Bookmarks menu, open the Bookmark List dialog box and choose the submenu name in the Menu Starts With list box.

♦ To choose the submenu to which Netscape will add new bookmarks, open the Bookmark List dialog box and choose the submenu in the Menu Adds After list box.

♦ To export your bookmark file so that a Netscape-using friend or colleague can import it, open the Bookmark List dialog box and click Export.

♦ To import a bookmark file that someone has given you, open the Bookmark List dialog box and click Import.

To add a bookmark for a page that's displayed on-screen (this is the recommended technique):

• From the Bookmarks menu, choose Add Bookmark

 or

• Press Command + D

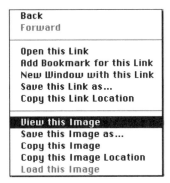

Figure 8.1   The pop-up menu lets you add bookmarks

After you add a bookmark, the bookmark you've added appears on the lower portion of the Bookmarks menu.

 After you've reorganized your Bookmarks menu with headers and submenus, as explained below, you use a different procedure to add bookmarks. For more information, see "Adding New Bookmarks to a Submenu," later in this chapter.

CHOOSING A BOOKMARK

After you've added a bookmark, you can choose it easily. Just open the Bookmarks menu, and highlight the bookmark you want. Netscape will download the document you've requested.

USING THE BOOKMARK LIST DIALOG BOX

If you want to perform operations more complicated than just adding or choosing bookmarks, you'll need the Bookmark List dialog box, shown in Figure 8.2. To access this dialog box, open the Bookmarks menu and choose View Bookmarks, or press Command + B. In this dialog box, you see the following:

- **Add Bookmark**   Click this button to add the current document to the bookmark list. Note, though, that it's a lot faster to do this by just choosing Add Bookmark in the Bookmarks menu.

- **Go To**   Click this button to go to the document that is currently highlighted in the bookmark list. (To change the highlighted item, use the down or up arrow keys, or click a bookmark name with the mouse.) Again, this is easier to do by just choosing the bookmark name from the Bookmarks menu.

- **Up Arrow**   Click this arrow to move the highlighted item up in the bookmark list. You will see this change on the Bookmarks menu.

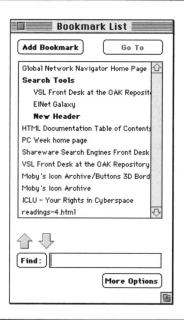

Figure 8.2   Bookmark List dialog box

- **Down Arrow**   Click this button to move the highlighted item down in the bookmark list. Again, you will see this change on the Bookmarks menu.

- **Find**   If you have a *really* lengthy bookmark list, you can use this box to find a bookmark name. For more information, see "Finding a Bookmark," later in this chapter.

- **More Options**   This button expands the Bookmark List dialog box, giving you more options.

Try clicking More Options now. You'll see the expanded version of the Bookmark List dialog box, shown in Figure 8.3. Much of the rest of this chapter deals with these options. Netscape shows additional information about bookmarks when they are highlighted in the list (see the "Name" box, and the boxes under it). If you like, you can add brief descriptions

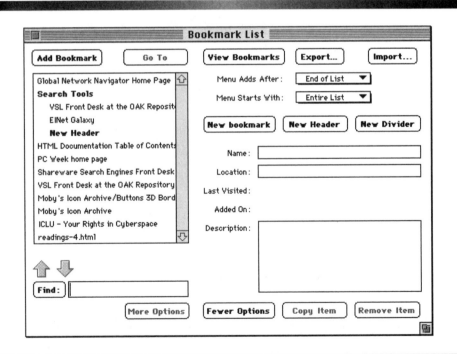

Figure 8.3   Expanded Bookmark List dialog box

of the bookmarks in the Description box. I haven't gotten around to this yet.

EDITING A BOOKMARK

You've just added a bookmark for a very useful Web document, but there's only one problem: The document's title ("Arnold's Page") doesn't convey very much about the contents of the document. On your Bookmarks menu, it would be nicer to see something like "Links to Sci-Fi Sites."

Here's another reason to edit a bookmark. Let's say you're accessing a bookmark that you haven't visited in a long time, and you see a message informing you that the site has moved to a new URL. If this happens, select the new URL, press Command + C to copy the new URL to the Clipboard, and follow the instructions below.

To edit a bookmark:

1. From the Bookmarks menu, choose View Bookmarks, or press Command + B. You'll see the Bookmark List dialog box.

2. In the bookmarks list, highlight the name of the bookmark you want to edit.

3. Click More Options. You'll see the expanded Bookmark List dialog box.

4. If you would like to edit the name, use the usual Macintosh text editing procedures to edit the Name box.

5. If you copied a new URL to the Clipboard, select all the text in the Location box, and press Command + V.

6. When you are finished editing, click the close box.

DELETING A BOOKMARK

The bookmark that once seemed so cool has lost its luster. Nuke it.
To delete a bookmark:

1. From the Bookmarks menu, choose View Bookmarks, or press Command + B. You'll see the Bookmark List dialog box.

2. In the bookmark list, highlight the name of the bookmark you want to delete.

3. Click More Options. You'll see the expanded Bookmark List dialog box.

4. Make sure you've highlighted the right bookmark—the Remove Item button doesn't ask for confirmation!

5. Click Remove Item.

6. Click the close box.

THE LITTLE BOOKMARK LIST THAT GREW

Very quickly, you will discover an unfortunate fact of life. Just as you get heavier when you get older, your bookmark list will get longer the more you use Netscape. Pretty soon, you've got the Bookmark List from Hell: 200 items, totally disorganized, won't even fit in the window. Ugh!

Very likely, you won't admit that You Have a Problem until you can't find a bookmark that you desperately need. If this happens, see "Finding a Bookmark," the very next section. And after that, it's time to get up in front of the group, and confess: "My name is Bryan. I have a disorganized bookmark list."

If you've gotten to this point, you're on the way to recovery. See "Reorganizing Your Bookmark List," which comes after "Finding a Bookmark."

FINDING A BOOKMARK

You've been adding bookmarks like crazy. Your Bookmarks menu is so big that it doesn't fit on the screen. You can't find that bookmark you saved last night, the one that contains the information vital to your term paper. The paper is due in two hours—you *must* find that bookmark, or your life will end. Isn't stress wonderful?

What you want is a quick solution, not a lecture. OK, I'll skip the lecture. (Besides, I just gave it.) And now for the quick solution.

The Find button and box, found in the miniature version of the Bookmark List dialog box, lets you search for text that appears in the bookmark name *and* the URL. For example, let's say you're looking for "Eppie's Useful Web Tools Archive" (at the fictitious URL "http://zylander.farout.com//~eppie/buttons.html"), which has lots of cool GIFs of buttons you can use in your HTML documents. Unfortunately, you can't remember Eppie's name, or anything else about the document's name; however, a search for "buttons" will work, since that word appears in the URL.

 You need one little bit of terminology before proceeding. The text you type in the Find box is called a *search string*. Why "string?" A *string* is a series of characters. And besides, computer people like to give incomprehensible names to everything they can.

To find a bookmark in a (poorly organized, overly lengthy, window-busting) bookmark list:

1. From the Bookmarks menu, choose View Bookmarks, or press Command + B. You'll see the Bookmark List dialog box.

2. In the Find box, type the part of the bookmark name that you're sure of. (If you *think* the bookmark name is "Daniel's Hot Icon Archive," but you're only sure about "Icon," type "Icon"). Netscape ignores capitalization, and it doesn't matter if you type just part of the bookmark name.

3. Click the Find button. Netscape searches down the bookmark list, and highlights the *next* item that matches your query. If this isn't the right one, click Find again.

4. To display the bookmark, click Go To, or just press Enter.

5. Click the close box.

 I couldn't find it! I know it's in there! If Netscape can't locate your bookmark, you see a cheerful message that says, "Search String not found." Does this mean you're dead? Don't let this old nasty computer get you down; sometimes these messages just aren't true. In this case, it's possible that the bookmark you're looking for is *above* the place where you started your search. Netscape only searches *down* in the list. **The solution:** Position the highlight at the top of the bookmark list, and try again.

Still can't find your bookmark? Check the Find box to make sure you've typed the search string correctly. If you did, try another variant on the bookmark's name, and search again. I'll bet you find it.

REORGANIZING YOUR BOOKMARK LIST

Netscape provides tools for reorganizing your bookmark list in a very useful way. In fact, if you read this section carefully, you will know how to create a Well-Organized Bookmark List, the type of thing you would want to show your mother when she comes for a visit.

And what does a Well-Organized Bookmark List look like? Take a look at Figure 8.4. Here, you see a Bookmarks menu that doesn't contain *any* bookmarks; instead, it contains *headers*—menu items that, when chosen, display a submenu. How do you know it's a header? Because of the little right arrow at the end of the header.

A header displays a *submenu*. A submenu is a little menu that appears when you choose the header item. Figure 8.5 shows the submenu that appears when you click "Icon Stuff" on the menu shown in Figure 8.4. Note that this submenu also lacks bookmarks. It contains two more headers, each of which displays its own submenu. You can keep adding headers and submenus to your heart's content. In this way, you can organize hundreds of bookmarks into a very useful resource.

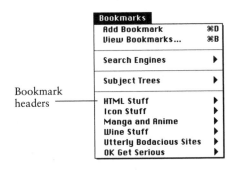

Figure 8.4   A well-organized bookmark list: top-level menu

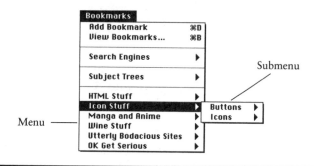

Figure 8.5 A submenu

Within Netscape's bookmarks list, the structure of headers and submenus is shown by using an outline format, as in the following example:

```
- Search Engines

    Lycos

    WebCrawler

- Starting Points

    Awesome List

    Meng Weng Wong's Home Page

    Planet Earth

- Subject Trees

    Whole Internet Catalog

    Yahoo

- Awesome Sites

    Internet Underground Music Archive

    You Will
```

In this example, the Bookmarks menu would show four entries: Seach Engines, Starting Points, Subject Trees, and Awesome Sites. If you click Starting Points, a submenu pops up with three options (Awesome List, Meng Weng Wong's Home Page, and Planet Earth).

I Can't Figure Out How This Works!

The good news is that Netscape's bookmark organization capabilities are very useful. The bad news is that the tools Netscape provides are somewhat difficult to understand, at least at first. You have to use the Up and Down arrow keys to move and indent bookmarks. I know lots of people who have used Netscape for six months and still don't have the vaguest idea how this works.

But don't worry. Once you get the basic idea, you won't have any trouble. And the best way to get the idea is to try it—so let's reorganize your menu right now.

Developing a Plan

Your first step in reorganizing your Bookmarks menu is to devote some thought to how you want it to work. You could alphabetize all the headers at the top-level menu. Or you could put your most frequently accessed menu at the top. Another option is to put *Cyberzombies from Hell* at the top, but then you couldn't show your reorganized bookmark list to your mother. Whatever your plan, it's essential to develop it now, since it's not convenient to change the order in which headers appear after you've added lots of bookmarks to them.

You will need some bookmarks to add to your header's submenu. Perhaps you already have some bookmarks on your bookmark list. If not, surf the Web for a while, and add some bookmarks now.

Creating the First Top-Level Heading

To get started, you'll add a top-level heading at the top of your Bookmarks menu. Here's how:

1. From the Bookmarks menu, choose View Bookmarks, or press Command + B. You'll see the Bookmark List dialog box.

2. Position the highlight at the top of the bookmarks list. To do this, click the first item.

3. Click More Options. You'll see the expanded Bookmark List dialog box.

4. Click New Header. Netscape adds the text "New Header" to the bookmarks list, and places this text in the Name box. If the New Header isn't at the top of the list, click the Up arrow until it is.

5. In the Name box, type the header you want to use.

Moving a Bookmark to a Submenu

To move a bookmark to a submenu beneath the header you just added, follow these steps:

1. In the Bookmark List dialog box, highlight the bookmark you want to move.

2. Click the Up arrow. As you see, Netscape moves the bookmark up.

3. Keep clicking the Up arrow until you have positioned the bookmark just beneath the header.

4. Click Up once more. This final click *indents* the bookmark under the header. The indentation shows that the bookmark has been added to the submenu.

Now you can see why I say that this procedure is a little difficult to understand. The Up arrow not only moves the header up; it also indents it when the bookmark bumps into a header. If you leave the bookmark indented, Netscape adds the bookmark to the header's submenu.

The Down arrow button works the same way, but in the opposite direction. When you move a bookmark down and bump into a header, the next click indents the bookmark beneath the header. This places the bookmark on the header's submenu.

It's pretty easy once you get the hang of it. Try positioning more bookmarks beneath your new header.

Adding a Header to a Submenu

If you have lots of bookmarks to put under a header, you may wish to create a submenu with headers in it. These items will display additional submenus, allowing you to pack more bookmarks into the tight confines of the Bookmarks menu.

To add a header to a submenu, follow these steps:

1. In the Bookmark List dialog box, highlight the header to which you want to add a submenu header. For example, if you want to add a submenu header called "Chardonnay" to the "Wine" header, highlight "Wine."

2. Click New Header. Netscape adds the "New Header" text to the bookmark list, positioned just beneath the header you selected.

Note, however, that it isn't indented. It isn't part of the submenu yet.

3. With "New Header" selected, click the Up arrow. This indents the New Header bookmark so that it will appear on the submenu.

4. In the Name box, delete "New Header" and type the name you want for the new submenu header.

5. Add bookmarks to the new submenu header, following the instructions in the previous section. You do this the same way you add bookmarks to the first-level header: Just use the Up or Down arrow buttons to indent the bookmark beneath the header.

Trivia buffs, you're probably wondering how many levels of submenus you can add. Lots, apparently, but the point is lost after adding 14 levels of submenus, because you can't see the names anymore on the bookmark list! Another practical minimum: the Macintosh doesn't do a very good job of displaying more than about three levels of submenus.

Expanding and Collapsing Headers

Once you've added lots of headers and bookmarks to your bookmark list (the one in the Bookmark List dialog box), it becomes difficult to read and use. However, there's help on the way. Like an outlining function in a word processing program, Netscape permits you to *collapse* all the bookmarks beneath a header, and to *expand* them if you wish. When you collapse the items beneath a header, Netscape hides all the items, showing you only the header. When you expand the items, Netscape displays all the items beneath the header.

To indicate that a header has been collapsed (and contains hidden items), Netscape changes the dash preceding a header into a plus sign, as shown in the following example. Note that the Starting Points header has been collapsed:

```
- Search Engines

    Lycos

    WebCrawler

+ Starting Points

- Subject Trees

    Whole Internet Catalog

    Yahoo
```

```
- Awesome Sites

    Internet Underground Music Archive

    You Will
```

To collapse a header, just double-click it. Do the same to expand a collapsed header.

 Are you planning to move a bookmark a long way in the bookmark list, say, from the bottom to near the top? Instead of clicking the Up (or Down) arrow six zillion times, collapse all the headers along the way. Once you've done so, you need far fewer clicks to move your bookmark.

Adding and Deleting Dividers

You can use *dividers*—lines that span the width of the Bookmarks menu—to organize a lengthy submenu of bookmark names. Using dividers makes sense when you can organize your bookmarks into logical groups, as shown in Figure 8.6. As you move the bookmark, Netscape just skips over the collapsed headers, because you can't add a bookmark to a collapsed header.

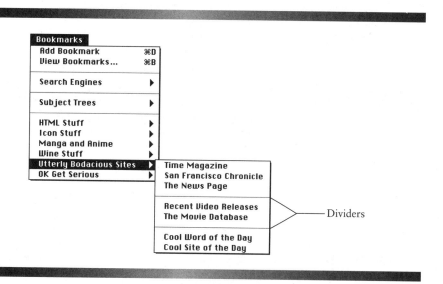

Figure 8.6 Dividers used to organize a submenu

When you get to the header to which you want to add the bookmark, be sure to expand it if it's collapsed.

To add a divider:

1. In the bookmarks list, highlight the item that is positioned just above the place where you want the divider to appear.

2. Click New Divider. Netscape adds a divider to the list, and selects it.

3. Reposition the divider, if necessary, using the Up or Down arrow buttons.

If you decide that a divider is unnecessary, you can delete it by selecting it and clicking Remove Item.

Deleting a Header

If you decide to remove a header, be aware that Netscape deletes all the bookmarks and headers that you've positioned beneath the header. This could be drastic—imagine, for example, that you've positioned 350 bookmarks under a header with three levels of submenus! For this reason, Netscape asks for confirmation before deleting a header, as shown in Figure 8.7. To delete the header and everything that's under it, click Yes. To cancel, click No.

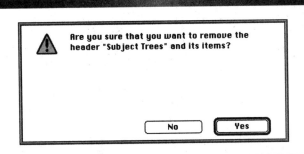

Figure 8.7　Think twice before clicking Yes

CHOOSING THE MENU TO DISPLAY

If you have created submenus, you can choose to display the entire bookmark list on the Bookmarks menu, or only a selected submenu. Normally, you will want to display the entire listing, showing you the headers of all the submenus. If you're working on a particular subject, however, you may wish to restrict the display to one of the submenus so that you can choose items more conveniently.

To choose the menu to display:

1. From the Bookmarks menu, choose View Bookmarks, or press Command + B. You'll see the Bookmark List dialog box.

2. Click More Options. You'll see the expanded Bookmark List dialog box.

3. Next to the Menu Start With list box, click the drop-down arrow. You'll see a list of the bookmark submenus you've created.

4. Click the submenu that you want to appear in the Bookmarks menu.

5. Click the close box.

To redisplay the entire bookmark list:

1. From the Bookmarks menu, choose View Bookmarks, or press Command + B. You'll see the Bookmark List dialog box.

2. Click More Options. You'll see the expanded Bookmark List dialog box.

3. Next to the Menu Starts With list box, click the drop-down arrow. You'll see a list of the bookmark submenus you've created.

4. Click Entire List.

5. Click the close box.

ADDING NEW BOOKMARKS TO A SUBMENU

Once you've created an organized Bookmarks menu with headers and submenus, a slight problem arises: How is poor Netscape to know where to add your new bookmarks? By default, the program adds new bookmarks to the top-level Bookmarks menu, but that's not very satisfactory. To be sure, you can move them later, but it would be better to add them to the correct submenu in the first place. Happily, Netscape enables you to do this.

To add new bookmarks to a particular submenu:

1. Display the Web document that you want to save as a bookmark.

2. From the Bookmarks menu, choose View Bookmarks, or press Command + B.

3. Click More Options. You'll see the expanded Bookmark List dialog box.

4. Next to the Menu Adds After list box, click the drop-down arrow. You'll see a list of the bookmark submenus you've created.

5. Click the name of the submenu to which you want to add new bookmarks.

6. Click Add Bookmark to add the current document to the submenu you've selected.

7. Click the close box.

After you have told Netscape to add new bookmarks to one of your submenus, the program continues doing so for the rest of the current Netscape session. After you quit Netscape and restart, the program returns to adding new bookmarks to the end of the Bookmarks menu.

EXPORTING BOOKMARKS

One of the nicer points of Netscape is the program's ability to export bookmarks to a bookmark file, which you can then give to friends and colleagues (or whomever). These fortunate persons can then import the bookmark file, and *your* bookmarks will magically appear on *their* Bookmarks menu. This has created a certain amount of Internet traffic in bookmark files, which we'll examine in a moment. First, the procedures.

To export your bookmarks to a bookmark file:

1. From the Bookmarks menu, choose View Bookmarks, or press Command + B.

2. Click More Options. You'll see the expanded Bookmark List dialog box.

3. Click Export. You'll see a Save As dialog box. Netscape suggests a file name of bookmark.html.

4. Type a filename. Try using your name, or part of your name, followed by a period and html (don't forget these). If your name is Arwen, for example, you'd type **arwen.html**. If your name is Aragorn, you'd type *aragorn.html*. Actually, if your name was either Arwen or Aragorn, you'd be in *The Lord of the Rings*, not in a computer book.

5. Click OK to save your bookmark file.

6. Click the close box.

To see what your bookmark file looks like, open it using the Open File command (File menu). You'll see a document such as the one in Figure 8.8. All the links work just fine, incidentally, so you can use this document just as you'd use any local file.

 Don't try to edit a bookmark file. It contains lots of secret, weird codes and other information that enables Netscape to import the file properly.

IMPORTING BOOKMARKS

If someone has given you a disk containing a Netscape bookmark file, you can import it so that the file's headings and bookmarks appear in your Bookmarks menu. Don't worry about losing your current bookmarks; when you import a bookmark file, Netscape adds the new bookmarks at the bottom of the existing list.

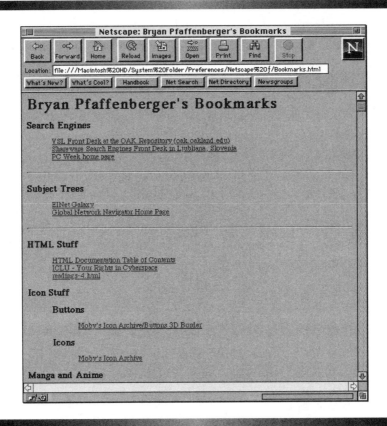

Figure 8.8   Bookmark file, loaded as a local file with Netscape

You can try this right now by importing HOTLIST.HTML, a bookmark file containing lots of extremely cool Web sites. There are dozens of them, organized in the following categories:

- Art
- Business
- Entertainment
- Environment
- Government
- Investing

- Kids on the Web

- Medicine and Health

- Music

- Sports

- Travel

To import HOTLIST.HTML, follow these steps:

1. From the Bookmarks menu, choose View Bookmarks, or press Command + B.

2. Click More Options. You'll see the expanded Bookmark List dialog box.

3. Click Import. You'll see an Open dialog box.

4. Select your CD-ROM drive.

5. In the Hotlist folder, locate and select HOTLIST.HTML.

6. Click OK to import this bookmark file. Netscape adds the bookmarks to the end of your bookmarks list.

7. Click the close box.

Have fun exploring the bookmarks you've just imported! They include some of the most interesting and fun sites on the Web. And as you discover new Web sites and new categories, you can add your personal touch and interests to an already impressive bookmark list.

FROM HERE

- You've mastered the essentials of Netscape for hopping around from link to link. To improve your nagivation skills, your next step involves mastery of trailblazer pages, subject trees, and search engines, the subjects of the next two chapters.

Chapter

9

Using Trailblazer Pages

I t's a big Web out there, with a couple of *million* documents. Whoops, make that three—and counting. One thing's for certain: You're going to need help finding information. Surfing alone won't do it.

Fortunately, there are plenty of people who are trying to help. In this chapter and the next, you'll learn how to make full use of Web documents that people have created in an attempt to help you find your way. I call these *trailblazer* pages. They don't attempt to be complete, up to date, or even 100% accurate—those URLs come and go—but they can be invaluable. Chapter 10, "Using Subject Trees and Search Engines," covers Web information resources that *do* try to be comprehensive. But for now, you're looking for good places to launch your exploration of the Web, and this chapter points the way to some very useful resources.

♦ To find useful or fun documents on the Web, you'll need help. Trailblazers are people—volunteers, mostly—who have created pages loaded with useful links.

♦ Starting points pages provide links designed for beginning Web users. Some of the best have been created by individuals rather than organizations.

♦ Some of the most useful sources on the Web are trailblazer pages, compilations of links focused on a specific subject area. If you can find one of these in an area of your interest, you'll be a very happy camper on the Web.

♦ You can access lists of the most popular sites, as well as lists of cool sites, the best sites, weird sites, and useless sites.

Don't know how to access the pages discussed in this chapter? Check out HOME.HTML, the home page provided on this book's CD-ROM. It contains all the hyperlinks mentioned in this chapter. Please note that some of the URLs mentioned in this chapter may have joined the dead byte heap of history by the time you read this—URLs do come and go. Still, I've chosen most of these documents because they appear to be more or less stable, so most of them should be up and running when you read this book.

INTRODUCING TRAILBLAZER PAGES

Pioneers, explorers, adventurers, helpful souls—whatever you want to call them, they're the saints of the hour. Often on a purely voluntary basis, they've gathered the best of the Web (and sometimes the weirdest of the Web) into collections of hyperlinks. I divide this fast-evolving class of documents into the following categories:

• **Starting Points** These are Web documents that are intended to help neophytes get started with the World Wide Web. Some are created and maintained by organizations, but the better ones are voluntary efforts by individuals.

- **Trailblazer Pages** These pages attempt to summarize all the links in a particular subject area. If you can find one in your area of interest, you will find it very helpful.

- **Most Popular Links** What everyone is accessing, largely because people read pages like this to find out what everyone is accessing.

- **Best of the Web** What some people (or more likely, one person) think the best hyperlinks are—a cyberspace Top Ten.

- **Cool Links** I'm not sure what the difference between "Best" and "Cool" is, but see for yourself by checking out these pages. Be prepared to waste at least five hours.

- **Worst of the Web** A relatively new and praiseworthy development, these pages list sites singled out for wasting Internet bandwidth with unnecessary junk (such as a list of some guy's T-shirts). I just hope my home page doesn't wind up on it.

- **Weird Links** Compilations of links to the Web underground. Forget sex, incidentally; there are too many dateless geeks out there looking for sex sites. When one appears, it gets inundated with several million accesses per day, which overloads the server and brings the computer to a halt. The service provider screams bloody murder, and the site gets shut down. A *Sports Illustrated* swimsuit site made a brief appearance, but after getting 7.2 million accesses in the space of 48 hours, it was withdrawn.

- **What's New** These resources try to keep track of the deluge of new Web documents.

STARTING POINTS PAGES

Starting points pages stem from the ancient past (maybe a year ago) when the World Wide Web was completely unfamiliar to people. Created by organizations such as the European Center for Particle Physics (CERN) and the National Center for Supercomputer Applications (NCSA), they provide a good point of entry for people accessing the Web for the first time. They include lots of links that introduce you to fundamental Web concepts, such as "What is a browser?" You'll also find links to subject trees, search engines, USENET FAQs ("Frequently Asked Questions"), Internet documents of all kinds, and What's New documents.

The World Wide Web Home Page

Does the Web have a home? Yes—according to CERN, the European Center for Particle Physics, it's located in Geneva, Switzerland. (The acronym CERN, incidentally, stands for the Center's name in French.) This isn't mere arrogance; CERN is actually the birthplace of the World Wide Web, which got its start in 1989 as an information system for physics researchers. To access the General Overview of the Web page, use this URL:

    http://www.w3.org/hypertext/DataSources/Top.html

The CERN home page's main claim to fame is the link to the Virtual Library, discussed in the next chapter. Apart from that, it's a bit of a yawner, although the By Service Type link takes you to a useful list of Internet resources accessible throughout the Web.

National Center for Supercomputing Applications Starting Points Page

The National Center for Supercomputing Applications (NCSA), located in Urbana-Champaign, Illinois, is the birthplace of Mosaic, the graphical browser that launched the Web into the big time. Its starting points document (Figure 9.1) is still one of the best. What's available here? You'll find a lot of information about the World Wide Web—its history, development, and future. Here's the URL:

    http://www.ncsa.uiuc.edu/SDG/Software/Mosaic/StartingPoints/
    NetworkStartingPoints.html

The Planet Earth Home Page

The Planet Earth Home Page (Figure 9.2) is arguably the Web's best starting point. It's loaded with basic information about the Web and the Internet, pointers to information resources, and much, much more. Here's the URL:

    http://white.nosc.mil:80/future_pc.html

The Planet Earth Home Page (PEHP) is the work of Richard P. Bocker, a physicist at the Naval Command, Control and Ocean Surveillance Center in San Diego, California. PEHP doesn't attempt to provide a comprehensive subject tree, like the ones discussed in the next chapter. It's just a wonderful

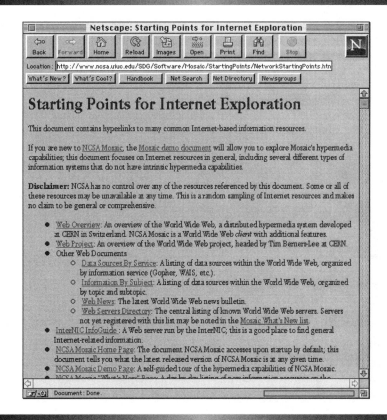

Figure 9.1   NCSA's Starting Points document

place to start your exploration of the Web—but do bear in mind that it's getting a bit long in the tooth; there are few signs of recent updates.

PEHP's offerings are organized into categories, which you select by clicking one of the on-screen buttons. After you do, you'll see additional pages crammed with graphics, URLs, and links to other resource-crammed pages. Explore—and have fun!

When you click one of PEHP's panels, you may see additional PEHP pages, or you may be transported directly to a distant site. You can also search PEHP by typing one or more words in the Search box and clicking the Search button. If PEHP finds any matches, you'll see a new page listing the documents that contain the words you typed.

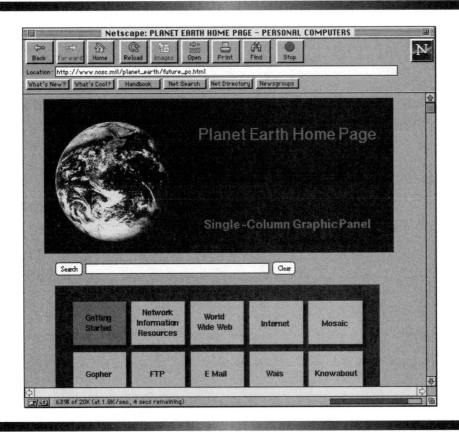

Figure 9.2   Planet Earth Home Page

John S. Makulowich's Awesome List

An Internet trainer, John Makulowich has assembled a list of what he calls "the glory and grandeur of the Internet, the sine qua non of Cyberspace, the main characters in the evolving drama ...," with special focus on the needs of journalists, trainers, and first-time Web users. Distilled down to the best of the Web, it's an excellent starting points document (Figure 9.3). Here's the URL:

http://www.clark.net/pub/journalism/awesome.html

The Awesome List contains lots of very useful URLs, and I'll bet it keeps you busy for a while. But its organization leaves a lot to be desired: The

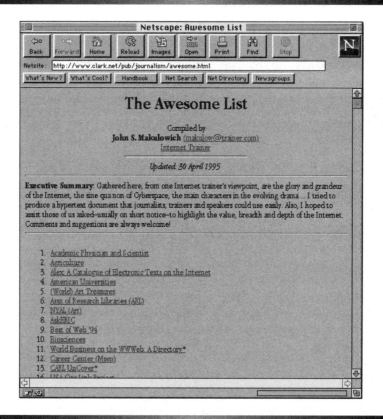

Figure 9.3   The Awesome List

numbers aren't really necessary, for instance, since the list is alphabetized. John, how about breaking the list down into categories?

John's Monster Hotlist

John's Monster Hotlist incorporates an unusual, innovative interface: You click on one of the upper-case headings located at the bottom of the screen, and the pertinent hotlist items appear at the top. The verdict? Not very artsy, but easy to use and packed with great information. Here's the URL:

http://wx.atmos.uiuc.edu/kemp/hotlist/INDEX.html

Internet Points of Interest

Maintained by Tony Sanders, this page (Figure 9.4) is what NCSA and CERN should be offering. It's an excellent list of essential introductory hyperlinks, including navigation catalogs, guides, general interest sites (including reference sources, on-line magazines, and Web storefronts), and Internet documentation resources. Here's the URL:

> http://www.bsdi.com/points-of-interest.html

More Starting Points Documents

Still looking for the perfect starting points document? Here are a few to try:

- **Spry City** (http://www.spry.com/sp_city/sp_city.html)   The home page of Spry, Inc., the makers of Air Mosaic. Lots of art, travel, computer dealers, education stuff, government links, and sports.

- **John December's Internet Index** (http://www.rpi.edu/~decemj/ index.html)   Lots of useful Internet information focusing on the analysis of computer-mediated communication. Lots of stuff focusing on John, too.

- **Special Internet Connections** (http://www.uwm.edu/Mirror/ inet.services.html)   Scott Yanoff's excellent starting points document; on its way to becoming a subject tree!

- **WWW Power Index**(http://www.webcom.com/power/ index.html)   A nice starting points selection: WWW information, pointers to search tools and subject indexes, and links to great sites in fields such as art, government, and education.

 As a source of good starting points, don't forget *personal home pages*, which were introduced in Chapter 6. These are essentially hotlists (bookmark lists) that certain individuals have made accessible to the public. Here are some more great personal home pages:

- **Bazik** (http://www.cs.brown.edu/people/jsb/hotlist.html) Lots of stuff on commercial sites, random cool things, government sites, and lots, lots more.

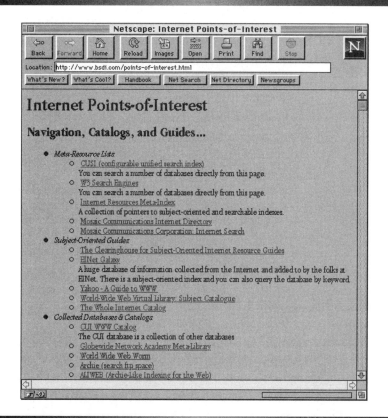

Figure 9.4   Internet Points of Interest

- **Bob** (http://www2.ncsu.edu/unity/users/a/asdamick/ www/weird.html)   The weird and the useful, with a great list of arts sites.

- **Cashman** (http://www.cs.odu.edu/~cashman/hotlist.html) Government, commercial, education sites and more, plus some fun.

- **Cybergrrl** (http://www.interport.net/~asherman/ surf.html) Music, people, good causes, and a link to Grrls on the Web; some great women's/feminist links.

- **Karen** (http://www.cs.cmu.edu:8001/afs/cs.cmu.edu/ user/kcf/www/me/newhot.html)   Very good entertainment links, plus a collection of cool home pages.

- **Lorrie** (http://dworkin.wustl.edu/pub/lorracks/ home.html)   Some good stuff on social issues facing the Internet.

- **Meng** (http://www.seas.upenn.edu/~mengwong/ meng.html)   The single most substantive page on the Web, if she does say so herself.

- **Ranjit** (http://oz.sas.upenn.edu/)   Toys for the amusement of travelers on the Information Superhighway.

- **Softlord** (http://www.interport.net/~softlord/kewl-links.html)   An impressive effort, sorted by category and containing over 40K of hyperlinks.

TRAILBLAZER PAGES

Chapter 6 introduced what I call *trailblazer pages*, which seek to sum up all the hyperlinks pertaining to a particular subject. Put together by volunteers who have personal interests in the area, they are gold mines of information. The following list provides some additional examples of useful trailblazer pages (for another list, see Chapter 6). Unfortunately, there's no real index of them; nobody's even sure what to call them (some people call them "home pages," while others call them "pointers pages," and still others call them "indexes"). You can try to discover a trailblazer page in your area of interest by using the search techniques introduced in the next chapter.

- **An Index to Electronic Journals and 'Zines** (http:// www.acns.nwu.edu/ezines/)

- **Backcountry Home Page** (http://io.datasys.swri.edu/Overview.html) Fishing, hiking, backpacking, climbing, and more.

- **Chronic Fatigue Syndrome** (http://huizen.dds.nl:80/~cfs-news/) Tons of information about this disabling disease.

- **FedWorld** (http://www.fedworld.gov/)   A very impressive list of U.S. Government Web resources.

- **Games Domain** (http://wcl-rs.bham.ac.uk/~djh/)   Everything you would ever want to know about computer games.

- **Human Languages Page** (http://www.willamette.edu/~tjones/Language-Page.html)   A treasure trove of information about human languages, past and present.

- **Legal Links on the Internet** (http://ssnet.com/~james5/business.html)   Emphasizing federal law and litigation.

- **Rockhounds Information Page**   (http://www.rahul.net/infodyn/rockhounds/rockhounds.html)   Everything on the Internet pertaining to rock collecting.

- **Science Fiction Links** (http://www.abdn.ac.uk/~u01rpr/sci-fi.html)   Tons of links to Star Trek, Star Wars, and science fiction sites.

- **Television Sites** (http://www.gu.edu.au/gwis/cinemedia/CineMedia.tv.html)   Grand Central Station for TV-related hyperlinks on the Web.

- **The Froggy Page** (http://www.cs.yale.edu/HTML/YALE/CS/HyPlans/loosemore-sandra/froggy.html)   An unbelievable assortment of frog-related items: pictures, songs, sounds, links to scientific studies, lists of famous frogs. Wow!

- **The Web as a Learning Tool** (http://www.cs.uidaho.edu/~connie/interests.html)   A very nice effort to bring together Web resources for K–12 education.

- **Ultimate Band List** (http://american.recordings.com/wwwofmusic/)   Links to all the rock bands—over 1200 of them—represented on the Web.

- **Wine Home Page** (http://augustus.csscr.washington.edu/personal/bigstar-mosaic/wine.html)   Dozens of links concerning wines, wineries, wine collecting, and wine accessories.

- **WWW Tennis Server** (http://www.cdf.toronto.edu/DCS/FUN/tennis.html)   Get the pun? Everything for the tennis fan, including ATP and WTA rankings, the code of tennis, and lots of tennis-related hyperlinks.

By far the best resource for subject-oriented trailblazer pages is the Virtual Library, a subject tree that is actually a compilation of volunteers' trailblazer pages. For more information on the Virtual Library, check out the next chapter.

WHAT'S POPULAR

Want to know what *everyone else* is doing with their Web browsers? Here's how to find out:

- **Most Popular Links at EINet Galaxy** (http://galaxy.einet.net/most-popular.html)   EINet Galaxy is a subject tree/search engine hybrid, to be discussed in the next chapter. This page links the most popular sites directly accessed from Galaxy.

- **The Top Ten Most Popular Fields in the Virtual Library** (http://info.cern.ch/hypertext/DataSources/bySubject/TopTen.html)   The Virtual Library is a subject-classified collection of metapages, put together by individual volunteers. Here's a list of the most popular subjects in the Virtual Library, which will be discussed in the next chapter.

- **The WebCrawler Top 25** (http://webcrawler.cs.washington.edu/WebCrawler/Top25.html)   The top 25 most popular pages accessed by means of the WebCrawler search engine, discussed in Chapter 10.

- **The Whole Internet Catalog Top 25** (http://nearnet.gnn.com/wic/top.toc.html)   The most popular sites in the Whole Internet Catalog's subject tree (discussed in Chapter 10).

- **Yahoo What's Popular** (http://www.yahoo.com/popular.html)   The most popular sites accessed from the Yahoo subject tree, also discussed in Chapter 10.

BEST OF THE WEB

What are the best sites available on the Web? Everyone has an opinion, but some have pages:

- **Best Commercial Sites on the Web** (http://www.pcweek.ziff.com/~pcweek/best_comm_sites.html)   Another award-bestowing effort from *PC Week*.

- **Best Home Pages** (http://www.ziff.com/~pcweek/best_homes.html) *PC Week's* line-up of the cool, the useful, and the truly puzzling.

- **Best of the British Web Page** (http://www.demon.co.uk/pcw/bob.html) Best sites in the U.K.

- **Best of the Web Contest** (http://wings.buffalo.edu/contest/)

- **Best Webs of the World** (http://www.sct.fr/net/ubest.html) A French view, and a nice, succinct list.

COOL LINKS

Frankly, I'm not sure what differentiates a "best" site from a "cool" site. You figure it out, and e-mail me (bp@virginia.edu), and I'll give you credit in the next edition. In the meantime, you're going to enjoy these pages:

- **Cool Site of the Day** (http://www.infi.net/cool.html) Glenn Davis selects a new site every day for this coveted distinction. You can browse a voluminous list of previous cool sites.

- **Creme de la Superhighway** (http://www.webcom.com/~ecola/megalist.html)

- **What's Cool** (http://home.netscape.com/home/whats-cool.html) At least according to Mozilla. I think this is verging on the "Best of the Web" territory. Or maybe it's a gallery of Netscape's business partners?

- **Yahoo Cool Links** (http://www.yahoo.com/Entertainment/COOL_links/) Definitely cool.

- **What's Hot and Cool on the Web** (http://kzsu.stanford.edu/uwi/reviews-l.html)

- **Webaholic's Top 50 List** (http://www.ohiou.edu/~rbarrett/webaholics/favlinks/entries.html) For the truly addicted.

WORST OF THE WEB

It had to happen. With all those "Best of the Web" pages, *somebody*, somewhere, would have had to come up with this idea.

- **Mirsky's Worst of the Web** (http://turnpike.net/metro/mirsky/
  Worst.html)   This is the worst worst-Web site.

- **Useless Web Pages** (http://www.primus.com/staff/paulp/
  useless.html)   This is actually one of the Web's best sites. With
  additions made on a daily basis, you'll find plenty of hysterically
  funny stuff here. Latest editions: A penis length chart, a dissertation
  on barbecue potato chips, and a shocking exposé of the lesbian Bar-
  bie doll scene.

- **Enhanced for Netscape Hall of Shame** (http://www.cs.dart-
  mouth.edu/~cowen/netscape.html)   Too many blinks spoil the
  broth.

WEIRD LINKS

It's the fringe. The edge. And if you're looking for it, here are the starting
points:

- **Anders' Weird Page** (http://www.nada.kth.se/~nv91-asa/
  weird.html)   Discordiana, very substantial collection of links to the
  Church of the Subgenius, Geek-related mysteries, and more; you figure it out, you let me know, OK?

- **Hyper-Weirdness by World Wide Web** (http://phenom.phys-
  ics.wisc.edu/~shalizi/hyper-weird/0.1.html)   An impressive compilation of weird links, spanning the gamut from fringe religions to
  weird science and unbelievable technology.

- **Justin's Links from the Underground** (http://raptor.sccs.swarth-
  more.edu/jahall/index.html)   The Lascivious Lurker's list of links,
  or as the Duke says, "When the going gets weird, the weird turn
  pro."

- **The Web's Edge** (http://kzsu.stanford.edu/uwi.html)   This is apparently the leading edge of some kind of worldwide conspiracy.

WHAT'S NEW PAGES

As if there weren't enough stuff on the Web to wade through, there are dozens—possibly hundreds—of new Web documents created daily. Here's how you can find out what's new:

- **Automatic News HREFs** (http://www.cs.cmu.edu/afs/cs.cmu.edu/user/bsy/www/auto_news/auto_news.0.html)   URLs culled automatically from USENET postings.

- **Global Network Navigator What's New** (http://nearnet.gnn.com/wic/nunu.toc.html)   GNN is a subject tree, to be discussed in the next chapter; this page lists the links that have been added recently to the subject index.

- **NCSA's What's New** (http://www.ncsa.uiuc.edu/SDG/Software/Mosaic/Docs/whats-new.html)   Probably the best What's New resource. Includes a Pick of the Week.

- **What's New** (http://home.netscape.com/home/whats-new.html)   Mozilla's very own list. Just click the "What's New" button on Netscape's button bar.

FROM HERE

- Take advantage of subject trees and search engines to find information on the Web. Both subjects are covered in the next chapter.

- Manage those Web documents—print 'em, save 'em, and cache 'em. Find out how (and what *cache* means) in Chapter 11.

- Put those helper applications to work! Chapter 12 documents all the multimedia helper applications included with this book.

Chapter
10

Using Subject Trees and Search Engines

L ooking for information on the Web? Let's start with the bad news. No single, up-to-date catalog of Web documents has ever been created. To do so would require a staff of hundreds of subject indexers working 'round the clock. Perhaps we'll see a Web Library someday, a service that would exhaustively catalog everything that's on the Web, but nothing like it exists right now.

 Now here's the good news. To find information on the Web, you can make use of the following tools:

- **Subject Trees**   A *subject tree* is an alphabetically organized list of *selected* Web resources, which is usually organized with major headings such as Arts and

Humanities, Business, Economy, Government, and the like. Within each category are found subheadings, which in turn display pages listing specific hyperlinks. Because subject trees are manually updated, they cannot hope to cover all of the Web—these services aren't the Web Library, or anything close. But they are very useful because they are selective; they list only those documents that would likely prove useful to you.

- **Search Engines**   A *search engine* enables you to search a database of Web documents using key words (such as "frogs" or "wine"). The search engine ransacks a database of Web documents. Where does this database come from? In most cases, the databases are created by Web-roaming programs called *spiders*. These programs seek out new URLs and add them to the database. Searching one of these search engines will very likely produce a lot of useless, junk URLs, but you may find some gold amidst the gravel.

This chapter shows you how to construct an effective Web search using Netscape, subject trees, and search engines. If it's out there, you'll know how to find it after reading this chapter.

For the Time-Challenged

◆ Subject trees try to classify Web documents according to subject. You can browse the subject tree. You can also search the subject headings and document titles. But bear in mind that subject trees classify only a small percentage of the total number of documents available on the Web.

◆ Search engines compile huge databases of Web documents, and you can search the databases using key words. The trouble is, you'll retrieve a lot of junk amidst the useful documents.

◆ A good search strategy uses both subject trees and search engines. To make sure you've found all the useful documents in a given subject area, you should repeat your search in several subject trees and search engines.

UNDERSTANDING SEARCH TECHNIQUES

In both subject trees and search engines, you can make use of key-word searches. In subject trees, you search the subject tree entries. In search engines, you search a huge database of URLs. In either case, you will find it helpful to understand a few basic concepts:

- **Choosing Key Words**   Try to think of one or more words that best describe the subject you're searching for. The more general the term, the more likely it is that you'll find something useful.

- **Choosing Portions of the Document to Search**   Some of the search tools discussed in this chapter let you specify which part of the document to search. For example, Yahoo enables you to search the document title, the URL, and the document description. It searches all three by default. You can perform a more focused search by restricting the search to the document title. This will eliminate irrelevant documents that just happen to include the key word in their descriptions.

- **Case Sensitivity**   Most of the search tools discussed in this chapter are *case-insensitive*, which means that they ignore the capitalization pattern you type. However, some offer the option of case-sensitive searching. If you choose this option, the search tool will match only those documents containing key words with the capitalization pattern you typed (if you type "MRI," the software will match "MRI" but not "mri").

- **AND Operator**   Most of the search tools you use will use the Boolean AND operator by default. If you type more than one key word, the software will not retrieve a document unless it contains *all* of the words you type. This is a very restrictive search and may not produce good results. However, it's a good approach when your initial search produces too many documents.

- **OR Operator**   Some search tools enable you to use the Boolean OR operator. If you type more than one key word, the software will retrieve documents that contain *any* of the words you typed.

- **Contiguous Strings**   A few search tools let you specify that the software should match the key words you type *only* if they occur in the precise order you typed them, with no intervening words. For example, if you type "Mesoamerican archaeology," the software will retrieve only those documents that contain these two words in this exact order, without any other words between them.

- **Substrings and Whole-Word Searches**   By default, most of the search tools discussed in this chapter search for *substrings*. A substring is a series of characters that might be embedded in a longer word. For example, if you search with the substring "very," the software will retrieve documents that contain "every" as well as "very." To restrict the search to whole words only ("very" only), you can sometimes choose a "whole word" or "complete word" option. If you choose this option, the search software will not retrieve documents in which the key word appears as a substring.

If the search doesn't produce any results, click the Back button to redisplay the search page, and check your spelling! This is the most common cause of search errors. If the search retrieves too many documents, try using more specific key words—and be sure to use the AND rather than the OR operator. To cut down on false drops, use whole-word searches instead of substring searches.

A GUIDE TO THE WEB'S SUBJECT TREES

There are several excellent subject trees available on the World Wide Web. Each has its own plusses and minuses, as you'll see in the pages to follow. We'll survey the top four: Yahoo, the Virtual Library, EINet Galaxy, and the Whole Internet Catalog.

Yahoo

Yahoo—short for Yet Another Hierarchically Officious Oracle—is the work of David Filo and Jerry Chih-Yuan Yang of Stanford University. Not overly academic, it's the best place to start your quest for Web information.

To access Yahoo, just click the Net Directory button, and click the Yahoo hyperlink. You'll see the Yahoo page, shown in Figure 10.1. Listed are Yahoo's main subject classifications (see Table 10.1), followed by the number of hyperlinks in each category. The word "new" signals categories to which new hyperlinks have been added.

Listing over 40,000 documents (at this writing), Yahoo offers a rich library of hyperlinks. To explore them, you can use two techniques, exploring the tree and searching.

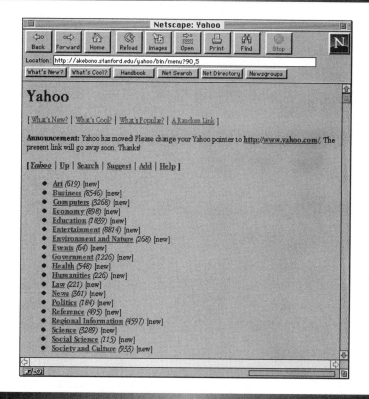

Figure 10.1   Yahoo

Table 10.1   Yahoo Subject Classifications

Art (770)	Humanities (283)
Business (9888)	Law (254)
Computers (3488)	News (342)
Economy (1015)	Politics (226)
Education (2004)	Reference (544)
Entertainment (10351)	Regional Information (5361)
Environment and Nature (288)	Science (3663)
Events (65)	Social Science (133)
Government (1296)	Society and Culture (1115)
Health (671)	

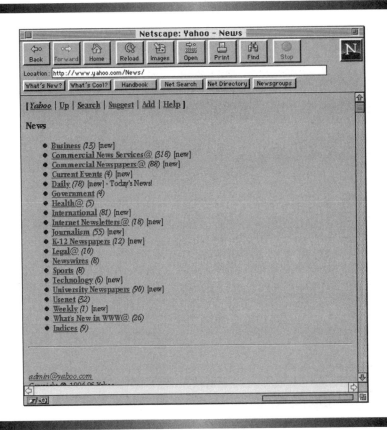

Figure 10.2   Top-level "News" category (Yahoo)

Exploring the Tree

The first way to use Yahoo is to navigate the subject tree by clicking on
hyperlinks. To do so, just click on one of the subject classifications, such as
"News." You'll see an additional page of hyperlinks, such as the one shown
in Figure 10.2. If you keep clicking, you'll eventually reach a page that
includes hyperlinks to Web documents. Unlike Yahoo's internal links, hyperlinks to Web documents aren't followed by a number, and many of them
include descriptions (see Figure 10.3). To access a hyperlink to a Web document, just click it.

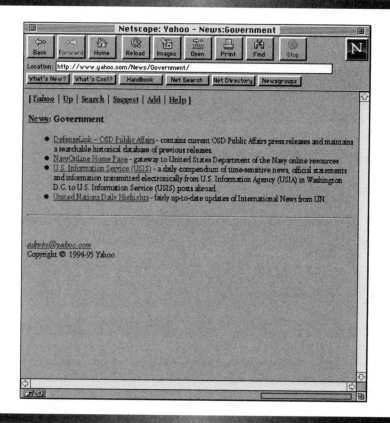

Figure 10.3 Hyperlinks and descriptions (Yahoo)

Yahoo's toolbar, positioned near the top of the screen, provides handy navigational aids. Here's what the options do:

Yahoo	Displays Yahoo's opening (top-level) page.
Up	Go up one level.
Search	Search for a document by typing key words.
Suggest	Mail your suggestions to the developers.
Add	Suggest a URL to add to Yahoo.
Help	Get help on using Yahoo.

Searching for Information

Another way to access the information in Yahoo is to perform a key-word search. To do so, click the Search button. You'll see a text box for entering key words, as shown in Figure 10.4.

Yahoo offers excellent search capabilities, allowing all of the search options discussed in "Understanding Search Techniques," earlier in this chapter. To search Yahoo, follow these steps:

1. If you don't see the Yahoo Search page, click the Search button. It doesn't matter at which Yahoo level you are; Yahoo searches the whole database no matter where you initiate the search.

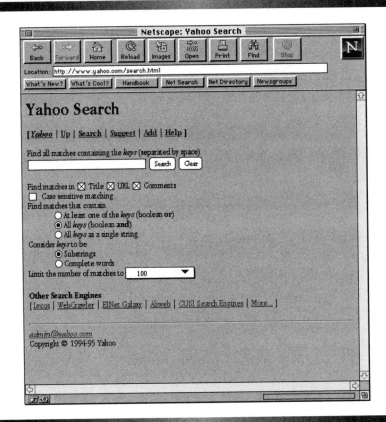

Figure 10.4 Searching Yahoo

2. In the text box, type one or more key words. Check your typing and spelling carefully.

3. If you would like to restrict the search to titles, URLs, or comments, use the check boxes in the Find Matches area. By default, Yahoo searches all three areas.

4. To match the capitalization you typed, click Case sensitive matching.

5. To perform a Boolean search, click the OR or AND button.

6. To perform a contiguous string search, click All keys as a single string.

7. To perform a whole-word search, click Complete words.

8. To specify the number of matches, choose a number next to Limit the number of matches.

9. To initiate the search, click Search.

The result of a Yahoo search is a list of Yahoo entries that match your key words (see Figure 10.5)—or, if there aren't any matches, a message that no match was found. You can browse the list and click the links as you please. To redo the search, click the Back button. Click the Clear button to clear the previous search and try again.

The Virtual Library

A center for particle physics research located in Geneva, Switzerland, CERN is the birthplace of the World Wide Web. Among its many contributions to the Web is the Virtual Library, one of the first subject trees to be developed and still one of the most useful and comprehensive.

Unlike Yahoo, whose administrators take upon themselves the arduous task of adding new URLS to the subject tree, the Virtual Library is a *distributed subject tree*. The Virtual Library's links (see Figure 10.6) are to pages maintained by individuals, who have been chosen to maintain only the page for which they are responsible. Many of the Virtual Library's pages got their start as trailblazer pages. They were incorporated into the Virtual Library after it became obvious that they had succeeded in achieving the most comprehensive collection of links in a given area.

You can browse the list of subject headings in numerous ways. The default list is more compact and somewhat easier to browse. If you click the

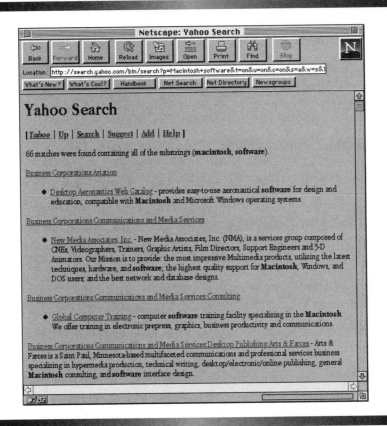

Figure 10.5 Results of a Yahoo search

Category Subtree hyperlink, you see a lengthier list of subject headings and subheadings. The Category Subtree gives you more of a sense of the riches stored within the Virtual Library's hyperlinks. In addition, you can display the subject headings according to Library of Congress subject classifications (to do so, click the Library of Congress Classification hyperlink). Alternative listings include Statistics, which orders subject fields according to their popularity, and Service Type, which orders the Library's resources by type of service (Web servers, Gopher, WAIS databases, etc.).

To access the Virtual Library, just click the Virtual Library icon in this book's home page (HOME.HTML), or use the following URL:

http://info.cern.ch/hypertext/DataSources/bySubject/Overview.html

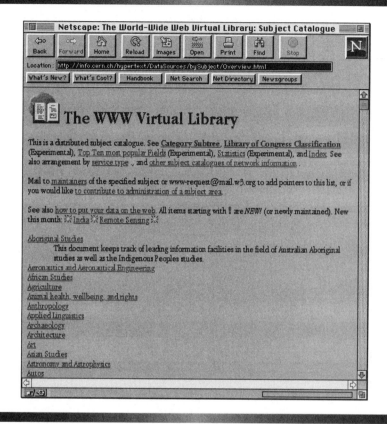

Figure 10.6 Top-level page of the Virtual Library

To access one of the pages in the Virtual Library, just click one of the subject hyperlinks. Figure 10.7 shows the African Studies page, which is maintained by the Schomburg Center for Research in Black Culture at the New York Public Library.

Like Yahoo, the Virtual Library can be searched, but the search is far more comprehensive: It searches not only the Virtual Library, but also the entire CUI W3 Catalog, a huge database that is automatically compiled by searching a number of What's New pages (see Chapter 9). To search the Virtual Library, follow these steps:

1. From the Virtual Library top-level page, click the Index hyperlink. You see the CUI W3 Catalog search page, shown in Figure 10.8.

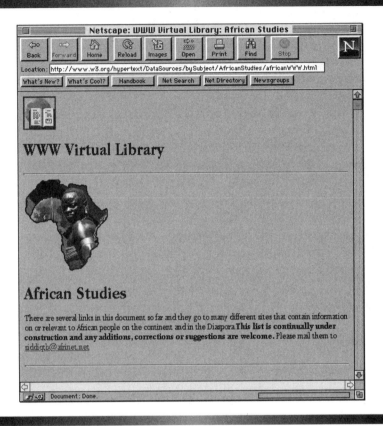

Figure 10.7   African Studies page (Virtual Library)

2. In the text box, type the key word or words to search for. By default, this search page is case-insensitive. If you enter more than one word, the search employs a Boolean AND (no document will be retrieved unless it contains *all* of the words you typed).

3. Click the Submit button. You'll see a list containing What's New and other items.

It says "Enter a PERL regular expression"! What's PERL?   You will frequently see this prompt when you are about to type key words for searching. PERL is short for

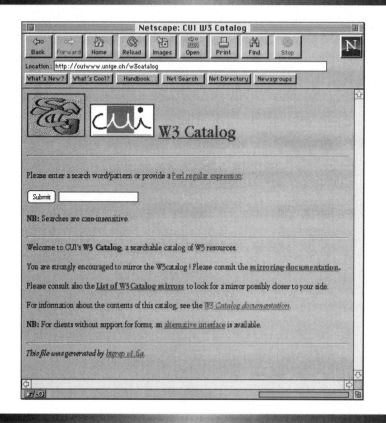

Figure 10.8 CUI W3 Catalog search page

Practical Extraction and Report Language. Developed by Larry Wall of Netlabs, it is a freely available scripting language designed for use on UNIX computers.

The Whole Internet Catalog

One of the most impressive publishing phenomena of the 1990s was the success of Ed Krol's *The Whole Internet*, published by O'Reilly & Associates. Formerly a sleepy, strictly low-volume publisher of obscure books on obscure UNIX topics, O'Reilly hit the jackpot with Krol's excellent book. The revenue led to all sorts of ventures, and the Whole Internet Catalog—based on the useful appendix included in Krol's book—is one of them. Now there's an on-line version (Figure 10.9) and you'll certainly want to make it part of your document-hunting strategy.

Like Yahoo, the Whole Internet Catalog is maintained manually, but the Catalog's staff doesn't even try to put in thousands of links. On the boundary between a starting points resource and a subject tree, the Catalog offers only about 1,000 links—but they're *good* links (Table 10.2).

To access the Whole Internet Catalog, just click the hyperlink in HOME.HTML, or use this URL:

> http://nearnet.gnn.com/gnn/wic/index.html

Solutions

PERL Search Tricks

CUI W3's search facilities seem primitive in comparison to Yahoo's: If you type more than one word, for instance, they're ANDed together. Moreover, only a substring search is permitted—apparently. But let us peer more deeply into the inner recesses of PERL.

To perform an OR search, so that the search software will match records that contain *any* of the words you type, separate the key words with vertical line characters, as follows:

> Asia|Africa

This expression will retrieve any records that mention either Asia or Africa, or both.

To perform a whole-word search, surround the word with \b commands, as follows:

> \bsex\b

This expression will retrieve "sex," but not "sexy," "sexuality," "asexual," or any other word in which "sex" is a substring.

You can use these techniques on any search page where you see the note "Enter a regular expression."

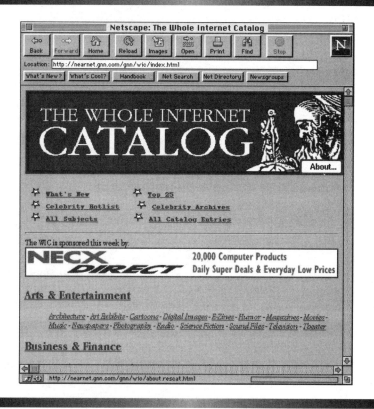

Figure 10.9 Whole Internet Catalog

Table 10.2 Whole Internet Catalog Subject Classifications

Arts and Entertainment
Art Galleries and Exhibits
Cartoons
Computer and Electronic Art
Dance
Electronic Magazines
Movies
Music
Science Fiction
Television
Theater

Business and Finance
Agriculture
Career and Employment
Entrepreneurship and Small Business
Government Information
Internet Commerce
Investment Management
Nonprofits
Personal Finance
Real Estate

Table 10.2 *Continued*

Computers
Artificial Intelligence
Computer Science
Dictionaries
Hardware
Publishing and Multimedia
Software
UNIX
Virtual Reality

Education
Dictionaries and Reference Guides
Educational Technology
Financial Aid
Government Information
Higher Education
Libraries
Teaching

Government
Executive Branch
Indexes to U.S. Government Resources
Foreign and International Government
Judicial Branch
Legislative Branch
State and Local Government
U.S. Agencies

Health and Medicine
Alternative Medicine
Cancer
Disability
Family Medicine
Health Care Policy
Nutrition
Professional Medicine
Safe Sex
Substance Abuse
U.S. and International Health Organizations
Veterinary Medicine

Humanities
Classics
Languages
Literature
Online Book Collections

Humanities (*cont.*)
Philosophy
Religion and Belief

Internet
Community Networks
HTML
Internet User Guides
Netiquette, Ethics, and AUPs
Resource Indexes
Search the Internet
Security
Standards and Technology
USENET
White Pages

Recreation, Sports, and Hobbies
Cooking
Food and Drink
Games
Gardening
Genealogy
Hobbies and Crafts
Outdoor Recreation
Pets
Sailing and Surfing
Spectator Sports
Sports and Fitness

Science and Technology
Aeronautics and Astronautics
Astronomy
Aviation
Biology
Botany
Chemistry
Engineering
Environmental Studies
Geography
Geology
Mathematics
Oceanography
Ornithology
Paleontology
Physics

Table 10.2 *Continued*

Science and Technology (*cont.*)	**Social Sciences** (*cont.*)
Psychology	History
Technology	Law
Transfer	Lesbian and Gay Studies
Weather and Meteorology	Politics and Political Activism
	Sociology
Social Sciences	Women's Studies
Anthropology	
Archaeology	**Travel and Culture**
Black and African Studies	Regional and Cultural Interest
Economics	Travel

To access one of the Catalog's subject pages, just click the hyperlink. You'll see a page such as the one shown in Figure 10.10.

 Look for those "INDEX" tags next to items in the Catalog's lists. They're what we call *trailblazer pages*—comprehensive collections of hyperlinks on a subject. You'll find these pages incredibly useful for finding high-quality documents!

SEARCH ENGINES

With more than three million documents on the Web and hundreds more arriving daily, there's no chance that Yahoo, the Virtual Library, or the Whole Internet Catalog can keep up. That's why your search strategy should include search engines.

Most search engines are based on robot-like programs called *spiders* (also called *worms*), which roam the Web looking for new URLs. Most of them do little more than catalog the words in the URL and the document's title and move on. Some spiders index the first few dozen words in the document itself, and a few index all the words in the entire document.

There's a tradeoff here. If the spider indexes only the title and words in the URL, it can index a lot of documents—the search goes quickly. But don't expect good results from your search. Web authors don't give much thought to their document titles, unfortunately, and URL words may have little or nothing to do with the document's content. Searching the database created by such a spider is sure to produce a lot of *false drops*, documents

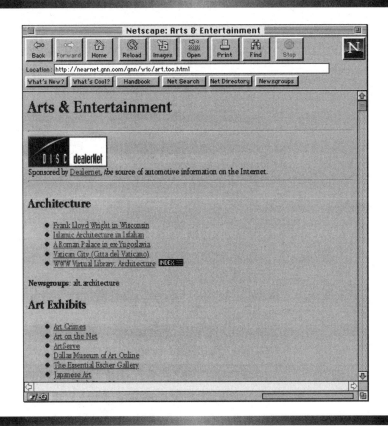

Figure 10.10 Arts and Entertainment page (Whole Internet Catalog)

that aren't relevant to your interests. On the other hand, if the spider indexes the full text of the document, don't expect the database to include more than a few hundred thousand documents—the search takes a long time. However, searching the database produces better results. Now that you know about this tradeoff, you can make a more informed choice among the various search engines that are available.

Some search engines (such as ALIWEB and DA-CLOD) do not rely on spiders. Instead, they search the contents of What's New pages, or use the submissions of Web authors. These search engines do not have voluminous databases, but they can search the document descriptions provided by the document's authors themselves. Generally, they produce useful results, although they may miss many relevant documents that were not reported through the What's New channels.

ALIWEB

ALIWEB (http://web.nexor.co.uk/public/aliweb/doc/search.html) relies on submissions from Web authors. As an incentive, all submissions to ALIWEB are automatically entered into the CUI W3 server, discussed earlier in this chapter. An ALIWEB search (Figure 10.11) provides many options that enable you to tailor the search to your needs.

To search ALIWEB:

1. In the ALIWEB search screen, type the key word or words in the Search Term(s) box.

2. If you wish, choose one or more of the following options:

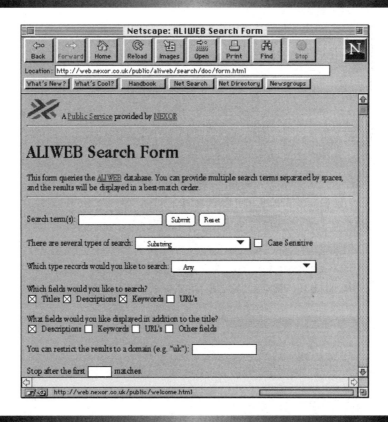

Figure 10.11 ALIWEB

By default, ALIWEB performs a substring search. To perform a whole-word search, choose this option in the text box next to "There are several types of search:".

By default, ALIWEB performs a case-insensitive search. To match the pattern of capitalization you typed, click the Case Sensitive check box.

To restrict the search to just one of the types of data records in ALIWEB, choose an option in the list box next to "What type records would you like to search:".

To restrict the fields on which ALIWEB searches, deselect one of the options below "Which fields would you like to search?"

To specify which fields you would like displayed in the search results, click one or more of the options below "What fields would you like displayed in addition to the title?"

To restrict the search to a certain Internet domain (such as com, edu, ca, or uk), type the domain name in the box next to "You can restrict the results to a domain".

To restrict the number of documents displayed, type a number in the box next to "Stop after the first... matches."

3. Click the Submit button to initiate the search.

The result of an ALIWEB search is a page of hyperlinks and document descriptions, if any were found that match your search interests. Just click one of them to jump to a document that looks interesting.

DA-CLOD

Short for "Distributedly Administered Categorical List Of Documents," DA-CLOD (http://schiller.wustl.edu/DACLOD/daclod) resembles ALIWEB in that users may add entries. But DA-CLOD does this much more directly than ALIWEB; there's no screening process whatsoever. As a result, DA-CLOD contains more than its share of the eccentric, the weird, the tasteless, and the lascivious. At the top level, DA-CLOD presents you with a huge list of subject categories. If you're bent on contributing to DA-CLOD, you can add your own category, or use one that somebody's already established.

If you're trying to find information in DA-CLOD, you have two choices: You can browse the user-created subject tree, a rather daunting task, or you can use DA-CLOD's search engine. To search DA-CLOD, click the Search Database hyperlink; you'll see a simple Search text box. You can type just one key word. And don't try anything fancy: DA-CLOD doesn't recognize

PERL expressions. The search software performs case-insensitive substring searches only, and that's that.

Lycos

Probably the best search engine on the Web, Lycos has one huge downfall: Its popularity. Overwhelmed by its own popularity, Lycos struggles to keep up with the load—and fails. Increasingly, Web wanderers are forced to conclude that Lycos is all but useless.

That's a shame, because Lycos offers by far the largest database of Web documents—more than 2.5 million, at this writing. Named after a particularly quick and agile ground spider, Lycos indexes the document's title, the headings and subheadings, the hyperlinks, the 100 most commonly used words in the document, all the words in the first 20 lines of text, and more. If you're really serious about finding information on the Web, it might be worth getting up in the middle of the night to access Lycos. Unfortunately, that's what it may take.

To access Lycos, just click the hyperlink on HOME.HTML, or use this URL:

> http://query1.lycos.cs.cmu.edu/cgi-bin/pursuit

You'll see a search form like the one shown in Figure 10.12. By default, Lycos performs a case-insensitive substring search.

To search Lycos:

1. Next to "Query," type one or more key words.

2. If you wish, search with one of these options:

    To exclude documents containing an unwanted word, type a minus sign followed by the word. For example, suppose you're interested in X Window software and you don't want to see documents about Microsoft Windows. Type the following key words: X Window –Microsoft.

    To perform a whole-word search, type a period after the key word (for example, "cat." retrieves "cat" but not "caterpillar," etc.).

3. To initiate the search, click Start search.

The results of your Lycos search appear in a new window (Figure 10.13), unless the server is too busy (an all-too-frequent result, I fear). You see your key words, plus a list of the words in Lycos' database that match the key

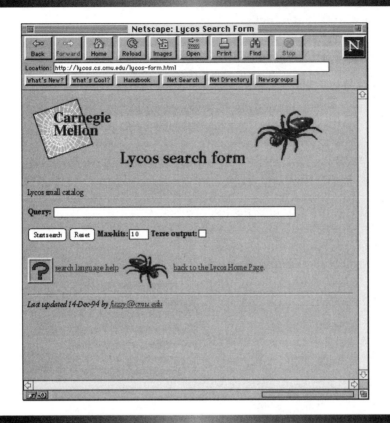

Figure 10.12 Lycos search form

words you typed. Following are the hyperlinks that Lycos retrieved, if any. Like the output of WAIS searches (see Chapter 17), Lycos ranks the output numerically: a document with the normalized score of 1,000 stands the best chance of meeting your criteria. If you find an interesting hyperlink, click it—or click the Back button to revise your search strategy.

This document's score is 1,000, but it isn't relevant to my interests! Just because a document scores 1,000 doesn't mean that it's going to contain material of interest to you. This calculation is done by mindless computers, blindly following their programming. They can't read the documents or understand the content—they can just match characters. Sometimes the result is laughably off the mark.

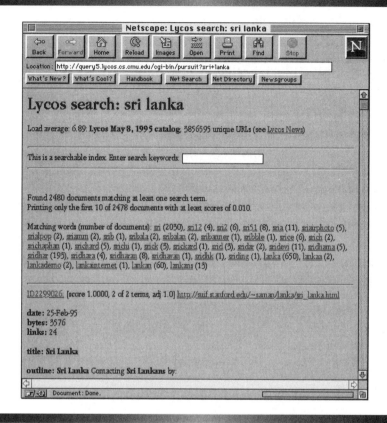

Figure 10.13 Results of a Lycos search

WebCrawler

Housed at the University of Washington, the spider-based WebCrawler doesn't have a very large database—at this writing, it indexes only 300,000 documents—but it amply compensates by indexing the full text of the document it analyzes. As such, WebCrawler is much more likely to retrieve that valuable document in which the key words appear only at the end of the document, buried deep within the document's text. Even though its database isn't very big, you should still include WebCrawler in your search. To access WebCrawler, click the hyperlink in HOME.HTML, or use the following URL:

http://webcrawler.cs.washington.edu/WebCrawler/WebQuery.html

You'll see the WebCrawler page, shown in Figure 10.14.

To search WebCrawler, follow these steps:

1. Type one or more key words in the text box.

2. If you would like to perform a Boolean OR search, deselect the "AND words together" check box.

3. If you would like to see more than 25 documents, choose a larger number next to "Number of results to return."

4. Click Search to initiate the search.

The result of your WebCrawler search is a page of hyperlinks. Like the results of a Lycos search, the documents are ranked numerically in order of relevance, with the top-scoring document (score: 1000) at the top.

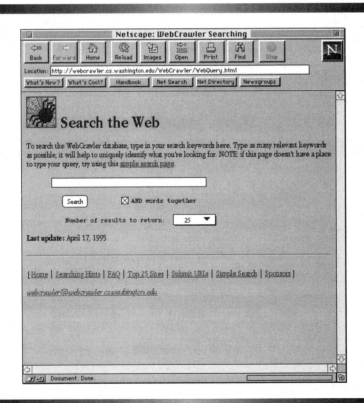

Figure 10.14 WebCrawler

THE BEST OF BOTH WORLDS: EINET GALAXY

Subject trees offer subject-classified indexes to Web resources, but they're a bear to maintain and often out of date. Search engines scour the Web and build searchable databases, but they throw huge amounts of irrelevant junk at you. To do a complete search, you need both.

That's the philosophy that underlies EINet Galaxy, one of the most impressive search services available on the Web. Galaxy was developed by the Enterprise Integration Network (EINet), a division of Microelectronics and Computer Technology Corporation. And the motivation wasn't just to provide a service to Web users: It's a prototype, supported by significant corporate funding, for a commercial information system. In the years to come, EINet Galaxy will evolve into a subject tree with both free and fee-based access; users will pay fees to access specialized versions of the database.

On first glance (Figure 10.15), Galaxy appears to be a subject tree like the Whole Internet Catalog. And it is: You can browse through the tree by clicking the subject categories (see Table 10.3). But beneath the subject tree look is a search engine of unusual breadth and power. It's capable of searching a huge database of Web documents as well as Galaxy's subject tree, all at the same time. The result is a document list that's almost certain to contain some useful information.

Table 10.3 EINet Galaxy Subject Classifications

Arts and Humanities	Community
Architecture	Charity and Community Service
Language and Literature	Consumer Issues
Performing Arts	Crime and Law Enforcement
Philosophy	Culture
Religion	Education
Visual Arts	Environment
	Family
Business and Commerce	Gender Issues
Business Administration	Health
Business General Resources	Home
Company Organization	Law
Consumer Products and Services	Liberties
Electronic Commerce	Lifestyle
General Products and Services	Networking and Communication
Investment Sources	Politics
Management	Religion
Marketing and Sales	US States

Table 10.3 *Continued*

Community (*cont.*)
Urban Life
Veteran Affairs
Workplace
World Communities

Engineering and Technology
Agriculture
Biomedical Engineering
Civil and Construction Engineering
Computer Technology
Electrical Engineering
Human Factors and Human Ecology
Manufacturing and Processing
Materials Science
Mechanical Engineering
Transportation

Government
Government Agencies
Laws and Regulations
Military
Politics
Public Affairs

Law
Administrative
Commercial
Constitutional
Criminal
Environmental
Intellectual Property
Legal Profession
Military
Personal Finance
Research
Societal
Tax

Leisure and Recreation
Amateur Radio
Beverages
Boating
Film and Video
Games

Leisure and Recreation (*cont.*)
Gardening
Humor
Music
Pets
Pictures
Radio
Reading
Recipes
Restaurants
Speleology
Sports
Television
Travel

Medicine
Community Medicine
Dentistry
Exercise
History of Medicine
Human Biology
Medical Applications and Practice
Medical Specialties
Medical Technologies
Nursing
Nutrition

Reference and Interdisciplinary Information
Census Data
Conference Announcements
Dictionaries etc.
Directories
Grants
Internet and Networking
Library Information and Catalogs
Publications

Science
Astronomy
Biology
Chemistry
Geosciences
Mathematics
Physics

Table 10.3 *Continued*

Social Sciences	History
Anthropology	Languages
Economics	Library and Information Science
Education	Psychology
Geography	Sociology

To search Galaxy, follow these steps:

1. On the toolbar at the top of the Galaxy screen (Figure 10.16), click Search. The document scrolls to the search box at the bottom of the screen.

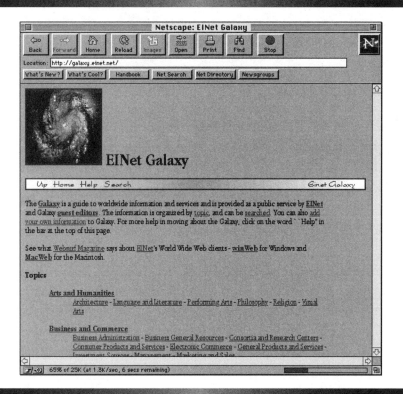

Figure 10.15 Galaxy subject tree

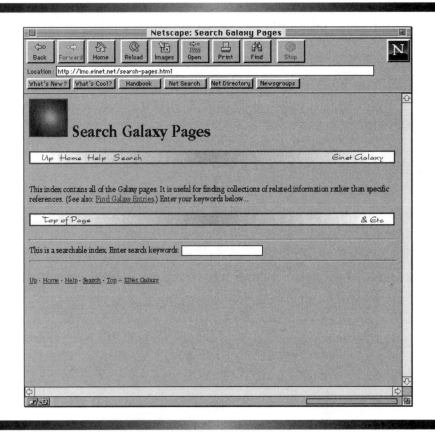

Figure 10.16   Searching EINet Galaxy

2. In the text box, type one or more key words.

3. Choose Galaxy Pages (search for Galaxy subject classification headings) or Galaxy Entries (Web documents). Normally, you'll choose Galaxy Entries to maximize the number of items you'll retrieve.

4. If you would like to search Gopher Jewels, a database of the best Gopher sites, click Gopher.

5. If you would like to search Hytelnet, a database of Telnet sites, click Hytelnet.

6. Choose World Wide Web (full-text search) if you would like to search Galaxy's full-text descriptions of Web documents, or World Wide Web Links to search the database of 100,000 URLs. The full text option searches fewer documents, but maximizes your chances of retrieving something valuable; the Links option searches more documents, but searches document titles only. Try one, then repeat the search and try the other!

7. If you would like to increase the number of hits (recommended), choose a larger number in the Hits list box.

8. Click Search to initiate the search.

The result of a Galaxy search is a new Web page. The documents are grouped into two categories, Galaxy documents and Web documents, and ranked numerically (the top-scoring document is at the top of each list). Chances are you'll find some good stuff, with a minimum of junk.

FROM HERE

• If you've gotten this far in this book, congratulations! You're a darned good Netscapist by now, and what's more, you know how to retrieve information in an orderly way. You'll be getting tons of useful documents, so you'd better learn how to cache, store, and print them—the subjects of the next chapter.

• Fire up those helper programs and dig multimedia. In Chapter 12, you'll find complete instructions for using all the helper programs included on this book's CD-ROM disc.

• What do they mean, "Access Forbidden?" Naughty, naughty! Find out what to do about this message and other Web surfing pitfalls in Chapter 14, "When the Surf Gets Rough."

Chapter
11

Managing Documents

A lthough Netscape can access almost any kind of information on the Internet, much of the information you'll be viewing is contained in World Wide Web documents. These documents are encoded with the HyperText Markup Language (HTML). Netscape decodes the HTML instructions and displays the documents on-screen, replete with fonts, in-line images, and hyperlinks to other documents as well as to hypermedia objects (such as MPEG videos). While you're viewing HTML documents with Netscape, you can search for text, save the document to your hard drive (in HTML or plain text), save in-line images to your hard drive, and print documents. To improve Netscape's handling of redisplayed documents, you can increase the size of the memory and disk caches. All these subjects are discussed in detail in this chapter—but, as the following explains, you can probably skip it or skim it.

For the Time-Challenged

♦ If you need to find text within a document you're displaying, click the Find button, type some search text, and click OK.

♦ Don't bother saving documents to your hard drive just so you can retrieve them more quickly. Netscape's disk cache does this for you automatically— *and* it saves the in-line images, too.

♦ To save an in-line image to your hard drive, hold down the mouse button and choose Save This Image As.

♦ To print the document you're currently displaying, click the Print button.

♦ To increase the size of the disk cache, open the Options menu and choose Preferences. Then select the Cache and Network options. Use the up or down arrows to change the size of the cache. Click OK to confirm.

If you already know the basics of saving and printing with the Macintosh, you might wish to skim this chapter. There's a discussion of memory and disk caches, but all you really need to know is that it's a great idea to increase their size, as long as you have sufficient room.

FINDING TEXT IN A DOCUMENT

You've just downloaded a humongous document, perhaps a USENET FAQ, and you *know* it contains something of interest to you... somewhere. Don't wear out your eyes searching the text manually; use the Find button.

To search for text in the document that's currently displayed:

1. Click the Find button, or press Command + F. You'll see the Find dialog box, shown in Figure 11.1.

2. By default, Netscape searches down in the document, and ignores capitalization. To search up, click the Find Backwards button. To

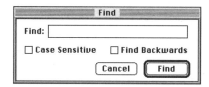

Figure 11.1   Find dialog box

match a capitalization pattern (for example, to find Robert *Frost* but not morning *frost*), click Case Sensitive.

3. In the Find box, type the text you want to match.

4. Click Find. Netscape tries to find the text you've typed. If the program finds a match, it scrolls to the text's location and highlights it.

5. To find another match, open the Edit menu and choose Find Again, or press Command + G.

SAVING DOCUMENTS

You can save any document that Netscape can display. It's easy to save documents in native HTML or plain text. But be aware that Netscape doesn't automatically save in-line images. To save a document with in-line images, you're in for some work, as the following sections explain.

Saving Documents in Plain Text

If you've downloaded a document that contains lots of interesting text that you'd like to save for future reference or use, you can save the document as plain text. With this option, Netscape removes all the HTML codes and hyperlinks.

If you just want a clean printout of the document, print it instead of saving it as plain text. Netscape's Print command produces an attractive-looking printout of the document, just as you see it on-screen—no ugly HTML codes.

To save a document as plain text:

1. From the File menu, choose Save As, or press Command + S. You'll see the Save As dialog box shown in Figure 11.2.

2. In the Format box, choose Plain Text.

3. In the folders list, choose the folder to which you would like to save the document.

4. In the Save As box, type a name for the document. Netscape suggests a name using the document's current title.

5. Click Save.

Saving Documents with HTML

The Web documents that Netscape displays are written in HTML, as you know. If you save a document in HTML format, you can reopen the document using Netscape's Open File command (File menu), and you'll see all the text formatting and hyperlinks the document contains. But you may not see the in-line graphics, as explained below.

 When should you save HTML documents? There's really only one good reason: You're learning HTML, and you want to study the HTML coding. Don't make disk copies of documents in an attempt to cut down on network retrieval delays;

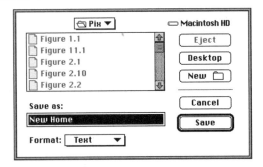

Figure 11.2   Save As dialog box

Netscape already does this job for you automatically (see "Understanding Netscape's Disk Cache" later in this chapter).

To save the document in HTML format:

1. From the File menu, choose Save As, or press Command + S. You'll see the Save As dialog box.

2. In the Format box, choose Source.

3. In the folder list, choose the folder to which you would like to save the document.

4. In the Save As box, type a name for the document. Netscape suggests a name using the document's current title.

5. Click Save.

Why don't you see in-line images when you open an HTML file you've saved? To understand, you need to know the difference between a *relative link* and an *absolute link*. A relative link displays a graphic or document that's stored in the same folder as the document; it doesn't contain any path information other than, in effect, "Look in the same folder for this." An absolute link displays a graphic or document that's stored on some other computer, and contains complete instructions on where it should be obtained.

Now let's say you download an HTML file to your Documents folder, and open the file. Almost certainly, all of the in-line images were created with relative links. Netscape goes hunting for the graphics in the Documents folder, but they're not there, so you see lots of placeholders. Web authors are loathe to use absolute links for in-line images, and for good reason: If you link to an image on somebody else's computer, what happens if that someone else decides to erase the image? Since you can't control this, it's easier and safer to use relative links for in-line images.

 Ugh! The background is black!   Did you save an HTML file that had a background? If so, the background graphic did not get saved along with the HTML document. When Netscape can't find the background graphic, you see a deep, rich black—which may appeal to some tastes, but not to mine (it's hard to read the colored text on a black background). You can try to obtain the background graphic (Netscape's server has most of the commonly used ones;

check out http://home.netscape.com/home/bg/index.html),
or you can just forget the whole thing and erase the file.

Viewing and Saving In-Line Graphics

Netscape's pop-up menu enables you to view in-line graphics in a new
Netscape document, or to save them to your hard disk, if you wish.

To view an in-line graphic:

1. Point to the graphic.

2. Hold down the mouse button until you see the pop-up menu
   shown in Figure 11.3.

3. Choose Load This Image. Netscape displays the image in a new
   document.

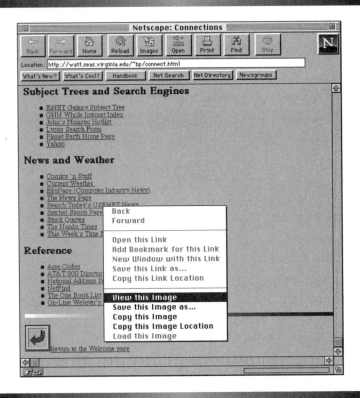

Figure 11.3   Pop-up menu for saving in-line images

To save an in-line graphic:

1. Point to the graphic.

2. Hold down the mouse button until you see the pop-up menu shown in Figure 11.3.

3. Choose Save This Image As. You'll see the Save As dialog box. Netscape has automatically placed the graphic's name in the file name box.

4. In the folder list, select the folder where you want to save the graphic.

5. Click Save.

 I can't save the background graphic! That's right. Click as hard as you might, you can't download the background graphic. If you're dead-set on getting your hands on one of these, you'll find most of them at http://home.netscape.com/ home/bg/index.html. You *can* save the versions of the background that you'll find in this document.

PRINTING DOCUMENTS

By far the best way to produce a permanent record of a Netscape-accessed document is to print it. Netscape prints all the fonts and graphics just as you see them on-screen.

Depending on your printer's capabilities, you can choose from a variety of printing options before printing. Options found in most printers include selecting the page range and the number of copies to print. After you choose your options, Netscape prints your document.

To choose print options and print your document:

1. Do one of the following:

    Click the Print button on the toolbar

    or

    From the File menu, choose Print

    or

    Press Command + P.

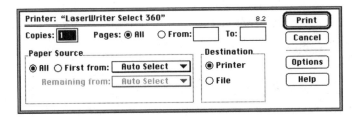

Figure 11.4   Print dialog box for LaserWriter Select 360

2. You'll see the Print dialog box, shown in Figure 11.4. Just what you'll see depends on which printer you're using.

3. If you would like to print just some of the pages in the document, select From in the Pages area, and type the beginning page number in the From box and the ending page number in the To box.

4. To make more than one copy, type the number of copies you want to make in the Copies box.

5. Choose Print to initiate printing.

UNDERSTANDING NETSCAPE'S DISK CACHE

A *cache* is a temporary storage location, like the ones thieves use to stash the loot until they get out of the pen. When you download a document, Netscape places the document in the cache. Should you wish to go back to a document you have viewed previously, Netscape locates and displays the document in the cache rather than retrieving it again from the network. Since cache retrievals are many times faster than network retrievals, this produces an impressive gain in Netscape's speed.

 Most readers of this book don't need to worry about Netscape's cache operation, which is automatic. But it's helpful to understand how cache operations work, and you may wish to increase the size of the cache, as explained in the next section.

Netscape for Macintosh employs a *disk cache*. This cache is a portion of your computer's hard disk that, like the memory cache, has been set aside for storing the most recently accessed documents. By default, Netscape sets aside 1 MB of disk space (about one million characters) for this purpose. As you retrieve additional documents, older documents are flushed from the cache. Unlike the memory cache, the disk cache retains documents between Netscape sessions. Up to one megabyte's worth of previously accessed Web documents are present on your disk, ready for fast retrieval should you access these documents again. By default, Netscape stores the cache in the Netscape Preferences folder within the System Folder—there's no reason to change this.

When Does Netscape Use the Cache?

The disk cache comes into play in the following situations:

- **When you access a visited hyperlink**   As you know, Netscape keeps track of visited hyperlinks, hyperlinks to documents that you have previously accessed. These hyperlinks appear in a distinctive color. When you access a visited hyperlink by any means (choosing a bookmark, clicking a visited hyperlink, or typing the URL directly), Netscape contacts the server and attempts to verify whether the document has been altered since its last retrieval. If the document has been altered, Netscape retrieves a new copy. If not, Netscape retrieves the document from the disk cache. By default, Netscape verifies visited hyperlinks every time you access one.

- **When you click the Back button**   If you click Back, you're returning to a document that you have accessed in the current Netscape session. For this reason, it's probable that the document has not been altered since its last retrieval, so Netscape does not contact the server to see whether the document has changed. Instead, the program retrieves the document from the memory cache or, if it has been flushed from the memory cache, from the disk cache.

 Here's a tip that may improve Netscape's performance and reduce unnecessary load on the Internet. From the Options menu, choose Preferences, and select the Cache and Network preferences. In the Check Documents area, click the Once Per Session option (the default is Every Time). With this setting, Netscape will attempt only once per session to

170　　　　　　　　　　　　　　　**Part III** • **Surfing the Web**

verify whether the document has been updated. Should you once again click this document's hyperlink or bookmark or type its URL in the same session, Netscape will retrieve the cache copy immediately, without accessing the server. This saves you time and reduces network load.

Should You Increase the Size of the Cache?

Do you have at least 50 MB of free hard disk space? Do you frequently access documents that have lots of in-line images, and redisplay them in subsequent sessions? If your answer to both these questions is "Yes," you may wish to increase the size of Netscape's disk cache. You won't notice any difference until you try to redisplay a document you accessed several weeks ago; the larger the cache, the less chance there is that this document has been flushed from the cache. If it's still in the cache, retrieval will be much faster than network retrieval, which is Netscape's only option if the document isn't present in either cache.

For information on modifying the size of the cache, see the next section.

Changing the Disk Cache Default Size

If you've decided to change the default size of the cache, follow these instructions:

1. From the Options menu, choose Preferences.

2. In the list box, choose Cache and Network. You'll see the Cache and Network preferences, shown in Figure 11.5.

3. To change the size of the disk cache, use the up or down arrows.

4. Click OK to confirm your preferences and exit.

Should You Flush the Cache?

Netscape provides a command, found in the Cache and Network dialog box, that permits you to erase (flush) the disk cache manually. There's no real reason to do this unless you suspect that, for some reason, the cache copy of a document has been corrupted by a transmission or storage error.

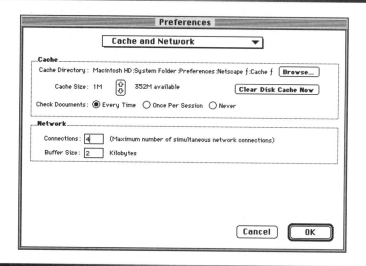

Figure 11.5 Cache and Network preferences

I've never experienced this, personally, but should it happen to you, follow these steps:

1. From the Options menu, choose Preferences.

2. In the list box, choose Cache and Network. You'll see the Cache and Network preferences, shown in Figure 11.5.

3. To flush the disk cache, click Clear Disk Cache Now. *Note:* This operation may take a few minutes.

4. Click OK.

 If you must think about security, remember that the cache contains a copy of every document you have recently accessed, up to the maximum size of the cache (1 MB by default). Anyone who knows this could sit down at your computer, open the Cache folder in the Netscape Preferences folder, and double-click the cached documents; this starts

Netscape, and—voila!—right on the screen is one of the Web documents you recently accessed. To cover your trail, be sure to flush the disk cache at the end of each session.

FROM HERE

- Now that you've learned how to manage documents, master those helper applications, as explained in Chapter 12.

- You can customize Netscape so that it works the way you want; check out Chapter 13 for the details.

- Having trouble? Chapter 14 surveys the most common error messages you'll encounter while using Netscape.

Chapter
12

Hypermedia Time!

Fire Up Those Helper Programs

Netscape can play sounds and videos, decompress files, display documents with rich on-screen formatting, and even help you navigate ancient mainframe computers via Telnet. The key lies in the helper applications you installed in Chapter 5. This chapter shows you how to listen to the sounds, view the videos, decompress files, and view richly formatted documents with the Adobe Acrobat reader.

This chapter assumes that you've installed the helper applications included on this book's CD-ROM disc, and configured Netscape to start them automatically. For information on installing these programs, see Appendix B. For information on configuring Netscape to use these programs, see Chapter 5.

For the Time-Challenged

♦ After Netscape downloads a sound, you'll see the SoundApp box and you'll hear the sound—just sit back and enjoy.

♦ After Netscape downloads a movie, you'll see the movie player. Look for a VCR-type Play button to start viewing the movie. You may wish to initiate continuous looping. Once you're finished watching the movie, exit the movie player.

♦ When you download a BinHex- or StuffIt-compressed file, StuffIt Expander starts and automatically decompresses the file.

♦ After Netscape downloads an Adobe Acrobat document, you'll see the Adobe Acrobat Reader. You can page through the document, zoom it to higher magnifications, search for text, and print, if you wish.

LISTENING TO SOUNDS

After you configure Netscape (see Chapter 5), the program automatically detects the type of sound you are downloading, and starts the appropriate player:

- Sun/NeXT (*.AU), Silicon Graphics/Apple (*.AIF, *.AIFF), Microsoft Windows (*.WAV): SoundApp

- MPEG audio (*.MP2): MPEG/CD

The following sections discuss the techniques you use to play the sound.

Playing the Sound

After you click a hyperlink containing a sound, Netscape starts the appropriate player and plays the sound. Just sit back and enjoy it!

Adjusting the Sound Volume

Normally, you adjust the sound volume by changing the volume setting on your speakers. SoundApp enables you to increase or decrease the volume of the sound by altering the disk file. This is useful if you notice that a given sound is fainter or louder than other sounds you have played.

To adjust the sound volume:

- **SoundApp** From the Sound menu, choose Volume Up or Volume Down. Alternatively, you can use the Command + Plus (+) or Command + Minus (-) keyboard shortcuts.

Saving the Sound

If you've just heard a sound that you want to save, you can do so by using the pop-up menu, as described in the following instructions.

To save the sound to a different file:

1. Display the page containing the sound hyperlink you want to save.

2. Point to the hyperlink and hold down the mouse button.

3. When the pop-up menu appears, choose Save This Link As.

4. In the dialog box, choose a folder in which to store the sound, and click Save. Netscape will download the sound to a file without playing it.

Playing a Stored Sound

Once you've saved a sound file as described in the previous section, you can play it whenever you wish.

To play a stored sound:

- **MPEG/CD** Drag the MPEG (*.mp2) sound to the MPEG CD icon, and release the mouse button.

- **SoundApp** From the File menu, choose Open, and select the sound using the Open dialog box.

 Like to find some cool sounds on the Web? Check out the "Sites With Audio Clips" trailblazer page at http://www.eecs.nwu.edu/~jmyers/other-sounds.html. The creation of Jennifer Myers, it's an awesome collection of aural resources that's sure to keep you busy for hours.

 It says "Cannot start Helper program"! You're out of memory. Close windows or quit one or more applications.

VIEWING VIDEOS AND ANIMATIONS

Most of the videos you'll find on the Web are in MPEG or QuickTime (Apple) format. Happily, Sparkle—the neat video application included with this book—can play both.

Playing the Video

After Netscape finishes downloading the video, Netscape starts the Sparkle player, and you can begin viewing the video.

> **To play the video:**   Click the Play button (the VCR-like right arrow; after you click this button it changes to a Stop button with two parallel lines).

> **To stop the video:**   Click the Stop button.

> **To play the video again:**   Drag the slider control back to the beginning of the bar, or choose Rewind to Start from the Video menu. Then click Play.

Playing the Video with Continuous Looping

When you play the movie as a continuous loop, it repeats over and over. Some movies are designed so that this produces a smooth illusion of continuous motion.

> **To play the video with continuous looping:**   From the Video menu, choose Loop, or use the Command + L keyboard shortcut.

Adjusting the Window Size

To get the best results, you should view the video using the size that you see it on-screen. However, you may wish to enlarge the video, particularly if the video seems to run too quickly. The larger the video, the slower the playback.

> **To adjust the window size:**   From the Image window, choose Grow Window (or press Command + Plus) to double the window size; choose Shrink Window (or press Command + Minus) to halve the window size.

VIEWING ADOBE ACROBAT DOCUMENTS

When you view HTML documents with Netscape, you see Netscape's interpretation of the underlying HTML tags. The formatting is simple and effective. Unfortunately, HTML does not include tags needed for more complex document formats, such as multiple-column text or footnotes.

To provide richer document formatting, some document authors prefer to encode their documents using a proprietary document format. One such format is the PostScript page description language, familiar to users of laser printers. PostScript can also generate richly formatted screen displays, but this requires a reader capable of decoding the PostScript commands. Such readers exist—GhostScript is an example—but Adobe, the originators of PostScript, has developed a set of extensions to PostScript, called Adobe Acrobat, that produce superior results on-screen. You will encounter growing numbers of Acrobat documents on the Web (for an example, see Figure 12.1), and you can read them with the Adobe Acrobat Reader software included with this book.

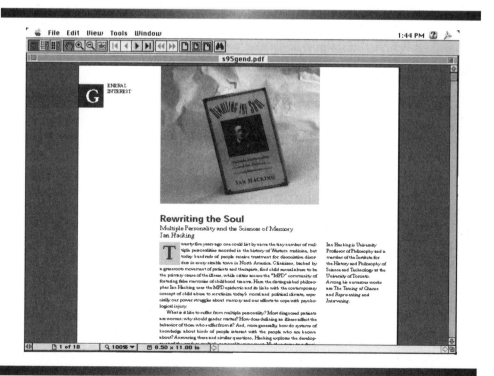

Figure 12.1 Adobe Acrobat document (Princeton University Press catalog)

When the Adobe Acrobat Reader displays a document, you will see one of the following display modes:

- **Page Only**   In this mode, the Adobe Acrobat document fills the window

- **Bookmarks and Page**   In this mode, you see a vertical list of bookmarks in the left panel of the page, with the document displayed in the right panel. These bookmarks are like hyperlinks. You can click them to display a page other than the one you are viewing. You may encounter some Acrobat documents that take advantage of this feature.

- **Thumbnails and Page**   In this mode, you see a vertical list of thumbnail (postage-stamp-sized) images of the document's pages in the left panel, while the document is displayed in the right panel. To go to one of the pages, click the thumbnail image.

You can change the display mode by using the following tools, which are located on the Reader's toolbar:

   Click this button to display the document in Page Only mode.

   Click this button to display the Bookmarks and Page view.

   Click this button to display the Thumbnails and Page view.

You can also change these options by choosing the appropriate command from the View menu.

Paging Through the Document

To page through the document, use these tools:

   Click this button to display the next page.

   Click this button to display the previous page.

Click this button to display the last page.

 Click this button to display the first page.

 Click this button to go back to the previously displayed page.

 Click this button to redisplay the page you were just viewing.

If you prefer to use the menus, you'll find paging commands on the View menu.

 Note that some Acrobat documents contain author-defined articles, which are designed so that you can page through them almost automatically. To find out whether the document has articles, open the View menu and choose Articles. You'll see a list of the articles the document contains, if any. To read an article, select it and click OK. The Reader will display the beginning of the article. Just click the mouse button to page through the article automatically.

Sizing the Document On-Screen

To get a closer look at a portion of the page, use one of the following tools:

 Click this button to increase the magnification.

 Click this button to decrease the magnification.

 Click this button to turn on the hand tool, which lets you bring hidden portions of the document into view.

To control the magnification by typing a zoom percentage, open the View menu and choose Zoom To. In the Zoom To dialog box, type a magnification and click OK.

You can also size the document by clicking one of the three page size buttons, which are situated near the right end of the toolbar:

 Click this button to display the page at 100% magnification.

 Click this button to fit the page to the window.

 Click this button to fit the width of the page to the window.

You'll find menu equivalents of these commands on the View menu.

Reading the Document in Full-Screen Mode

You can also read Acrobat documents in full-screen mode, in which the page takes up the whole screen. From the View menu, choose Full Screen. To view the next page, press Enter, the right arrow key, or the down arrow key. You can also click the mouse button. To view the previous page, press the left arrow or up arrow key. When you are finished paging through the document, the program switches back to the normal display mode (you see the Adobe Acrobat Reader in a window).

Finding Text in an Acrobat Document

If you would like to search for text in an Acrobat document, click the Find tool (the button with binoculars). In the Find What dialog box, type the text for which you want to search. Click the Match Whole Word Only option to avoid retrieving embedded strings, and click Match Case, if desired, to match the capitalization pattern you have typed. To search backwards, click the Find Backwards option. Click Find to initiate the search. If the program finds a match, it highlights the matched text on-screen.

If no match is found, you'll see a dialog box asking whether you want to continue searching from the beginning of the document. If you click OK, the program continues the search. Should this search fail to retrieve a match, you'll see an alert box informing you that the text could not be found.

Copying Text and Graphics to the Clipboard

If you find text in an Adobe Acrobat document that you would like to copy to another document, click the Select button (the one with "abc" on the button face), and select the text. Then open the Edit menu and choose Copy, or press Command + C.

You can also select and copy graphics. To do so, open the Tools menu and choose Select Graphics. Then drag a selection box around the graphic you want to copy. From the Edit menu, choose Copy, or just press Command + C.

Printing the Document

To print the Adobe Acrobat document you are viewing, follow these steps:

1. From the File menu, choose Print.

2. In the Print dialog box, choose printing options, if you wish. You can print all the pages (the default setting), the current page, or a range of pages. You can also choose to print more than one copy. Additional options may be available, depending on your printer's capabilities.

3. Click OK to start printing.

 I can't save this document! You're right—there's no Save option on the Reader's File menu. What gives? Simple—there's no need. Netscape has already downloaded the Acrobat document to the directory listed in the Temporary Directory box (Applications and Directories page of the Preferences menu). Unless you deliberately erase it, there it will stay. Even after you quit Netscape, you can open the Adobe Acrobat Reader and load this document using the Open command in the File menu.

 For an introduction of the extremely cool things that can be done with Adobe Acrobat and the Web, check out the following URL:

http://www.adobe.com:80/Acrobat/PDFsamples.html

You'll find Acrobat versions of Shakespeare's plays and son-
nets, the Declaration of Independence and other historical
documents, Aesop's fairy tales, and lots of other very interesting things. Don't miss Sun Tzu, *The Art of War.*

FROM HERE

- Want to soup up Netscape so that it runs the way you want? See
  Chapter 13.

- Running into horrendous problems on-line? See Chapter 14.

Chapter
13

Customizing Netscape

N etscape is more fun when it works the way you want. You can choose the fonts you like, and you can also paint the screen with colors and even graphics backgrounds. On the Options menu and the Preferences dialog boxes, you'll find many more options that will make Netscape run your way.

If you're just learning Netscape, I'd suggest leaving the default options in place. As your knowledge grows, you may wish to choose fonts and colors, to hide the Directory buttons, and change the Security option that displays a pop-up warning every time you upload text.

For the Time-Challenged

♦ Netscape doesn't give you much control over fonts. In the Fonts and Colors page of the Preferences dialog box, you can select the base font and font size for the proportionally spaced font (which applies to most of the text on the screen) and fixed fonts (plain text documents and computer code). For the proportionally spaced font, choose one that you find highly readable.

♦ You can mess around with colors all you like, but I'll bet you get sick of seeing pink text on a chartreuse background and want the defaults back. Save yourself the trouble.

♦ In the Options menu, leave all the options on except Show Directory Buttons (which you can access in the Directory menu anyway).

♦ In the Images and Securities page of Preferences, choose After Loading if you want the text to appear more quickly in downloaded documents. Also, de-select the Submitting a Form Insecurely check box to ensure that Netscape doesn't bug you about insecure uploads at inappropriate times.

FONTS!

Unlike some graphical browsers, Netscape doesn't enable you to assign distinctive fonts to HTML tags, such as Heading 1 (<H1>), Heading 2 (<H2>), and body text (<P>). Instead, you can assign fonts only to the following:

• **Proportionally Spaced Base Font**   This is the font used for almost all of the text you'll see on-screen. In a proportionally spaced font, each character is given a width proportional to its size ("m" gets more space than "l"). The default proportionally spaced font is Times Roman.

• **Fixed (Monospace) Base Font**   This is the font used for plain-text documents (such as README files in FTP file archives) and text marked with the <CODE> tag in HTML. (The <CODE> tag is used to give examples of computer programming code.) In a monospace font, each character gets the same amount of space, producing the effect of a typewriter. The default monospace font is Courier.

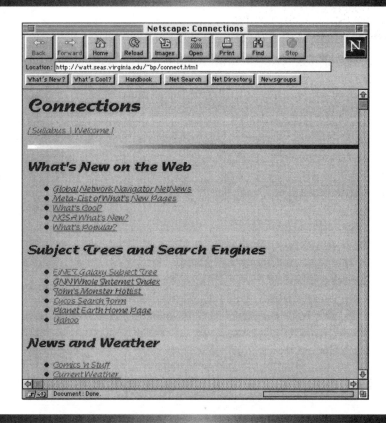

Figure 13.1   Web document displayed in 14-point Nadianne font

There's no need to change the fixed (monospace) base font; Courier works just great. But do consider changing the proportionally spaced base font. Times Roman is a beautiful font, but it's designed to fit as many characters as possible in a given space (after all, it was designed for use in newspapers). For this reason, it's hard to read on-screen. Try choosing a less compact font such as New Century Schoolbook or Bookman. In Figure 13.1, you see a Web document shown in 14-point Nadianne. Cool, huh? I'll bet I get sick of it pretty fast.

To change the base proportional font:

1. From the Options menu, choose Preferences.

2. In the list box, choose Fonts and Colors (see Figure 13.2). In the For the Encoding Box, the current setting is Latin1, which is the correct choice for English or European languages.

3. In the list box next to the proportional font setting, click the down arrow to see a list of fonts. Choose the font you want, and release the mouse button.

4. In the list box next to Size, click the down arrow to see a list of font sizes. Choose the font size you want, and release the mouse button.

5. Click OK.

To change the base monospace font:

1. From the Options menu, choose Preferences.

2. In the list box, choose Fonts and Colors (see Figure 13.2).

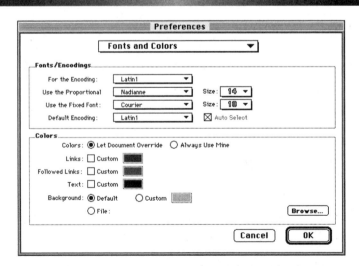

Figure 13.2   Fonts and Colors preferences

3. In the list box next to the fixed font setting, click the down arrow to see a list of fonts. Choose the font you want, and release the mouse button.

4. In the list box next to Size, click the down arrow to see a list of font sizes. Choose the font size you want, and release the mouse button.

5. Click OK.

COLORS!

Ah, color. Kiss that yucky gray background goodbye! Pick up your paintbrush, and get ready to liven things up a bit. What about a shocking pink background? Or one of those cool backgrounds you can get from Netscape's server? The sky's the limit. You can always restore the defaults once your choices start getting on your nerves.

You can choose colors for the following:

- **Links**   Hyperlinks you haven't visited appear in this color. By default, they're blue.

- **Followed (Visited) Links**   Hyperlinks you've already visited. By default, they appear in lavender.

- **Text**   All other document text. By default, it's in black.

- **Background**   The default background is battleship gray. You can choose colors or, to make things even more visually confusing, a background graphic.

To change the default colors:

1. From the Options menu, choose Preferences.

2. In the list box, choose Fonts and Colors. You'll see the Fonts and Colors preferences, shown in Figure 13.2.

3. To choose a color for Links, click the check box after Links, and double-click the color box. You'll see the Pick a Color dialog box, shown in Figure 13.3.

4. Drag the pointer to change the color. You can also experiment with the Hue and Saturation levels; click More Choices to find even more ways to waste time.

5. To change the followed links and text colors, repeat steps 3 and 4 for the Followed Links and Text areas.

6. To set the background, click Custom and choose a color, or click File and use the Browse button to select a JPEG or GIF graphic.

7. In the Colors area, click Always Use Mine if you really want Netscape to override incoming documents' color choices. I'd suggest leaving this option set to the default, Let Document Override.

8. Click OK to confirm your choices.

For a super collection of background patterns, check out http://home.netscape.com/home/bg/index.html. You can download any of the patterns by pointing to the pattern you want, holding down the mouse button, and then choosing Save This Image As.

What does a custom-colored screen look like? It's hard to show in black and white, but Figure 13.4 shows the blue_rock.gif background with white text, yellow links, and red followed links.

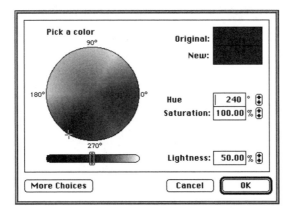

Figure 13.3   Pick a Color dialog box

Figure 13.4   After coloring the screen

I'm sick of this! I want the defaults back!   No problemo. Just open the Fonts and Colors preferences again, deselect all the Custom check boxes, and click Default in the Background area. Click OK to confirm, and you're back to boring-old-gray background with boring-old-black text. Want your colors back again? Sheesh, make up your mind! Well, you can get them; the Preferences dialog box retains your color choices. Open the Fonts and Colors preferences again and select the Custom boxes, and restore your background by clicking File. Click OK to confirm your choice.

OPTIONS GALORE!

In addition to fonts and colors options, you can choose additional options on the Options menu and in the many pages of the Preferences dialog box.

Options on the Options Menu

You can choose the following options on the Options menu:

- **Show Toolbar** With this option selected, Netscape displays the Toolbar. When it's turned off, the Toolbar is removed.

- **Show Location** With this option selected, Netscape displays the Location box. When it's turned off, the Location box is removed.

- **Show Directory Buttons** With this option selected, Netscape displays the Directory buttons. When it's turned off, the buttons are removed.

- **Auto Load Images** With this option selected, Netscape displays in-line images automatically. With this option turned off, in-line images do not appear unless you hold down the mouse button and choose Load This Image. You can select further in-line image options in the Images and Security page of the Preferences dialog box (choose Preferences from the Options menu, and then select the Images and Security page). You can choose to display images while loading (the default) or after loading.

- **Show FTP File Information** With this option selected, Netscape shows cool little icons that tell you what type of information is listed in an FTP file directory, such as text files, folders, and binary files. With this option turned off, you just see the directory listings without icons.

What are the best options? It's partly a matter of taste, but most Netscape users like to see the Toolbar and the Location box, which tells you the URL of the document you're viewing (in addition, you can use the Location box to type a URL directly). You can dispense with the Directory buttons, since the same choices are available in the Directory menu.

When you are finished choosing options on the Options menu, be sure to choose Save Options. Unless you do, Netscape won't save your choices for the next Netscape session.

Options in the Preferences Dialog Boxes

- **The Window and Link Styles Page**   In the Window Styles area, you can choose to display the Toolbar as pictures and text (the default), text only, or pictures only. Options for hyperlinks are also found on the Styles page. You can choose to remove the underlining from links (deselect the Underlined check box), and you can also choose expirations for visited (followed) links. You can choose between Never Expire and Expire after a number of days that you choose (the default is 30 days). You can also click the Expire Now button to cause all the links to expire immediately.

- **The Fonts and Colors Page**   See "Fonts!" and "Colors!," earlier in this chapter, for a discussion of these options.

- **The Mail and News Page**   For information on configuring these options, see Chapter 18.

- **The Cache and Network Page**   For information on cache options, see Chapter 11. This page also contains two options that control Netscape's communications with the Internet. You can set the network buffer size (the default is 31 KB), and change the maximum number of simultaneous Netscape connections that can occur at the same time (the default is four). If you increase these, you'll consume more RAM memory, so I don't recommend that you change these settings.

- **The Applications and Directories Page**   For information on configuring these options, see Chapter 5.

- **The Images and Security Page**   In the Colors area, you can choose to display images While Loading (the default) or After Loading, which makes the text appear more quickly. Security notification options are also found in the Images and Security page. These options display a pop-up alert box when entering a secure document, leaving a secure document, viewing a document with a secure/insecure mix, and submitting a form insecurely.

- **The Proxies Page**   The Proxies page contains settings that you would use only if your Mac is connected to a firewall-protected network. A firewall is a security device that prevents outsiders from accessing internal resources. Unfortunately, it also prevents insiders from accessing external resources! As a solution to this problem,

Netscape can interact with *proxy servers*, which mediate between your computer and the wider Internet beyond the firewall. For information on how to configure the Proxies page, consult your network administrator. If you're using a SLIP/PPP connection or working on a network that isn't protected by a firewall, just ignore this page.

- **The Helper Applications Page**   For information on configuring these options, see Chapter 5.

What are the best options to choose in the Preferences pages? You'll probably want to display both text and pictures on the Toolbar, at least until you've memorized what the pictures mean. Documents will seem to load faster if you choose the After Loading option in the Images area of the Images and Security page. You should probably leave all the Security options turned on, with the possible exception of Submitting a Form Insecurely; this option ensures that an alert box will pop up when you're supplying information for searching purposes, which is annoying. One glance at the key/broken key icon will let you know whether it's safe to upload your credit card number.

FROM HERE

- Run into problems with Netscape? Check out Chapter 14, "When the Surf Gets Rough."

- Get ready to explore the Internet! With Netscape as your companion, you'll explore the far reaches of the Web, send electronic mail, access Gopher menus, obtain files from FTP archives, search WAIS databases, and join USENET newsgroups. It's all found in Part IV, "Exploring the Internet."

Chapter 14

When the Surf Gets Rough

N etscape is loads of fun to use, but the Web isn't perfect. This chapter discusses the things that can go wrong while you're surfing the Web—the black holes, the forbidden zones, the unplugged sockets, and more.

Even if you haven't run into the problems discussed in this chapter, it's still a good idea to skim it. It surveys the most commonly encountered network errors, and tells what to do about them.

I CLICKED THE HYPERLINK — AND NOTHING HAPPENED!

The site you're trying to access is busy, busy, busy—so busy in fact, that it can't even transmit a message that it's too busy! Pathetic. Try again later—like at 2:30 AM.

If you're determined to get through to a site, open a new window in Netscape and let the original window keep on tryin'. Maybe the document you want will appear after a few minutes. Maybe not.

A site that just never responds is known to Web surfers as a Black Hole. If you've never had this experience, but would like to give it a try, there is a Black Hole simulation at the following URL:

http://www.ravenna.com/blackhole.html

Please do not click the Black Hole link (Figure 14.1). You will be caught in the Hole and unable to get out. Somehow, resist the temptation!

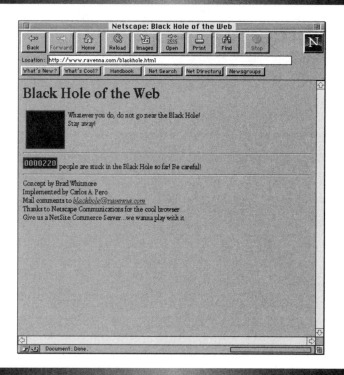

Figure 14.1 *The* Black Hole

IT SAYS THE DNS LOOKUP FAILED!

Netscape tried to access a Web site, but nothing happened, and then you see a dialog box with the message that the DNS lookup went awry (Figure 14.2). There are several possibilities here:

- Are you using a SLIP or PPP connection? Check to make sure that you're still connected. Many dial-in systems are programmed to hang up on you if there is no activity for a specified period of time, such as 10 minutes. (After all, other people are trying to access the system, and as far as anyone knows, you've probably gone fishing or something.) Use your SLIP/PPP dialer to re-establish the connection, and click the hyperlink again.

Figure 14.2   A DNS lookup gone astray

- Did you type the URL? You may have mistyped the domain name part of the URL (the part that contains the name of the computer you're trying to access).

- The computer you're trying to access may have gone "Whoomp!" (That's the noise a computer makes when it's taken out of service and permanently disconnected from the Internet, in case you were wondering.)

IT SAYS "404 NOT FOUND"!

The domain name's all right, but—sorry to say—there's no document by that name located on the machine you've accessed (Figure 14.3). Did you type the URL yourself? If so, carefully check your typing and make any corrections, if necessary, right in the Location box. Press Enter to try again.

If you get the 404 Not Found message again, it's probable that the document has been withdrawn from the server.

WOW! "FORBIDDEN"!

Naughty, naughty! You weren't trying to access a *sex* site, were you? Sites with naughty pictures tend to get shut down by system administrators, thanks to the fact that there are, apparently, about 20 million Web users with nothing

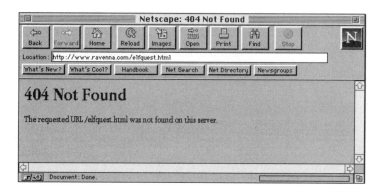

Figure 14.3 404 Not Found

better to do than hunt down erotic Web sites. With so many people trying to access the document, its host system can't function. Irate, the system administrator removes the offending document and places a restriction on its access, producing this sternly worded message (Figure 14.4).

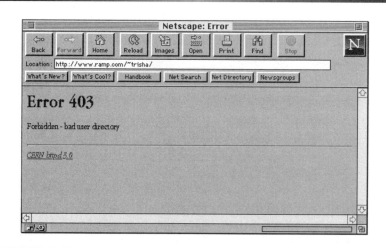

Figure 14.4 403 Forbidden

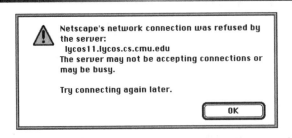

Figure 14.5　Connection refused

CONNECTION REFUSED!

The server's too busy, probably, to deal with your request (Figure 14.5). Chances are good it's a temporary problem. Just click the hyperlink again. Or try later—like at 2:30 AM.

IT SAYS "THIS SITE HAS MOVED!"

Well, make a note of the new hyperlink. Usually, pages such as this one include something you can click to get to the right place (see Figure 14.6).

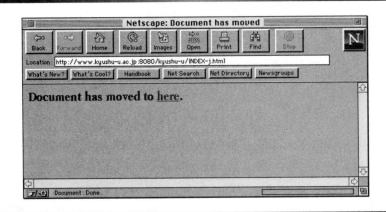

Figure 14.6　Forwarding address

THEY'RE DEMANDING A PASSWORD!

They can do that, if they like. And you can't access the page unless you type the correct login name and password (Figure 14.7). Probably, there's information on how to register—do it.

IT SAYS "THE INFORMATION YOU HAVE SUBMITTED IS NOT SECURE"!

And it isn't (Figure 14.8). Any message you send on the Web can be quite easily intercepted and read. That's why you should never, never, never send

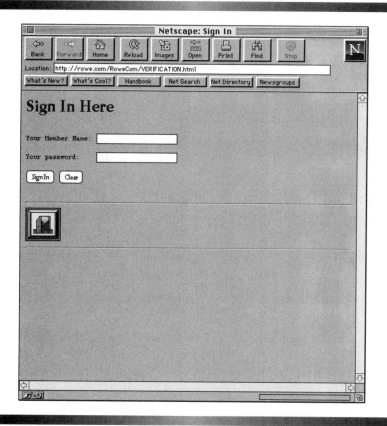

Figure 14.7   To get past this, you'll need a login name and a password

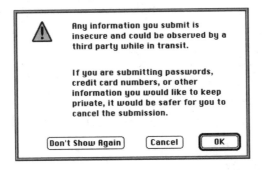

Figure 14.8 Warning about uploading information to an "insecure server"

your credit card information, or any other personal information, via forms that you fill out in Web documents—unless, that is, you're accessing a secure document (see Chapter 21). This message is telling you that you're uploading (sending) information to a server that isn't secure. (Netscape knows.)

This message gets a bit boring after a while. If you're tired of seeing it, and know better than to upload sensitive information to servers that aren't secure, you can stop Netscape from displaying it. From the Options menu, choose Preferences, and select the Images and Security page. In the Security Alerts area, deselect "Submitting a Form Insecurely." Click OK to confirm the change, and choose Save Options from the Options menu just to make sure Netscape gets the message.

FROM HERE

- At this point, you're an accomplished Web surfer. Ready to take on the rest of the Internet? Flip to Part IV.

Part IV

EXPLORING THE
INTERNET

Chapter
15

Digging Around in Gopher

Gopher got its start as a campus-wide information system at the University of Minnesota, the mascot of which is—you guessed it. It enables people to access all kinds of different information with the same easy menu-based browsing system. Those nice University of Minnesota folks made the program freely available, and what do you know? Colleges and universities everywhere used Gopher to make information available. A few private organizations did, too.

Before the Web came along, Gopher was the Latest Best Thing for accessing Internet resources, and it grew wildly. But the Web's success has choked off Gopher's growth. Still, there are lots of useful resources available in Gopher menus, mainly because people haven't had the time to put them on the Web yet. But no matter; clever Netscape can navigate Gopher menus directly. You can also use services called Veronica and Archie to find Gopher-based information.

For the Time-Challenged

◆ Gopher is a menu-driven information system that Netscape can access directly. Gopher menus may contain links to Gopher submenus, documents, binary files, graphics, or search utilities.

◆ If you've gone "down" into a Gopher submenu, click the Back button to get out of the "hole."

◆ Check out EINet Galaxy's Gopher Jewels list for some terrific Gopher sites.

◆ You can search Gopher directory titles and document names with Veronica, but you'd be wise to access this overloaded service in the wee hours of the morning.

◆ It isn't obvious from Veronica's search screen, but the software has some very sophisticated search capabilities.

This chapter covers the use of Gopher menus with Netscape. Although Gopher is easy to use, this chapter includes some yummy tips for locating great Gopher sites and searching Gopherspace effectively. Even if you've navigated Gopher already, you'll still want to skim this chapter.

ACCESSING GOPHER SITES

To access a Gopher site, you have two options:

• **Click a Gopher hyperlink**   A hyperlink to a Gopher site looks like any other hyperlink. After you click the link, you'll see a Gopher menu instead of a Web page.

• **Type a Gopher URL directly**   A Gopher URL looks like a Web URL, except that it starts with gopher:// instead of http://, as in the following:

gopher://gopher.well.sf.ca.us/

UNDERSTANDING GOPHER MENUS

After you've accessed a Gopher site, you'll see a Gopher menu, such as the one shown in Figure 15.1. As displayed by Netscape, a Gopher menu is a list of hyperlinks—but they're of different kinds. You may see one or more of the following items, each with its own icon:

 Another Gopher Menu — Click this item to display the items in this folder.

 A Document — If you click this link, you will see a plain-text document, which you can read on-screen.

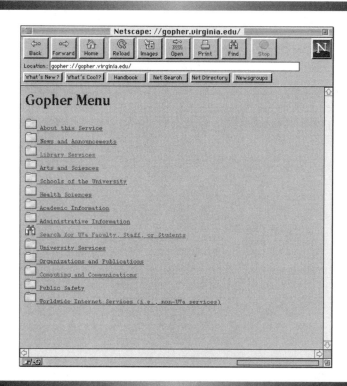

Figure 15.1 A Gopher menu

A Binary File   If you click this link, Netscape will begin down-loading the file.

 A Graphic   If you click this link, Netscape will display the graphic.

 Perform a Search   If you click this link, you'll see a search document. Type one or more key words, and click the Search button to initiate the search.

 Access a Telnet Session   If you click this link, Netscape will start your Telnet helper application. For more information on Telnet, see Chapter 19.

When you've gone "down" to a Gopher submenu (otherwise known as a "Gopher hole"—get it?), you can go back "up" again to the menu you just viewed. To do so, click the Back button.

GOPHER JEWELS

Looking for good stuff on Gopher? Check out Gopher Jewels, accessible via EINet Galaxy (http://galaxy.einet.net/GJ/). You'll see a list of hyperlinks to great Gopher sites, which are classified by subject; there are over 2,300 Gopher sites accessible in this way. Table 15.1 lists the subject categories currently found in the Gopher Jewels list. Have fun!

SEARCHING GOPHER: VERONICA

Veronica is a search engine that's designed to find resources in Gopherspace (the world of accessible Gopher items). To do so, Veronica scans an automatically compiled index of titles of Gopher directory titles and document names. Note that this index does *not* include words found within the text of these files. Jughead is essentially a version of Veronica that searches for directory titles only.

Table 15.1 Subject Categories in Gopher Jewels (EINet Galaxy)

Agriculture and Forestry

AIDS and HIV Information

Anthropology and Archaeology

Architecture

Arts and Humanities

Astronomy and Astrophysics

Biological Sciences

Books, Journals, Magazines, Newsletters, and Publications

Chemistry

Computer Related

Country Specific Information

Disability Information

Economics and Business

Education (Includes K–12)

Employment Opportunities and Resume Postings

Engineering Related

Environment

Federal Agency and Related Gopher Sites

Free-Nets and Other Community or State Gophers

Fun Stuff and Multimedia

Genealogy

General Reference Resources

Geography

Geology and Oceanography

Global or World-Wide Topics

Grants

History

Internet Cyberspace Related

Internet Resources by Type (Gopher, Phone, USENET, WAIS, Other)

Internet Service Providers

Journalism

Language

Legal or Law Related

Library Information and Catalogs

List of Lists Resources

Manufacturing

Math Sciences

Medical Related

Meteorology

Military

Miscellaneous Items

Museums, Exhibits and Special Collections

News Related Services

Patents and Copyrights

Physics

Political and Government

Products and Services—Store Fronts

Psychology

Radio and TV Broadcasting

Religion and Philosophy

Safety

Social Sciences

State Government

Technical Reports

Technology Transfer

Travel Information

To access Veronica, click the Veronica hyperlink in HOME.HTML, or use the following URL:

gopher://gopher.ed.gov:70/11/other_gopher/veronica

You'll see a Gopher menu such as the one shown in Figure 15.2. Note that you can search two ways:

1. **Directory Titles Only (Jughead)** This is a good place to start your search. If you're lucky, you'll find a Gopher menu that groups a lot of resources pertaining to the subject in which you're interested.

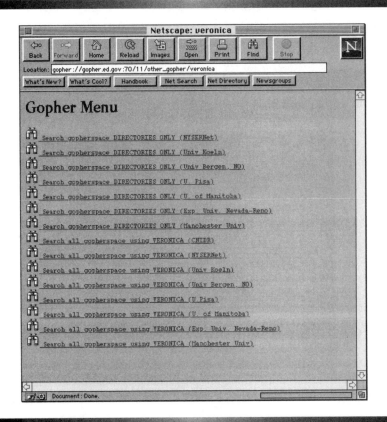

Figure 15.2   Veronica

2. **Searching All Gopherspace (Veronica)**   This search examines Gopher document names as well as directory titles. You'll get a lot more items from this search, but much of it will be irrelevant junk.

To initiate the search, decide whether you're going to search directory titles or Gopherspace, and click a server name. You'll see a search page, such as the one shown in Figure 15.3.

It says "Too many connections—Try again soon"!   What, you're trying to search Veronica during the *day*? With so many gazillions of people using the Internet, Veronica has become an early-morning-hours service, unless you're very lucky.

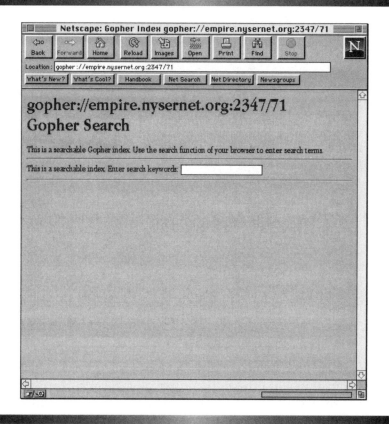

Figure 15.3 Veronica search page

On some Veronica servers, you'll see an item called "Simplified Veronica Search." This option uses automated techniques to find an available server. It gives you the best chance of actually getting something out of your Veronica search.

If the search is successful, you'll see a Gopher menu containing the items the server has retrieved (Figure 15.4). You can navigate this Gopher menu just like any other Gopher menu.

If the search is unsuccessful, you'll see a message informing you that the server returned no data. Try again, using more general key words.

Solutions

Veronica Search Tips

Like many of the Internet's search services (see Chapter 10), Veronica searches are more capable than you'd think, looking at that simple search page. By default, Veronica performs a case-insensitive search; if you type two or more words, Veronica ANDs them (no document is retrieved unless *all* of the key words are present in the document title). In addition, Veronica performs a whole-word search; if you type "cat," you'll get documents with the word "cat" in the title, but not "concatenate."

You can override Veronica's default search settings in the following ways:

- **OR Operator**   To search with an OR operator so that Veronica retrieves documents that have any of the key words in their titles, separate the words with OR ("cats or dogs").

- **NOT Operator**   To exclude documents containing a certain word in their titles, type NOT followed by the word you want to exclude ("cats not dogs").

- **Parenthetical Statements**   For a finely honed search, you can embed Boolean operators in parentheses. For example, a search for "recipes and (indian or thai)" retrieves Indian as well as Thai recipes, but nothing else pertaining to India or Thailand.

- **Searching for Resources of a Certain Type**   The -t operator enables you to restrict the retrieval list to certain types of documents. For example, the following retrieves graphics (GIFs) and sounds pertaining to Star Trek: Star Trek -tgs. To restrict the search in this way, type **-t** followed by a code and the text you're searching for. For a list of the -t codes, see Table 15.2.

- **Specify the Maximum Number of Hits**   By default, Veronica retrieves 200 hits. To increase this number, use the -m operator. The following retrieves 1,000 Star Trek documents: Star Trek -m1000. (You can combine this code with the -t code, if you wish: Star Trek -m1000 -tg retrieves 1,000 Star Trek GIFs, which is assuredly more than you'll ever need.)

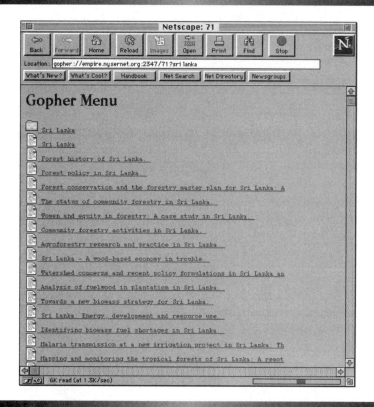

Figure 15.4   Result of a Veronica search

Table 15.1   Codes for Restricting Veronica Searches with the -t Operator

0	Text file	s	Sound
1	Directory	e	Event (not in 2.06)
2	CSO name server	I	Image (other than GIF)
4	Mac HQX file	M	MIME multipart/mixed message
5	PC binary	T	TN3270 session
7	Full Text Index (Gopher menu)	c	Calendar (not in 2.06)
8	Telnet session	g	GIF image
9	Binary file	h	HTML, Hypertext Markup Language

FROM HERE

- Hunt down some files with FTP; you'll find the lowdown in Chapter 16.

- Learn how to search WAIS databases with the best of them in Chapter 17.

- Join the tumult on USENET newgroups with Netscape's excellent newsreading and mail capabilities; check out Chapter 18 for the details.

- See Chapter 19 for information on using Telnet with Netscape.

Chapter

16

Ransacking FTP File Archives

F FTP is short for File Transfer Protocol, which pretty much describes what it does. Using FTP, you can exchange program or text files with anyone connected to the Internet. Netscape gives you partial FTP capabilities—specifically, to *get* files. (You can send files with Netscape's mail capabilities, as discussed in Chapter 18, but this is mail, not FTP—there *is* a difference.)

You can't just browse around in anyone's computer in search of files. Normally, you need an account and a password to access someone else's computer on the Internet. But some kind people have created *publicly accessible file archives*. This is also called "anonymous FTP," since you had to log into these computers as "anonymous" when you were using one of those old, clunky FTP programs. Netscape logs you in automatically.

For the Time-Challenged

◆ Netscape accesses anonymous FTP file archives smoothly, showing you a graphical version of UNIX file directories. Just click the items you want. To go back up to a parent directory, be sure to use the hyperlink, not the Back button.

◆ Archie searches a database of thousands of FTP archives. With Netscape, you can access Archie through a gateway such as ArchiePlex.

◆ The Virtual Shareware Library (VSL) provides an easy way to obtain software from the largest and best shareware archives. Don't miss this!

Most of the files in these publicly accessible file archives are programs. You can obtain these and soup up your computer to just an incredible degree. (Mine shows a picture of the Starship Enterprise on start-up, plays the theme from Star Trek, and then you hear a "beam-me-up" transporter sound.) These programs are either *freeware* (copyrighted but freely copiable as long as you don't sell them) or *shareware* (you really ought to pay that registration fee, you know). The moral: *Use FTP to get your hands on extremely cool programs, and they're free (or really cheap)*. Netscape gives you wonderful tools for browsing FTP file archives, and the StuffIt Expander software included with this book automatically decompresses the files after you download them.

If you're interested in obtaining software from the Internet, this chapter's for you!

ACCESSING ANONYMOUS FTP FILE ARCHIVES

FTP is smoothly integrated with Netscape. You can access anonymous FTP file archives in two ways:

1. **Clicking an FTP Hyperlink**   You see an FTP file directory.

2. **Typing the URL Directly**   To access an anonymous FTP archive, you can type **ftp://** followed by the archive's name, such as **ftp:// ftp.virginia.edu/**.

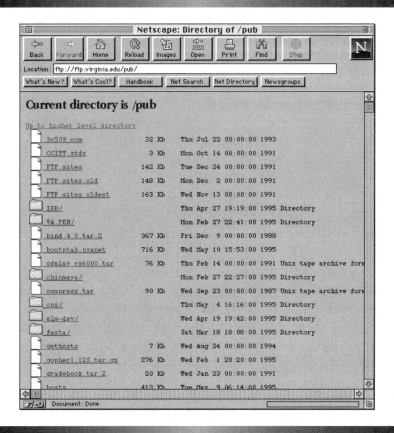

Figure 16.1 Anonymous FTP file archive displayed by Netscape

NAVIGATING FTP DIRECTORIES

You can think of UNIX directories as folders within folders, like the Mac's folders in the Finder. In Figure 16.1, for example, the folder icons represent directories.

To navigate within FTP directories, do the following:

- To open a subdirectory, click one of the folders.

- To go back to the parent directory (the next directory up in the directory tree), click "Up to higher level directory," a hyperlink you'll find at the top of the file list. *Do not click the Back button.* If you do, you'll get disoriented, and lose track of the directories' hierarchical arrangement.

WHAT'S IN THE FILES?

Netscape uses little icons to tell you which kind of file you're viewing. Here's a handy guide:

 A Text Document   Click here to read the document. If it's called README, chances are it contains important and useful information about the files in this directory.

 A Graphic   Click here to download the graphic.

 A Document or File that Netscape Couldn't Identify   Click it and see what happens.

 A Program   Click here to download the software.

 A Subdirectory   Click here to see another directory of files, and possibly additional subdirectories.

FINDING FTP RESOURCES: ARCHIE

There are thousands of anonymous FTP file archives out there—but how do you find them? A service called Archie enables you to search for a file, but there's a rub—you pretty much need to know the name of the file you're looking for. Suppose someone tells you about a file called uudecode.exe that you just *have* to have. Since you know the name, Archie can help you find an anonymous FTP file archive that contains it, if there is one.

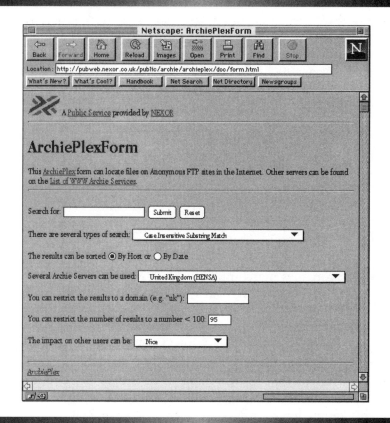

Figure 16.2 ArchiePlex (Archie Gateway)

Archie is a UNIX program, but there are lots of Web gateways that enable Netscape and you to communicate with Archie. One of the best is the ArchiePlex gateway, at the following URL:

http://pubweb.nexor.co.uk/public/archie/archieplex/archieplex.html

After accessing ArchiePlex, you'll see the page shown in Figure 16.2.

 If you haven't already read Chapter 10, take a look at the section called "Understanding Search Techniques." It will help you use ArchiePlex more effectively.

To use ArchiePlex, follow these steps:

1. In the Search For box, type the name of the file you want to retrieve. If you don't know the whole name, that's OK—type as much as you know for sure. The default search setting, Case Insensitive Substring Match, is a good one for Archie.

2. If you wish, change the default output sort order (click By Date to see the most recent version of the file first).

3. Next to "Several Archie servers can be used," pick the Archie server nearest you.

4. Choose other options, if you wish, although the defaults are fine. In particular, be nice to other users.

5. Click Submit.

If Archie finds any files matching your request, you'll see a new page (Figure 16.3) listing the anonymous FTP sites that have the file you're looking for.

It says "Server timed out"! Welcome to the club. Here, unfortunately, is yet another of those overloaded Internet services that is becoming increasingly difficult to access. If the server is busy, you're likely to see this message. As the saying goes, "try again later"… like at 3:30 AM.

LOOKING FOR SHAREWARE WITH THE VIRTUAL SHAREWARE LIBRARY

Archie has grown somewhat long in the tooth, and there's a new game in town: the Virtual Shareware Library (VSL). VSL permits you to search the text of file descriptions, and provides very nice search tools.

VSL isn't a complete replacement for Archie, though. Archie's database includes files in thousands of anonymous FTP archives worldwide. VSL is designed to search only certain shareware repositories, such as the renowned CICA archive at the University of Indiana, the world's largest repository of Microsoft Windows software. Still, VSL will keep you plenty busy.

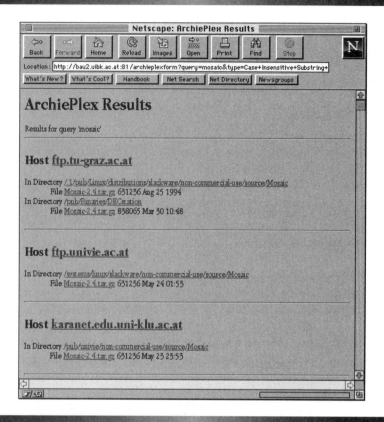

Figure 16.3 Results of ArchiePlex Search

To access VSL, click the hyperlink in HOME.HTML, or use the following URL:

> http://www.acs.oakland.edu/cgi-bin/shase

You'll see VSL's beautiful welcoming screen, shown in Figure 16.4. To search for files in VSL, follow these instructions:

1. Below the document's title, you'll see a number of icons. To search for Macintosh files, click the Apple icon. You'll see the VSL search page, shown in Figure 16.5. VSL has automatically selected the best archives for Macintosh software.

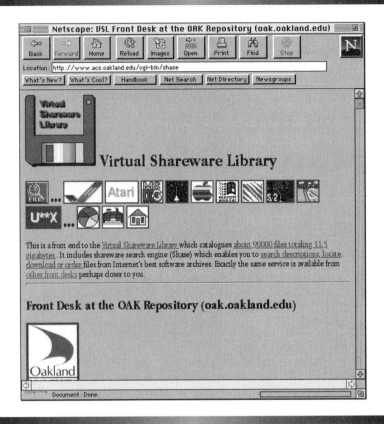

Figure 16.4   Virtual Shareware Library

2. In the "search for" box, type the first word you want to match. VSL searches the text that describes each program as well as program and file names.

3. If you would like to perform an AND search, type a second key word in the "and for" box. VSL will retrieve a file only if it matches both the key words you have typed.

4. If you would like to exclude files with certain words in their descriptions, type the unwanted word in the "and not for" box.

5. If you want to perform a case-sensitive search, click the "match case" check box.

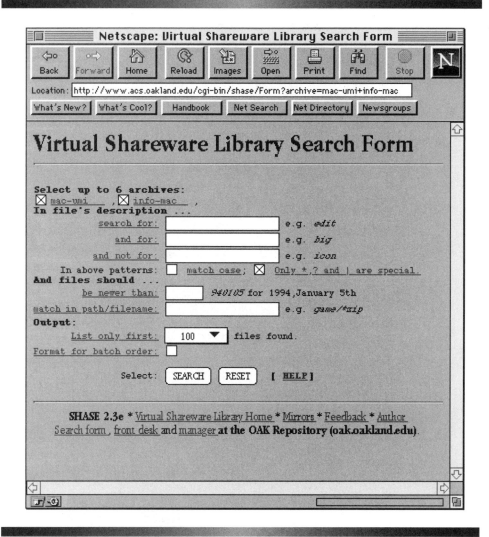

Figure 16.5 VSL search page

6. To search for files of a certain age, type a date (using the format 950105 for January 5, 1995) in the "be newer than" box.

7. To increase the number of files retrieved, choose a larger number in the "list only first" list box.

8. Just leave the setting in the "Only *, ? and | are special" check box the way it is, unless you really want to search with a PERL expression.

9. Unless you know exactly which directories you want to search, leave the "match in path/filename" box blank.

10. Leave the "Format for batch order" check box deselected. This is only for automated downloading of lots of files.

11. Click Search.

You'll see a new page reporting the results of your search (Figure 16.6). If VSL couldn't find any files, you won't see any file names. If you do see file

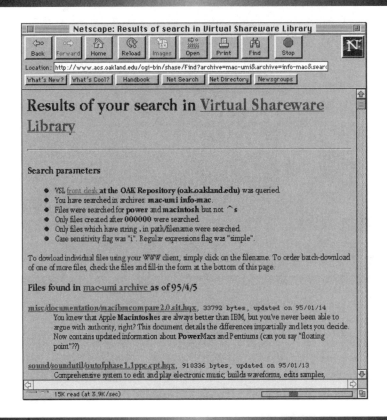

Figure 16.6   Results of VSL search

names, click the one that looks like it meets your needs. You'll see another page of hyperlinks for downloading the file; click the one nearest you to begin downloading.

FROM HERE

- You've done Gopher, you've done FTP. How 'bout WAIS? It's in the next chapter.

- Feeling brave? Venture into the wilds of USENET, with Netscape as your helper. See Chapter 18.

- Don't forget you can access Telnet sessions with Netscape, as you'll learn in Chapter 19.

Chapter
17

Searching WAIS Databases

S earching for information in Web and Gopher documents? You use search terms called key words, as you've learned. But good luck finding a document if the search term is buried deep within the document, discussed only peripherally, and omitted from the title. With Web searches, you'll be lucky if you find it—and you'll have to use a search engine such as WebCrawler, which indexes the full text of the documents it finds. But WebCrawler has indexed only a small fraction of the Web documents available. With Veronica and Gopher, you might as well forget it—Veronica searches directory titles and document names, but not document content.

Due to the difficulty of retrieving information on the Internet, there's a role to play for WAIS. Short for "Wide Area Information Server," WAIS consists of programs that index a collection of documents, called a *database*, and produce an index listing *all* the words these documents contain. When you perform a key-word search using the WAIS search engine, the software will retrieve any document that contains the key word for which you're looking, even if the word is used peripherally in the document.

Netscape can't search WAIS databases directly. Thanks to *WAIS gateways*, you can access Web pages that give Netscape (and most other graphical browsers) access to these databases. In this chapter, you'll learn how to search WAIS databases using the best WAIS gateway of them all, WAISGATE (a WAIS gateway maintained by WAIS, Inc.).

UNDERSTANDING WAIS

WAIS sounds great, but it hasn't exactly taken the Internet by storm. In fact, it's probably the slowest-growing Internet service. Part of the problem is that it's a hassle to set up and maintain a WAIS server (software that enables WAIS searches). Also, WAIS isn't very intuitive and it's somewhat difficult to learn and use. A final reason: WAIS database coverage is spotty. On some subjects, there's a ton of information; on others, zilch. Here's a sampler:

- **ERIC Digests**   Periodically, a U.S. Department of Education office publishes a summary of new developments in education, including the results of education research, new tools for educators, and new perspectives on education. More than 1,000 *ERIC Digests* have been published, and they're searchable by means of WAIS.

- **Recipes**   An amazing database, compiled from the contributions to the USENET newsgroup rec.food.recipes. Yum, let's have a look.

- **Speeches of Bill Clinton**   Want to track Bill's speeches, starting from his days as Governor of Arkansas right through his presidency? Find out whether his positions on words such as "tax," "environment," and "defense" have changed over time.

- **U.S. Congressional Record**   Want to find out what your representative has been saying about endangered species, NASA, or GATT? Find out by searching the full text of the *Congressional Record*.

For the Time-Challenged

♦ Netscape can't access WAIS databases directly, but several WAIS gateways have been established. Essentially, these are Web documents that mediate between Web browsers (such as Netscape) and WAIS databases.

♦ To find information in WAIS, you start with the directory of servers. This is a database of WAIS databases. Use general search terms (such as "education" or "environment") to search these pages. Note that WAIS performs whole-word searches by default ("recipe" won't match "recipes"). Use the truncation (wild card) operator, an asterisk, to make sure you match as many databases as possible ("environment*" will match "environmental" as well as "environment").

♦ After you've identified a WAIS database of interest to you, search using more specific words and phrases. When you have discovered a document that's pertinent to your interests, return to the list of retrieved documents, click the check box next to this document's name, and click the Search button again. This will retrieve any other documents that closely match the document's analytical profile.

ABOUT THE DIRECTORY OF SERVERS

How do you find out whether there's a WAIS database containing information of interest to you? You can search a service called the *directory of servers*. This is really just a WAIS database in which the individual items are database descriptions. The directory of servers does *not* search the complete indexes of all the databases. When you search the directory of servers, therefore, you should use general subject terms, rather than the specific key words you're trying to find. For example, suppose you're looking for seafood pasta recipes. In the directory of servers database, you should search for "recipes." You'll discover the Recipes database. In the Recipes database, you can search for "seafood pasta."

 Want to see a current list of WAIS databases and their descriptions? Check out the following URL:

http://www.wais.com/wais-dbs/

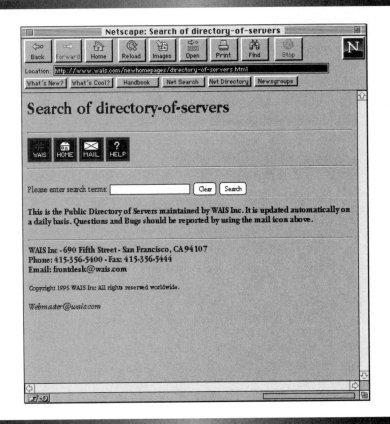

Figure 17.1   Result of directory of servers search

To view one of the database descriptions, just click on the
database name.

To access the WAISGATE directory of servers, click the hyperlink in
HOME.HTML, or use the following URL:

http://www.wais.com/newhomepages/directory-of-servers.html

Like so many of the search engines accessible via the Web, the WAISGATE
main page (Figure 17.1) gives you a text box in which you can type one or
more key words.

Before you initiate your search in the directory of servers, open a new Netscape window and access the database description page (http://www.wais.com/wais-dbs/). This will enable you to make sense of the database names that WAIS retrieves.

When you're using the directory of servers, remember to type *general* subject words ("recipes," not "squid pasta"). You're searching brief database descriptions rather than the full indexes of WAIS databases. To initiate the search, type the key word or words in the text box, and click the Search button. Note that, by default, WAIS performs a case-insensitive whole-word search (for more information on search terminology, see Chapter 10). Watch out for the "whole word" part: a search for "recipe" will *not* retrieve the database recipes.src.

 To get around the restrictions of WAISGATE's whole-word search setting, you can use the asterisk wild card character (*), which works just like it does in MS-DOS (it stands for one or more characters). If you search for "recipe*," WAIS will succeed in retrieving "recipes" (and it will also retrieve entries for "recipe," should any exist).

The result of a directory of servers search is a ranked list of WAIS databases, all of which contain all or some of your key words in the database description (Figure 17.2). Here, you can see what I mean when I said earlier that WAIS is difficult to use: Many of the database names provide no clue about their contents. To view the database description for a database that looks interesting, switch to the window you opened earlier, and use the Find command (Edit menu) to locate the database name. Then click the database name to view the description.

If you see an item ranked 1,000, it means that WAIS's analysis puts it at the top of the list. This document not only contains the key words you typed, but it also contains them in important places, such as the title and first few lines. However, other documents—even those with lower rankings—could contain information of interest to you, so don't ignore them. Should WAIS come up empty-handed, you'll see a message informing you that no matching items were found.

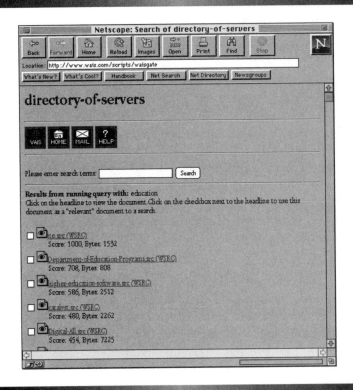

Figure 17.2   Result of directory of servers search

SEARCHING A WAIS DATABASE

If you find an appropriate database in the directory of servers' output list, click its name. You'll see a database search page, such as the one shown in Figure 17.3. Type one or more key words in the text box, and click Search.

The result of a search is, again, a list of ranked documents. To see a document, click its name.

 A unique feature of WAIS software is the ability to search by document matching. If you find a document that perfectly matches your interests, click the Back button to redisplay the list of retrieved documents, click the check box next to the document's name, and click the Search button to redo the

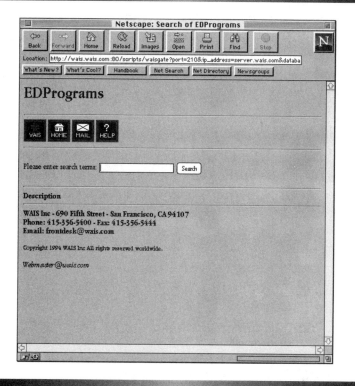

Figure 17.3 Database search page

search. WAIS will examine the document that you have
clicked and attempt to find other documents that match its
analysis profile.

ADVANCED WAIS SEARCHING

WAISGATE enables you to search for documents using a variety of
advanced search techniques, including the following:

- **Contiguous Strings** To match two or more words in the exact
order in which you type them, enclose the search words in quotation

marks. "Sierra Club", for example, matches only those two words in that precise order.

- **Boolean Operators (AND, OR, NOT)**　WAIS recognizes Boolean operators (see Chapter 10 for more information on Boolean operators and their use).

- **Adjacency Operator (ADJ)**　To find only those occurences of a word that are immediately followed by another word, use the ADJ operator. For example, "cellular ADJ telephone" retrieves documents only if "telephone" immediately follows "cellular."

- **Parenthetical Expressions**　You can use parentheses to tell WAIS which parts of the search question to resolve first. Consider the following: (California OR Oregon) AND (Pinot Noir or Merlot). This question will retrieve documents pertaining to California Pinot Noir, Oregon Pinot Noir, California Merlot, and Oregon Merlot.

FROM HERE

- Why leave yourself out? Get on USENET, and throw in your two cents' worth. Chapter 18 shows you how.

- Want to find out what's available via Telnet sessions? Find out in Chapter 19.

Chapter

18

Ranting and Raving in USENET Newsgroups

U SENET is a computer-based discussion system that's widely distributed on the Internet. The idea underlying USENET is devilishly
clever: The USENET software works behind the scenes, copying and
relaying the messages users contribute, so that in time every participating
computer (called a *USENET site*) has an exact copy of every message contributed to the network. The software knows how to organize these messages into topical categories, called *newsgroups*, which you can read. In
addition, you can contribute your own messages to these newsgroups. With
more than 160,000 USENET sites connected to the network worldwide,
more than 7,000 newsgroups, and an estimated 7 million regular users, contributing to USENET may be the ultimate act of self-publishing—or self-
immolation, if you break any of USENET's none-too-explicit rules or guidelines. Whatever else you do with USENET, read newsgroups for a good
while before attempting to post your own messages.

USENET got its start in 1979 as a method of sharing information about UNIX computer systems, and the network still plays a major role in providing computer support. From its earliest days, though, participants showed even more interest in discussing social and political issues, including controversial ones such as abortion and the death penalty Since then, USENET has grown wildly, but the growth has not been without controversy. USENET's strong points lie in the discussions of computer hardware and software, hobbies, entertainment, and recreation. But many people have concluded that USENET is not very well suited for the discussion of controversial social issues. It's just too easy for obnoxious twerps to ruin the discussion, leading to a "low signal-to-noise ratio," as experienced USENET hands term it. I'll promise you one thing: After reading USENET for a while, your estimate of the number of obnoxious twerps in the world will go up by a very substantial percentage.

One of USENET's worst problems is its own success. Every day, USENET contributors post the equivalent of 80,000 pages of text—the days are long gone, obviously, when anyone could hope to read all or most of the newsgroups. Most people follow just one or two of them, and ignore the rest—but even so, many newsgroups receive dozens or hundreds of messages per day.

Still, USENET is a wonderful resource. Many newsgroups offer intelligent discussion—particularly the *moderated* ones, in which all submissions must pass the scrutiny of a human moderator, who checks to see whether they are relevant to the newsgroup's goals. Generally speaking, the technically oriented newsgroups are of the greatest value; there's a real spirit of information exchange and resource sharing One of the best things about USENET are the *FAQs* ("Frequently Asked Questions"), which attempt to provide answers to the questions people are most likely to ask. There are hundreds of these, and some of them are among the best sources of information on a topic that you can obtain anywhere.

To read and contribute to USENET newsgroups, you need software called a *newsreader*. But don't go out on the Net hunting down FTP sites—you already have one of the best newsreaders available: Netscape. Whether you want to join in the hue or cry or just access FAQs, Netscape provides wonderful tools for accessing USENET. You can read messages, post your own messages on a new subject, or reply—either by a follow-up post or an e-mail message—to messages others have left. Compared to the most powerful newsreading programs, Netscape lacks only a few advanced functions. It's the perfect tool for reading USENET on a daily basis. This chapter thoroughly explores Netscape's USENET capabilities.

For the Time-Challenged

♦ To get started with USENET, you must name your NNTP server in the Mail and News page of the preferences menu. Then you download the names of all the newsgroups and choose the ones to which you want to subscribe.

♦ To read a newsgroup, click its name in the Subscribed Newsgroups window. You'll see a list of current article titles. To read an article, click its title.

♦ While you're at the article level, you can use the buttons to view the next or previous articles in a thread, or the first article in the next or previous thread. You can also mark all the articles as read, return to the article list (This Newsgroup button) or return to the Subscribed Newsgroups page (Subscribed Newsgroups).

♦ Don't even think about posting until you fully understand the rules of netiquette.

♦ Create your signature file before posting. This is a text file that you reference in the Mail and News page of the Preferences menu.

♦ To post an article, click the Post New Article button at the newsgroup's article title level.

♦ Consider posting an e-mail reply instead of posting a follow-up message to the group.

Netscape provides excellent tools for USENET navigation and posting—in fact, you may not need any additional software. If you're interested in USENET, you should read this chapter.

Please do not post messages to a USENET newsgroup until you fully understand the newsgroup's purpose and the range of acceptable discussion subjects. Most of all, please do not post questions that have already been answered in the newsgroup's FAQ ("Frequently Asked Questions"), if there is one (not all newsgroups have FAQs). This chapter shows you how to access USENET FAQs; please read this section carefully and obtain the FAQ for any newsgroup to which you're thinking of posting a message. Carefully observe the rules of "netiquette," which boil down to good manners, basically: be polite, don't "shout" (using all capital letters), give credit where credit is due, and don't post anything in anger.

INTRODUCING USENET NEWSGROUPS

With at least 7,000 USENET newsgroups available from most servers, some kind of organization is needed to make sense of the lengthy list of newsgroup names. This organization is *hierarchical*, and works in the following way:

- Every newsgroup is part of a top-level hierarchy, such as comp (computer-related subjects), rec (recreation), or soc (social newsgroups).

- Every newsgroup has at least one other part to its name, with the parts separated by dots (such as misc.test or alt.censorship).

- Many newsgroups are further subdivided by adding additional names, as in the following examples:

    alt.fan.tolkein
    alt.fan.woody-allen
    comp.sys.mac.games.action
    comp.sys.mac.graphics

Newsgroups are organized into two broad categories:

1. **Standard Newsgroups**   These newsgroups have been established by a formal voting procedure. Every USENET site is expected to carry the standard newsgroups; not all do, however, owing to problems with disk storage space.

2. **Alternative Newsgroups**   Anyone who knows the correct UNIX command can create a newsgroup in the alternative (alt.*) hierarchy—but no USENET site is obligated to carry it. However, many sites offer all or many of the alt newsgroups, which range from important and useful (alt.censorship) to completely silly (alt.barney.dinosaur.die.die.die).

The standard newsgroups fall into the following hierarchies:

bionet	Biology and the environment
biz	Business discussions and advertising
ClariNet	A do-it-yourself on-line newspaper consisting of feeds from major wire services, such as UPI and AP
comp	Computers and computer applications
K12	Primary and secondary education)
misc	Anything that doesn't fit into the other categories
news	Newsgroups about USENET itself
rec	Hobbies and sports
sci	The sciences generally
soc	Social issues and socializing
talk	No-holds-barred controversy, flaming, verbiage— and occasionally, interesting discussion and debate

USENET may be among the world's most ephemeral communications media: Every article is set to expire after a certain period (usually, two weeks), in which case the message simply disappears from the net. With hundreds of megabytes of new articles streaming in daily, many USENET sites have no choice but to decrease the expiration period down to as little as 24 hours. If you don't read the newsgroup regularly, then, you'll miss the action—and you won't have a clue about why a certain topic has become the day's *cause celebre*.

WHAT'S IN A NEWSGROUP?

A newsgroup consists of *articles*, which have been contributed by USENET's participants. They fall into two categories:

1. **Posts** An original message, with a new topic, that somebody contributed.

2. **Follow-up Posts** A reply to the original message, which usually contains some quoted text from the original message. The title of a

follow-up post usually echoes the original post's title, with the addition of "re:" at the beginning of the title.

To enhance your ability to follow the "thread" of discussion, USENET software can organize posts and follow-up posts into groups (called *threads*). Not all newsreaders are *threaded*, though, in which case they throw the messages at you in chronological order. Happily, Netscape can thread the messages—and that makes it an above-average newsreader. Other features take it into the "very good" category, as you'll see in the pages to follow.

READING USENET

All USENET newsreaders, Netscape included, operate at three distinct levels:

1. **Newsgroup Level**   At this level, you select the newsgroup you want to read (from a list of 5,000 or more). You can also *subscribe* to individual newsgroups, so that they appear on a shorter, more accessible list.

2. **Article Title Level**   At this level, you see a list of the current articles' titles in the newsgroup you've selected to read.

3. **Article Level**   By clicking an article title, you go "down" to this level, where you see the text of the article you clicked. You can stay at this level to see the next or previous articles, if you wish, or you can go back "up" to the article title level.

When you display and then close a USENET article, Netscape marks the article as read, and its name doesn't appear on the article list anymore. There's a way you can see it again, though, if you act quickly; as explained in the section entitled "Using the Button Bar," you can click the Show Read Articles button to redisplay articles you've read, as long as they haven't expired.

CONFIGURING NETSCAPE TO ACCESS USENET

To configure Netscape to access USENET, you must do the following: Supply the program with the domain name of your NNTP (USENET) server

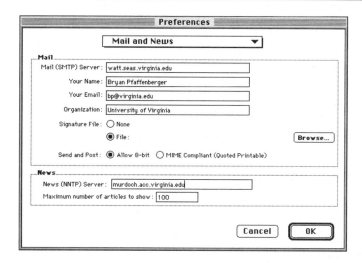

Figure 18.1 Mail and News preferences

and download the current newsgroup list. The following sections detail these procedures.

Telling Netscape the Domain Name of Your NNTP Server

To access USENET, you need access to an *NNTP server*, a program that makes USENET newsgroups accessible to newsreading software. Generally, access to an NNTP server is included with Internet service subscriptions. If you're not sure, call your service provider, and be sure to get the NNTP server's domain name.

To tell Netscape which NNTP server to use, follow these steps:

1. From the Options menu, choose Preferences.

2. In the list box, choose Mail and News. You'll see the Mail and News page, shown in Figure 18.1.

3. In the News (NNTP) Server box, type the domain name of your NNTP server. Get this information from your service provider, if you don't already have it.

4. Click OK.

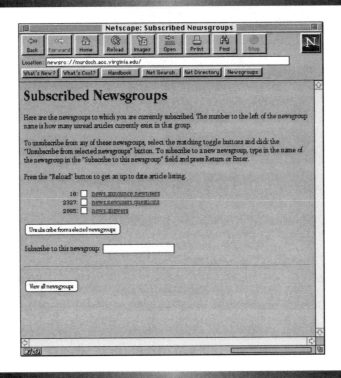

Figure 18.2   Minimal subscription list

Downloading the Newsgroups List

After you have told Netscape the domain name of your newsreader, you can begin downloading the list of newsgroup names. Since your server may offer as many as 7,000 newsgroups, this process may require a few minutes.

To download the newsgroups list:

1. From the Directory menu, choose Go to Newsgroups. You'll see a message indicating that Netscape is creating a newsrc file for you; just press Enter to continue. The newsrc file will contain your newsgroup subscription list. You'll see a minimal list consisting only of newsgroups that new users should read, as shown in Figure 18.2.

2. Click the View All Newsgroups button, located at the bottom of the document you are currently viewing. You'll see a window informing you that this procedure will take a few minutes.

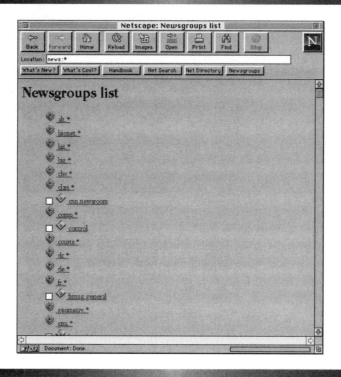

Figure 18.3   List of all the newsgroups available from the NNTP server

> 3. Click OK to proceed. Netscape downloads the list of newsgroups. When the program finishes downloading the newsgroups list, you'll see the document shown in Figure 18.3.

Subscribing to Newsgroups

Once you've downloaded the newsgroups list, as described in the previous section, it's time to select the newsgroups that you think you'll want to read on a regular basis. With more than 7,000 groups, that's a daunting job, but there's help available. Your humble author's book on USENET (called, by an odd coincidence, *The USENET Book* [published by Addison-Wesley]), contains reviews of the top USENET newsgroups. I also recommend the magazine *NetGuide*, which includes newsgroup reviews in every issue.

The newsgroups list (see Figure 18.3) has two kinds of icons next to the listed items:

 A Newsgroup Hierarchy

Click here to see lots more newsgroup hierarchies and newsgroup names.

 A Newsgroup

To subscribe to the newsgroup, click the check box, and then click the Subscribe to Selected Newsgroups button.

To navigate the newsgroups list, click hierarchy names to see the lists of newsgroups within the hierarchy. Subscribe to as many groups as you like by clicking the check box next to their names. To go up to a higher level, just click the Back button.

You can also search for newsgroups. To do so, follow these steps:

1. Scroll down to the bottom of the newsgroups list. You'll see a search box.

2. In the search box, type the word you're looking for, such as "politics" or "beer." Don't type more than one word.

3. Press Enter. You'll see a list of just those newsgroups that contain the word you typed in their names.

4. To subscribe to a newsgroup, click its check box, and click the Subscribe to Selected Newsgroups button.

5. Each time you click the Subscribe to Selected Newsgroups button, you'll see the Subscribed Newsgroups page again; in front of each newsgroup's name is a number informing you how many articles are available to read. To subscribe to more newsgroups, click the View All Newsgroups button, and repeat the above procedure.

There's another way you can subscribe to newsgroups: By typing their names. In the Subscribed Newsgroups page, note the search box next to "Subscribe to this newsgroup." If you know the exact name of the newsgroup to which you want to subscribe, type it here and press Enter.

READING THE NEWS

To read the articles in a particular newsgroup, click its name in the Subscribed Newsgroups list. You'll see Netscape's article selector level, shown in Figure 18.4. Listed are article titles; by default, Netscape displays the 100 most recently received articles. If there are more than 100 articles available, you'll see hyperlinks to Earlier Articles and Earliest Articles.

Note how Netscape has grouped the articles into threads. Where a subject has received two or more posts, you see the subject in bold and the posts grouped below the subject.

Often, the article list does not show the original post because it has expired. USENET postings are temporary; to make room for incoming

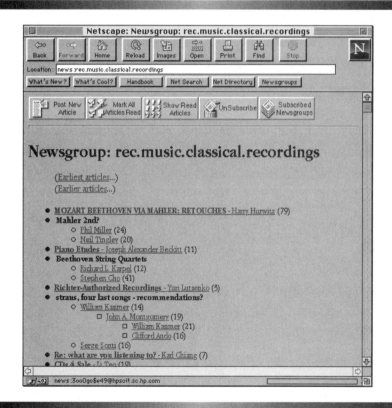

Figure 18.4 Article selector level

posts, the news software automatically deletes postings after a period set by the USENET site administrator. Depending on the amount of available disk space, this could be as brief as a few days. So don't count on finding the original article in a thread. If you open one of the posts in a thread, however, you will find a section called References at the top of the message. Here, Netscape provides numbered hyperlinks to previous articles in the thread; try clicking 1 to see if the original post is still available. If not, you'll see a page informing you that the article may have expired.

By default, Netscape displays the most recent 100 articles—a manageable chunk. At the top of the page, you'll see the following hyperlinks:

- **Earliest Articles**   Click here to see the first 100 articles that are currently available.

- **Earlier Articles**   Click here to see the next-most recently received chunk of 100 articles.

Once you have clicked Earliest Articles or Earlier Articles, you'll see the following hyperlinks at the bottom of the article selector page:

- **Later Articles**   Click here to see the next 100 articles.

- **Latest Articles**   Click here to see the most recently received articles.

If you'd like to see more articles at a time, open the Mail and News page of the Preferences menu, and type a larger number in the Show box.

Using the Button Bar

At the top and bottom of article selector pages in Netscape, you'll see the following button bar:

Click here to post an article to the newsgroup.

Click here to mark all these articles as read so that they do not appear in the article list again.

Display all the articles, even the ones you've read. This is a great feature if you've read an article (which removes it from the list) and want to read it again.

 Remove this newsgroup from the subscription list.

 Return to the Subscribed Newsgroups page.

Reading an Article

To read an article, just click it. You see the article on its own new page (Figure 18.5).

Note the following features of the article page:

Button Bars	A new button bar appears, both at the top and the bottom of the article.
Header	Every USENET message has a header that tells you the subject, the date of posting, the e-mail address of the person doing the posting, the poster's organization, and the newsgroup(s) to which the article was posted.
Message Body	Here's the text of the message.

Here's a quick guide to the buttons:

 Next Article Read the next article in this thread, if there is one (if not, this button is dimmed).

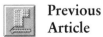 **Previous Article** Read the previous article in the thread, if there is one (if not, this button is dimmed).

 Next Thread Display the first article in the next thread.

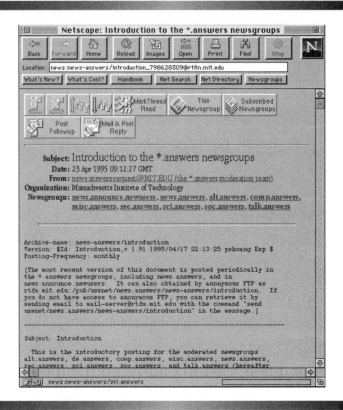

Figure 18.5 Article displayed by Netscape

  Previous Thread   Display the first article in the *previous* thread.

Mark Thread Read   Mark all the articles in the thread as read.

This Newsgroup   Display the list of article titles in this newsgroup.

Subscribed Newsgroups   Go back to the Subscribed Newsgroups page.

Post Follow-up Post a follow-up message.

 Mail and Post Reply Post a follow-up mesage and also send a reply by e-mail. *Don't* click this button if you only want to send an e-mail reply! Open the File menu and choose Mail Document instead.

Navigating at the Article Level

As you read the news, you'll commonly perform the following actions:

- **Go to the next article in this thread** Click the Next Article button.

- **Go to a previous article in this thread.** Click the Previous Article button.

- **Read the article that started all this ruckus.** If you're reading a follow-up article, look in the header for a References field, and click the first number you see. The original article may have expired, though.

- **Bag all the articles in this thread and go on to the next thread.** Click the Mark Thread Read button. Netscape displays the first article in the next thread.

- **Redisplay the article list for this newsgroup.** Click the This Newsgroup button.

- **Leave this newsgroup entirely and choose another newsgroup.** Click the Subscribed Newsgroups button.

 If you've recently accessed a newsgroup, Netscape will read its cache instead of downloading the latest articles. To see the latest articles, click Reload.

Printing a Message

You can print the text of any USENET post you see. Just open the File menu and choose Print. Uncharacteristically, Netscape prints the posting's text in plain Courier—no icons, no graphics. But, it's fast.

POSTING YOUR OWN MESSAGES

Be sure to read a newsgroup for a couple of weeks before posting, so that you understand the type of subjects that are discussed. And please, contribute something of value, not just your opinion, and familiarize yourself with *netiquette*, the rules of proper comportment on-line. So that people can tell who you are, create a *signature*. When you post you can choose between an original message (post on a new subject) or a follow-up post. The following sections detail these points.

Netscape thoughtfully subscribes you to three basic news-groups: news.announce.newusers, news.newusers.questions, and news.answers. These first two newsgroups contain basic information about USENET. Read the posted articles carefully before attempting to post your own articles to USENET. In particular, read Mark Moraes' "Emily Post-news: Rules for Posting to USENET."

Netiquette

Before you post to USENET, you should make sure you know what you're doing. If you don't, you may find yourself on the wrong end of lots of angry posts and e-mail messages. USENET people aren't difficult to get along with—as long as you follow the rules, called *netiquette*. Here's a quick overview:

- Don't *crosspost* (post to more than one newsgroup) unless there's a compelling reason to do so. Since you're a beginner, you wouldn't know any such reasons, so don't do it.

- Make sure you are posting to the right newsgroup.

- Read the newsgroup for at least two weeks before posting.

- Read the FAQ. Don't ask questions that have already been answered in the FAQ.

- Do not criticize anyone's spelling and grammar. Lots of people who post to USENET speak English as a second or third language.

- Keep your cool. Never post in anger.

- Don't quote a lengthy message and end it with "Me too." You'll get some sizzling flames in your mailbox!

- Ignore messages that contain obvious inaccuracies ("Francis Ford Coppola directed *Star Wars*"). These messages may be a trap (called a *troll*) to tempt you to make a fool out of yourself.

- Do not post a follow-up message if an e-mail reply will do.

- Don't post anything you wouldn't want to see on your boss's desk tomorrow morning—or your mother's.

- Do not post "test" messages to an ordinary newsgroup. There are newsgroups for this purpose, such as alt.test.

Creating Your Signature

It's not strictly necessary, but you may wish to create a *signature*, a text file containing your name, address, phone, and fax numbers, so that people can find out how to contact you (other than through e-mail).

To create a signature file, follow these steps:

1. Open your word processing program or SimpleText.

2. Type a signature of no more than four lines. Include your name, title, organization, city, state, zip, phone, and fax. Don't get cute.

3. Save the file to Netscape's folder. If you're using your word processing program, be sure to save the file as ASCII text (plain text).

4. In Netscape, open the Options menu and choose Preferences.

5. Choose the Mail and News option.

6. Click the Browse button, locate your signature file, and click OK.

Posting an Original Message

Assuming you've carefully read the "Netiquette" section above, and you're confident you know what you're doing, you can use Netscape to post a message to USENET. For your first post, use alt.test.

To post your message:

1. Open the newsgroup to which you want to post.

2. Click the Post New Article button. You'll see the Send Mail/Post News window, shown in Figure 18.6. If you've identified a signature file in the Mail and News dialog box (Preferences menu),

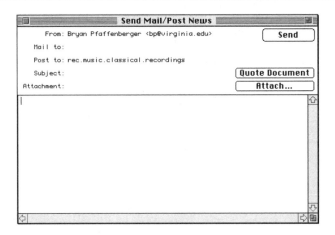

Figure 18.6 Send Mail/Post News window

Netscape will insert your signature into the message. In addition, the program will automatically place the current newsgroup's name in the Post To line.

3. In the Subject area, type a brief but descriptive title for your document. This is what people will see in the newsgroup's article title list. Don't type "Help" or "A Question." Titles such as this will be ignored. Be specific.

4. Type the message above the signature.

5. Carefully proofread your post for spelling and typographical errors. You can't get it back once it has been sent!

6. Click Send. Netscape posts your message.

I don't see my message on the article list! Don't worry, everything's OK with your post. USENET software has a low priority for processing; the posts you contribute are kept in a storage area until there's enough computer capacity to take care of them. This might be minutes, or even hours, from the time you actually post the message.

REPLYING BY E-MAIL

If you want to reply to somebody's post, consider sending an e-mail reply rather than posting to the group. Suppose, for example, that somebody has posted a question, and you know the answer. Do you think the whole group would be interested? If so, then post a follow-up reply, as explained in the next section. If you think only the person asking the question would be interested, then send an e-mail reply.

To send an e-mail reply, follow these steps:

1. Display the article to which you want to reply.

2. From the File menu, choose Mail Document. You'll see the Send Mail/Post News window, like the one shown in Figure 18.6. Netscape has echoed the person's e-mail address.

3. If you would like to quote the text of the document to which you are replying, click Quote Document. By all means edit this text down to just the part to which you want to respond. In particular, edit out the person's signature.

4. Type your reply. You can insert this within the quoted text, if you like.

5. Carefully check your typing and spelling, and make sure once more that you deleted the newsgroup name from the Post Newsgroup field.

6. Click Send.

 Oh no! My e-mail reply got posted to the whole group! And it was probably something private, wasn't it? Here's what happened—you clicked the Post Mail and Reply button instead of choosing Mail Document from the File menu. This is a very dangerous button, and I wish Netscape would remove it. With advanced newsreaders, you can cancel a message. Your system administrator might be able to help you do this; call for help, and do so fast.

POSTING A FOLLOW-UP MESSAGE

Post a follow-up message only if you're sure you want the whole newsgroup to see your reply. That's OK, as long as you really think that it's worth reading and that it falls within the newsgroup's guidelines.

To post a follow-up message, follow these steps:

1. Display the article to which you want to reply.

2. Click the Post Reply button. You see the Send Mail/Post News window, like the one shown in Figure 18.6. Netscape has echoed the subject, and placed "Re:" before it.

3. If you would like to quote the text of the document to which you are replying, click Quote Document. By all means edit this text down to just the part to which you want to respond. In particular, edit out the person's signature.

4. Type your reply. You can insert this within the quoted text, if you like.

5. Carefully check your typing and spelling.

6. Click Send.

SEARCHING TODAY'S USENET POSTINGS

If you're looking for specific information on USENET, you can easily go nuts trying to search manually through the thousands of postings that appear each day. Why not let the computer do it for you? A gateway document entitled Search Today's USENET News allows you to do just that. Click the hyperlink in HOME.HTML, or use the following URL:

http://ibd.ar.com/News/About.html

The result of your search is a new page listing the results, which you can directly access by clicking the listed hyperlinks.

SEARCHING USENET FAQS

To make sure you don't post a question that others have asked before, you should read the FAQ for a newsgroup to which you want to post. Not all newsgroups have FAQs, but you should make an effort to find one in case there is.

Happily, it's easy to search for USENET FAQs. To do so, click the USENET FAQs hyperlink in the Reference section of HOME.HTML. Alternatively, use this URL:

http://www.cis.ohio-state.edu/hypertext/faq/usenet/FAQ-List.html

Just follow the on-screen instructions to browse or search for the FAQ you want.

What's Missing?

Netscape is a capable newsreader, but it's missing a couple of features you'll find in the best programs:

- **Decoding of multi-part sound and graphics files**   Some newsreaders have this capability built in. With Netscape, you'll need to save the files and decode them with a uudecode program that's compatible with the Macintosh.

- **Kill files**   Wouldn't you prefer to never see the message "Make Money Fast" again? In advanced newsreaders, a feature called a *kill file* intercepts unwanted messages before you ever see them. You can add selected words and even individual's names to the file, which results in a net decrease of the obnoxious twerp quotient. Maybe the next version, eh, Mozilla?

From Here

- Want to see what the Web's future looks like? Check out Part V, "The Netscape Marketplace." Shop 'til you drop!

Chapter 19

Surviving Telnet and 3270 Sessions

S ome computers cannot connect to the Internet. Among the worst offenders are IBM mainframe computers, which don't speak the same language that most other computers do. In addition to mainframe computers, the roster of Telnet sites includes thousands of bulletin board systems (BBSs) all over the world, and a good sprinkling of freenets (community information services). All in all, there's a lot of interesting stuff out there, as long as you're willing to forgo multimedia—Telnet is strictly text-only.

In order to access the information stored on Telnet resources, you need a Telnet and a 3270 helper application, as discussed in Chapter 5. Basically, a Telnet helper application turns your computer into a primitive, dumb VT100 terminal, which allows you text-only access to mainframe computer data. A 3270 session is virtually the same species of beast, save that your computer is taught to emulate an IBM 3270 terminal. Like Telnet, 3270 sessions are text-based, but 3270 sessions can include text with varying colors (wow!) and even primitive ASCII-style graphics.

This chapter isn't of much value unless you really need to access a Telnet resource, such as a university library card catalog. If so, read on, and good luck.

USING NCSA TELNET

When you see a hyperlink that leads to a Telnet session, you can access the data contained in this resource. To do so, follow these instructions:

1. Click the Telnet hyperlink. You may see a dialog box telling you what to type after your Telnet client starts. Click OK to proceed.

2. After NCSA Telnet appears on-screen (Figure 19.1), you may need to press Enter once or twice before things start happening.

3. If you were instructed to type something special to log on (see step 1), do so now.

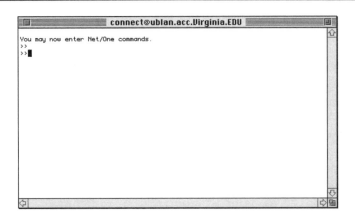

Figure 19.1   NCSA Telnet

For the Time-Challenged

♦ By means of Telnet and 3270 links, you can access the resources of thousands of mainframe computers, bulletin board systems, and freenets worldwide. But it's strictly text-only.

♦ When you click a Telnet hyperlink, Netscape starts NCSA Telnet. Watch for a dialog box telling you how to log on. If nothing happens, press Enter. To quit the Telnet session and return to Netscape, choose Quit from the File menu or type Command + Q.

♦ When you click a 3270 hyperlink, Netscape starts TN3270. If you have an extended keyboard, you may be able to use your computer's function keys (F1 through F12) to perform certain functions; these keys are also available in the Function Keys menu. The application may paint the screen with vivid colors and text-based graphics.

---

4. If the Telnet server asks you what type of "terminal" you are using, type **VT100** and press Enter.

5. To end your Telnet session, choose Quit from the File menu or type Command + Q.

 In most Telnet sessions, you can type a question mark (?) and press Enter to see an on-screen list of your options.

From here on out, you're at the mercy of the mainframe programmer who created the application you're using. Each Telnet session you encounter will have its own unique user interface, which might be very good or very bad. In Figure 19.2 for example, you see the Telnet screen of VIRGO, the University of Virginia's library card catalog. VIRGO's user interface is reasonably easy to use; the commands you need to know appear on a menu near the bottom of the screen, and help screens are provided.

 Here are some things to remember about Telnet sessions:

• If the screen is blank, press Enter.

• If you need to correct a typing mistake, you can usually do so by pressing the Backspace key to rub out what

```
┌─────────────────────────────────────────────────────────────┐
│ ▓▓▓             connect@ublan.acc.Virginia.EDU          ▓▓ │
│ ▓      ■  University of Virginia Library          H7GH  ⬆ │
│             VIRGO Database Selection Menu        5.1.1      │
│                                                             │
│ Type CHOose, followed by the database code, and press <Enter>.│
│            CHO VCAT                  CHO WILS               │
│                                                             │
│                                                             │
│      VCAT        UVA Library Catalog                        │
│     *WILS        Wilson Periodical Indexes                  │
│     *CART        Current Contents Articles                  │
│     *CCON        Current Contents Journals                  │
│     *NABS        Newspaper Abstracts                        │
│     *ABII        ABI/INFORM Business Abstracts             │
│     VIRTUAL      Other Library Catalogs                     │
│                                                             │
│                           * Databases that require Sign-On. │
│ ─────────────────────────────── + Page 1 of 2 ──────────── │
│      HELp        Select a database label from above  <F8>  FORward │
│                  NEWs  (Library System News)               │
│                                                             │
│ Database Selection:                                       ⬇ │
│ ⬅                                                      ⇨ ▣ │
└─────────────────────────────────────────────────────────────┘
```

Figure 19.2   VIRGO session (Telnet)

you've typed. If this doesn't work, open the Configure menu and activate the Backspace option.

• If you get lost or confused, just quit the session by choosing Quit from the File menu or typing Command + Q. You'll see the Web page containing the Telnet hyperlink; you can start over, if you wish.

Using TN3720 (3270 Telnet Sessions)

3270 sessions closely resemble their Telnet brethren, save that your computer emulates an IBM 3270 mainframe terminal. Generally, that's good news—you'll see colored text and even some primitive graphics, which may make the application easier to use. As in all things Telnet, though, that depends on the programmer's skill.

If you click a hyperlink to a 3270 session, Netscape starts TN3270, the application you installed in Chapter 5. You'll see the TN3270 screen, as shown in Figure 19.3. You can't see the colors very well in this book's screen shot, admittedly, but it's much better than garden-variety Telnet: you see colored text against a black background, and it all adds up to an easier-to-use interface. In addition, the Function Keys menu gives you access to a variety of function keys (if you have an extended keyboard, you can press the F1 through F12 keys). You can click these buttons or function keys to perform special tasks (just what they do depends on how the programmer set up the application you're accessing). Otherwise, TN3270 looks and works pretty much the same way NCSA Telnet does.

Here are some things to remember about 3270 sessions:

- If the interface tells you to press a PF key to do something, press the corresponding function key on your keyboard. For example, PF1 corresponds to F1.

- If the interface tells you to press a PA key to do something, open the Function Keys menu and click the appropriate PA button.

- If you need to correct a typing mistake, you can usually do so by pressing the Backspace key to rub out what you've typed.

- You can move the cursor by pressing the arrow keys on your keyboard.

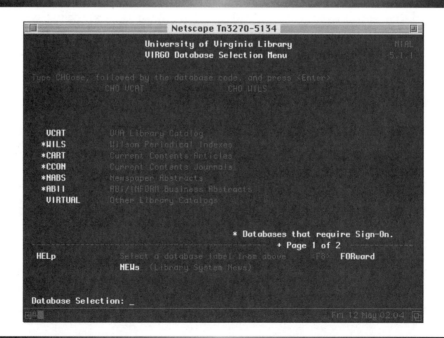

Figure 19.3   TN3270 at work

SEARCHING FOR TELNET RESOURCES WITH HYTELNET

What's out there in Telnet-land? To find out, you can search a database of Telnet and 3270 gateways called HyTelnet. To access HyTelnet's search page, use the following URL:

http://galaxy.einet.net/hytelnet/HYTELNET.html

The result of a HyTelnet search is a Web page that lists Telnet sites that include your search words in their descriptions. To access one of these sites, click the hyperlink; you'll see another Web page with the Telnet site's description. Included is a Telnet or 3270 session link.

FROM HERE

- You've surfed the Web and explored the Internet. So what's left? How about the future? Check out Part V for the exploding world of on-line commerce, which you can access by means of Netscape's secure protocols.

Part V

THE NETSCAPE
MARKETPLACE

Chapter
20

Understanding Secure Transactions

A revolution's about to happen: The Web is going commercial. In the coming years, more and more businesses will open shop on the Web, allowing you to access on-line catalogs and providing the means for you to order on-line. And for payment? Use your credit card. Thanks to Netscape's security technology, you can rest assured that nobody can intercept your credit card number or expiration data while it's in transmission via the Internet.

This chapter is for anyone who would like to understand Netscape's security capabilities, but it's not really necessary to read: This technology functions in the background. If you access a secure site, you see a message and the broken key becomes a whole key. You can have confidence at this point that your transmissions cannot be intercepted or read by a third party.

♦ Security actually involves three different aspects: authentication (knowing who's sending you something), confidentiality (knowing that no third party can intercept and read the information you exchange with someone), and integrity (knowing that your message has not been tampered with or altered while en route).

♦ Public key cryptography, the technology that underlies Netscape's security features, enables any two people to exchange undecipherable messages without needing to exchange decoding keys via a secure channel.

♦ Netscape's security standard, called Secure Socket Layer (SSL), uses public key cryptography to enable you to establish a secure connection with a Web server.

♦ There is no single Web security standard yet; in fact, there are several competing standards. In the years to come it is likely that a single standard will emerge.

♦ Your credit card information cannot be intercepted en route, but you still need to use common sense when ordering via the Web. Order from trusted, well-established firms and make sure you understand their policies.

WHAT IS "SECURITY"?

In the computer world, *security* has three distinct shades of meaning: *authentication*, *confidentiality*, and *integrity*, as the following sections discuss. Of greatest interest to you, as a potential customer of commercial Web services, are confidentiality and integrity.

Authentication

In brief, *authentication* ensures that you are really who you say you are when you log on to a server. Most Web servers demand no authentication at all—they just let you in. However, virtually all Web servers support simple protection by password: You must type a login name (user name) and password to access the service. An example of a Web service that requires password authentication is HotWired, the on-line version of *Wired* magazine.

When you access HotWired for the first time, you're asked to create a login name and password and to supply your e-mail address. You then receive an automatically generated e-mail message that includes an authorization number. You must then supply this authorization number to access the system. What's gained from this? A modicum of assurance that you aren't accessing the site using someone else's name and e-mail address.

Confidentiality

Confidentiality refers to the protection of information while it is en route to its destination. It's not nice to think about, but none of the information you are transmitting via the Web is free from prying eyes. Hackers, criminals, or investigators can easily intercept, record, and print all the information you transmit.

Integrity

Integrity refers to the exact preservation of the transmitted data so that it reaches its destination without any alteration, accidental or deliberate. As with confidentiality, the Web provides absolutely no means of ensuring the integrity of transmitted data. It could be altered while en route, either by chance or deliberate interference, and the receiving computer would have no way of knowing.

THE NEED FOR ENCRYPTION

The solution to the Web's confidentiality and security problems lies in the use of *encryption*. In essence, encryption is the process of converting a *plaintext* message (a message that could be read by anyone) into an unreadable *ciphertext*, by means of a *key* (a method of transforming the message so that it appears to be gibberish). The message can be read only by the intended recipient, who possesses the key and uses it (in a process called *decryption*) to make the text readable again. A simple encryption technique is ROT-13, which "rotates" all letters 13 characters to the right in the alphabet. The ciphertext looks like gibberish, but it is easily decrypted by rotating the letters 13 characters left. Encryption ensures integrity as well as confidentiality; if anyone or anything has altered the message en route, it won't decode 100% correctly, so you'll know that something has gone wrong.

ROT-13 is a poor encryption technique because its key is so simple. In fact, it's used on USENET only to keep adult-oriented material away from the eyes of children or those who would rather not have such material thrown in their faces. More complicated keys are needed to ensure confidentiality and integrity. With more complicated keys, though, another problem arises: How to transmit the key to the recipient. Traditionally, this has been done by courier, but this is costly and time-consuming.

A new cryptographic method called *public key cryptography* eliminates the need to deliver the key and raises the possibility that people who have never previously exchanged messages could send encrypted messages to each other that could not be intercepted by a third party. In public key cryptography, there are two different keys, an encryption key and a decryption key:

- **Public Encryption Key**   You make your encryption key public; people use it to send an encrypted message to you.

- **Decryption Key**   This key is kept private. You use it to decode the messages sent to you. Nobody else can read the message without this key.

With public key cryptography, there is no need to establish a secure channel to exchange the decryption key; the person who wishes to send an encrypted message to you merely obtains the public encryption key, encrypts the message, and sends it to you. Nobody along the way can decode the message, even if they have intercepted the encryption key: they would need the decryption key, and you keep that secret. Rightfully, public key encryption has been described as a revolution in cryptography. It will make cryptography available to ordinary people.

INTRODUCING THE SECURE SOCKET LAYER SECURITY PROTOCOL

To provide secure transactions via the World Wide Web, Netscape Communications Corporation has proposed a standard called the Secure Socket Layer (SSL) protocol. This proposed Internet standard seeks to provide secure public key encryption capabilities so that people can exchange information securely via any established Internet protocol, including not only the

Web but also Gopher, FTP, Telnet, and others. What is more, SSL seeks to do this without placing undue demands on users; much or all of the SSL processing goes on in the background, without requiring any intervention from the user.

An SSL session begins when an SSL-capable client (such as Netscape Navigator) contacts an SSL-capable server (such as Netscape's secure Web servers). A brief exchange of public keys occurs; from that point on, the client and server can exchange secure, encrypted messages, and no third party can intercept them. In addition, SSL includes integrity-checking features that assure both parties that the message has not been tampered with or altered during its transmission.

WHAT ABOUT STANDARDS?

As of this book's writing, there is no "official" standard for the secure transmission of sensitive data on the World Wide Web. In an effort to gain acceptance for its SSL protocol as the standard security protocol for the Web, Netscape has published SSL's specifications and made the technology widely available. However, competing firms are attempting to do the same. The worst-case scenario is that two or more competing but incompatible security standards will exist. If this happens, the Web's budding commercial ventures could die on the vine: a user of Netscape would be able to access only Netscape-friendly secure sites, while users of competing browsers (such as Spyglass's Enhanced NSCA Mosaic) would be able to access only those sites conforming to Spyglass's protocol.

The most likely outcome of this struggle, in the short run, is that two or three competing security standards will exist and Web servers will have to recognize them all. Netscape has announced its plans to support S-HTTP, a competing Web protocol, in addition to its own SSL, in both Netscape Navigator and its server products. In the long run, it seems likely that the Web community will be able to agree on a single standard for secure Web transactions. Most likely, it will include many features from SSL plus additional ones from Netscape's competitors. The *Wall Street Journal* reported in 1995 that Netscape Communications had invested in Terisa Systems, which is developing a Web security standard that would unify all the competing security technologies. A solution to the standardization dilemma may be very near.

ACCESSING A SECURE SERVER

You'll know when you access a secure server: You'll see the dialog box shown in Figure 20.1. This dialog box informs you that you are accessing a secure document. In addition, the broken key on the status bar is suddenly made whole.

Another way you can tell that you've accessed a secure server is to look at the Location box: A secure server's URL begins with https//.

To get more information about the document you have accessed, open the File menu and choose Document Information. This command displays the dialog box shown in Figure 20.2. When you access a secure document, you'll see the server's authentication certificate, which tells you that you really are accessing the service you think you're accessing (and not some clever hacker's "mock" service). This dialog box also indicates the level of security that has been established.

IS MY CREDIT CARD INFORMATION REALLY SAFE?

Once you've accessed a secure server, you can transmit your credit card number without fear of its being intercepted along the way. Does that mean your credit card information is safe? With Netscape's security features, you can be assured that nobody can obtain your credit card number by tapping

Figure 20.1   Message displayed when contacting a secure server

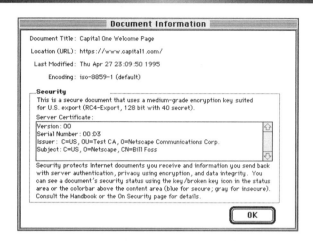

Figure 20.2 Document Information dialog box

your Internet connection. But sending your credit card number via a secure link is very much like giving it to somebody over the telephone: You're still dependent on the honesty and integrity of the person on the other end. In the end, ordering on the Web won't be any safer than any other form of mail order.

 If you're thinking about ordering something by credit card on the Web, use all the common-sense rules that you would when ordering by telephone or mail. Order from well-established firms with good reputations. Make sure you fully understand the firm's policies regarding the delivery of ordered goods, returns and exchanges, and refunds.

FROM HERE

• Want to take a look at some Web commerce pioneers? Check out the next chapter.

Chapter
21

Let's Go Shopping!

Secure Web Commercial Sites

To promote Web vendors who have adopted Netscape's secure server technology, Netscape Communications has developed a Galleria page featuring growing numbers of commercial Web servers. To access the Galleria, open the Directory menu and choose Netscape Galleria. What you'll find, as this chapter attests, is that Web commerce is still in the experimental phase. What's going to sell on the Web? Are there some types of merchandise that aren't well suited to the Web commercial idiom? Do you offer just a few high-profile items, or your whole catalog? Are Web commercial sites best deployed for one-of-a-kind, special-interest items, or for huge shopping enterprises on a department store scale? As of yet, nobody knows—but there are plenty of experiments in all directions.

For the Time-Challenged

◆ If you run into a secure Web commercial site, scope it out one step at a time. Be sure to display and read the fine print—when will your order be delivered, and how? What happens if you want to return it? Don't shut off your shopping smarts just because you're ordering on-line.

◆ You won't find full on-line catalogs—at least, not yet. The dominant philosophy seems to be, "Let's offer a few good deals, and see who bites."

◆ Don't assume that the price is right—at least, not without checking around. Is it really worth the thrill to order something on-line if you could get the same article for less money at a local retail store?

This chapter provides an in-depth look at a few of the most interesting commercial Web sites that were on-line at the time of this book's writing; the Galleria page will certainly list additional vendors, so take a look.

Don't be shy about browsing these sites—there's no obligation. You can even fill out order forms, and then change your mind and cancel at the last moment.

CAPITAL ONE

Need a Visa card? Well, how about getting one on-line? Capital One (https://www.capital1.com/CapitalOne/c1-home.html; see Figure 21.1), one of the top credit card issuers in the country, offers an on-line Visa card application. If you're interested in applying, click the hyperlink to display the application form (Figure 21.2). Or maybe you'd like to find out how much you could save by transferring existing credit card debts to Capital One's card, with its low, introductory-offer interest rate (Figure 21.3). But be forewarned: The interest rate goes up after the first year. To its credit, Capital One makes this abundantly clear by sticking its terms in your face—you can't get to the application form without having at least seen the fine print. A class act, all around.

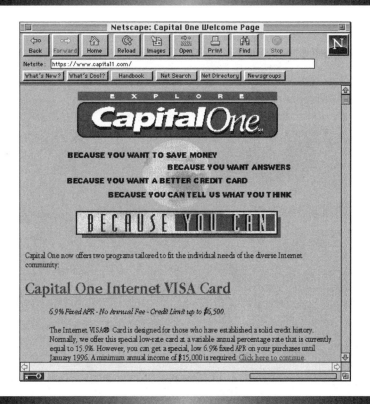

Figure 21.1 Capital One

SOFTWARE.NET

As an indication of what software retailing might be like in the future, software.net (Figure 21.4) goes the whole nine yards—not only can you take advantage of on-line ordering via secure Netscape transactions, but you can also obtain some programs via electronic links. No packaging to fill up landfills, no old buggy versions to worry about, no truck making its way across the United States, no week-long delay—just instantaneous, environmentally responsible delivery. Don't think that the software distributed electronically is strictly no-name, low-quality stuff: For those taxing moments before April 15, you can obtain H &R Block's TaxCut or Novell's TaxSaver.

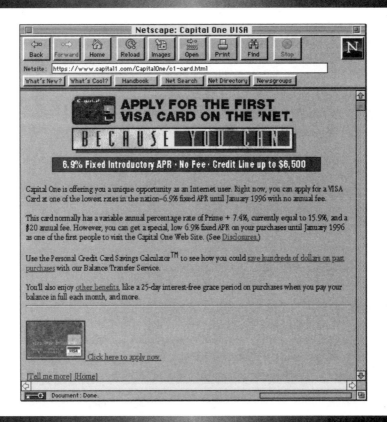

Figure 21.2   Capital One's on-line Visa card application

software.net illustrates the First Rule of Web Marketing: Provide some freebies that make the site attractive to people. Not a site to mince words, software.net offers a Freebies page, full of genuinely interesting stuff. At this writing, you could obtain the latest version of the Norton virus-scanning software, and a half-dozen sampler programs (full-featured but with built-in expiration dates). There's even a USENET-like discussion system for software.net's products and services.

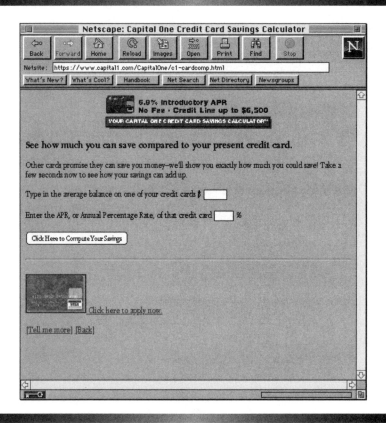

Figure 21.3 Clever use of forms (calculating your savings)

INTERNET SHOPPING NETWORK

It had to happen: cable TV's Home Shopping Network is one of the first commercial ventures on the Internet, and it figures. After all, who else has more experience in high-tech marketing? After you've had some experience with the Internet Shopping Network (ISN), though, you may wish ISN (Figure 21.5) had stuck to TV. It's not that there aren't good deals—I saw some hard drives that looked like good buys—but ISN is just a little too pushy about requesting personal information from you.

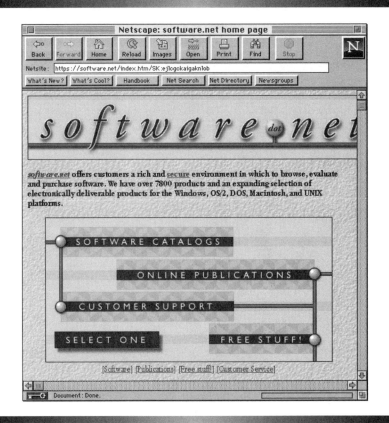

Figure 21.4   software.net

When you access ISN, you discover that you're supposed to become a member—and that you'll need to supply your credit card information up-front. If you leave the credit card information out, as I did, you'll see a message that you haven't filled out your credit card information completely. This in-your-face demand leaves one with a queasy feeling, at best, about what's to follow. But cheer up—if you really want to explore ISN, you can; there's a "tour" option that lets you look around without committing your personal information. ISN, how about putting this option up front, and letting people supply their information when they're ready to order?

Assuming you're brave enough to supply your credit card information up front, what does ISN offer? At this point, the vendor's emphasis is clearly on computers. You'll find hard drives galore, software for kids, modems, CD-ROM discs, and much more.

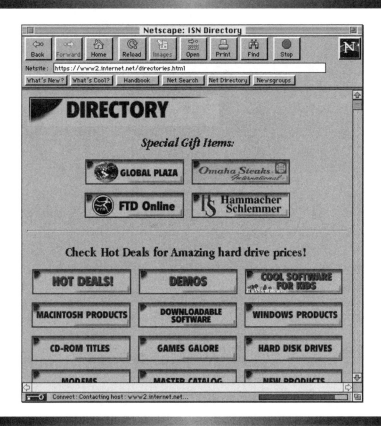

Figure 21.5   Internet Shopping Network

VIRTUAL VINEYARDS

It's an interesting match: a technology that dates back at least 2,500 years (wine-making) and the Web, which is just celebrating its sixth birthday. Virtual Vineyards makes it happen.

Don't look to Virtual Vineyards for well-known, widely distributed wines: Virtual Vineyards specializes in low-volume, high-quality vineyards, as well as limited production bottlings from larger concerns. Like other high-quality commercial Web sites, Virtual Vineyards offers freebies that attract you to the site: in this case, a glossary of wine terms, something that even experienced sippers can appreciate. What's more, you can (virtually) tour the small, interesting vineyards that VV features, and read biographies of the owners and winemakers (no pictures, though). Navigation among the site's many pages is easy, thanks to navigation buttons, tables of contents, and other well-designed features. The bottom line, though, is whether the wines are any good—and whether they're reasonably priced. On these points, I'm no wine connoisseur, so I'll have to defer, but an advertised Sanford Chardonnay—a pretty nice wine, I think—was selling for only about $1 less than the price at my local (and rather high-priced) wine shop.

MARKETPLACEMCI

The Web shopping arm of internetMCI, the long-distance company's foray into the Internet service provider sweepstakes, marketplaceMCI (Figure 21.6) offers a number of storefronts. Each of them is accessible by means of Netscape's secure communications technologies. Here's what's available at this writing:

- **Art Access** Fine art celebrating nature
- **Covey Leadership Center, Inc.** Leadership training featuring the "Seven Habits of Highly Effective People"
- **DAMARK** Electronics, sporting goods, housewares, and more
- **Doneckers** Fine women's apparel, restaurant, guest houses and more
- **Dun & Bradstreet Information Services** Global business intelligence
- **FTP Software, Inc.** Go anywhere networking
- **Hammacher Schlemmer & Co.** Since 1848, a wide range of products as unique as their name
- **Intercontinental Florist** Flowers available for worldwide delivery
- **The Mac Zone and The PC Zone** Low prices and overnight delivery of the hottest computer products
- **MCI Store** Communications products and services

Figure 21.6 MarketplaceMCI

- **OfficeMax OnLine**   Grand opening specials on office supplies, computers, accessories and business machines

- **Proxima, Inc.**   Internet applications, technologies, design, and commerce

- **QUALCOMM Incorporated**   Eudora (Internet-native) e-mail software

- **Reiter's Scientific & Professional Books**   60,000 books in stock, established 1936, world-wide shipping

- **Reveal Computer Products**   Computer hardware, software and accessories

DAMARK

I'm sure you've received a DAMARK catalog—you know, the mail-order catalog with all those great electronic close-out items. The Web incarnation of DAMARK appears in marketplaceMCI, and it's worth a visit—if only to see how a well-endowed direct-marketing firm conceptualizes the possibilities of the Web market. Plus, you might find a bargain or two!

Like other marketplaceMCI retailers, DAMARK is going for the "hit-'em-with-a-few-good-deals" approach (Figure 21.7) rather than producing a true on-line catalog. Most of the pages list two or three items, with full-color graphics; you can click on a hyperlink to get more information or to place an order.

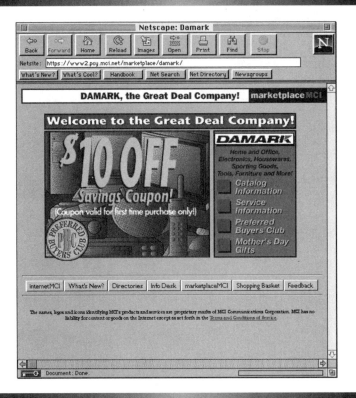

Figure 21.7 Deals from DAMARK

FROM HERE

- With this chapter, we've come to the end of this book—but don't forget the appendices! Appendix A provides a quick, handy reference to Netscape's menu commands and Appendix B shows you how to install all those helper programs that you'll find on the CD-ROM disc.

Part VI

APPENDICES

Appendix

A

Netscape Quick Reference

FILE MENU

The File menu (Figure A.1) enables you to manage Web documents—specifically, you can open additional windows or open documents by typing the URL directly or loading them from disk. You can save files, both in HTML and plain text; you can even mail documents to other Internet users. To preview and print documents, you can view hidden information about a document, including its security status. To preview and print documents, you can display the printed appearance of a document on-screen, and then print. A final option enables you to save all your preferences and exit Netscape.

```
┌─────────────────────────────────┐
│ File                            │
│ New Window              ⌘N      │
│ Open Location...        ⌘L      │
│ Open File...            ⌘O      │
│ Save As...             ⌘S       │
│ Mail Document...       ⌘M       │
│ Document Information...          │
│                                 │
│ Page Setup...                   │
│ Print...               ⌘P       │
│                                 │
│ Close                  ⌘W       │
│ Quit                   ⌘Q       │
└─────────────────────────────────┘
```

Figure A.1   File menu

New Window

Opens a new Netscape window and displays the default home page. *Note:* By default, you can open a maximum of four Netscape windows. To increase this number, type the number of windows you want to open in the Connections box of the Cache and Network Preferences (see Options menu).

Open Location

Displays a dialog box that enables you to type a URL directly. This is all very nice, but it's much easier just to type the URL in the Location box. Just drag over the existing URL to select it, type the URL you want to connect with, and press Enter.

Open File

Displays an Open dialog box that enables you to open a local file. Netscape can display HTML documents, JPEG and GIF graphics, and text files.

Save As

Saves the current document to a local disk drive. You can save the document with the HTML formatting (source), or as plain text (HTML codes are stripped from the document).

Mail Document

Displays a Send Mail/Post News dialog box, which enables you to send electronic mail. You must specify the recipient's e-mail address. Optionally, you can quote the text of the document you are currently viewing. By clicking the Attach button, you can include a copy of the currently displayed document (in source HTML or plain text). If you have specified a signature file, Netscape includes this automatically. To specify a signature file, display the Mail and News page of the Preferences dialog box (Options menu) and type the location of your signature file (a plain text file) in the Signature File box.

Document Information

Displays a dialog box providing information about the document you are currently displaying. For all documents, the dialog box displays the document title, the location, the date of last modification, and the encoding method. The Security Information panel displays additional information when you access a secure server.

Print

Displays the Print dialog box, which prints the document you are currently viewing. You can select from a variety of print options, including number of copies, page range, and others (depending on your printer's capabilities).

Close

Closes the current window.

Quit

Saves the current configuration and quits Netscape.

EDIT MENU

The Edit menu (Figure A.2) includes the standard Macintosh commands for editing text.

Edit

Can't Undo	⌘Z
Cut	⌘X
Copy	⌘C
Paste	⌘U
Clear	
Select All	⌘A
Find...	⌘F
Find Again	⌘G

Figure A.2   Edit menu

Undo

Reverses the last editing action, if possible. For example, suppose you type a new URL in the Location box. If you choose Undo, you see the previous URL. *Note:* This command is available only when it is able to reverse the last action.

Cut

Deletes the current selection and places a copy of the selection on the Clipboard. *Note:* This command is available only when it is possible to delete the selection (for example, you may use it within the Location box, but not within a Web document).

Copy

Copies the current selection to the Clipboard.

Paste

Pastes the Clipboard's contents at the insertion point's location. *Note:* This command is available only when it is possible to paste text (for example, into the Location box).

Clear

Deletes the current selection, but without placing a copy of the deletion on the Clipboard (unlike Cut).

Select All

Selects all the text in the current editing area (such as the Location box).

Find

Displays the Find dialog box, which enables you to search for a word or phrase within the currently displayed document.

Find Again

Repeats the search using the current settings in the Find dialog box.

VIEW MENU

The View menu (Figure A.3) enables you to choose options for the display of Web documents. You won't use it much, though, because the most commonly accessed commands have more convenient equivalents on the Toolbar.

Reload

Retrieves a fresh copy of the current document from the cache or, if the original document has changed, from the Web server.

Load Images

If you have turned off the automatic display of in-line images (see Options), this command reloads all the in-line images in the current document. To

Figure A.3 View menu

load in-line images selectively, point to the image you want to see, hold down the mouse button, and choose View This Image.

Source

Displays the HTML source code of the document you are currently viewing. In the Source window, you can scroll through the document. You can also copy text to the Clipboard (select the text and press Command + C).

GO MENU

The Go menu (Figure A.4) provides navigation commands. You won't use it much, though, because the Toolbar offers a more convenient way of choosing these commands.

Back

Displays the previous document (same as clicking the Back button). This option is dimmed if the current document is the first you've displayed in a new Netscape window.

Forward

Displays the document that was displayed prior to clicking the Back button or choosing Back from the Go menu (same as clicking the Forward button). This option is dimmed if you have not chosen Back or clicked Back.

Figure A.4   Go menu

Home

Displays the default home page (the document listed in the Home Page Location field of the Styles page, Preferences menu).

Stop Loading

Stops the retrieval of the current document (same as clicking Stop).

View History

Displays the History dialog box, from which you can redisplay previously viewed documents (as long as they are in the current lineage).

Documents Listed at Bottom of Go Menu

Choose one of these document names to redisplay previously viewed documents.

BOOKMARKS MENU

The Bookmarks menu (Figure A.5) enables you to add, view, edit, and organize bookmarks. Bookmarks that you've added appear on the lower portion of the menu.

Add Bookmark

Adds the current document to the bookmark menu that is currently selected in the Menu Adds After list box (Bookmark List dialog box).

View Bookmarks

Displays the Bookmark List dialog box, which has the following buttons and text boxes:

- The bookmark list shows all the current bookmarks; information about the currently selected bookmark is shown in the Name, Location, Last Visited, Added On, and Description boxes. You can edit

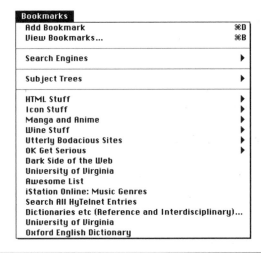

Figure A.5 Bookmarks menu

the text in these boxes, which may be necessary if the item's URL changes (as sometimes occurs).

• **Add Bookmark**   Adds the current document to the bookmark menu listed in the Menu Adds After list box.

• **Copy Item**   Copies the currently selected bookmark item and places the copy below the selected item.

• **Down Arrow**   Moves the currently selected bookmark down in the bookmark list.

• **Export**   Displays the Export Bookmarks dialog box, which you can use to export your bookmarks to a file so that others may use your bookmarks.

• **Find**   Searches down in the bookmark list for text that you specify in the text box next to this button.

• **Go To**   Displays the document that is named in the currently selected bookmark.

• **Import**   Displays the Import File As Bookmarks dialog box, which you can use to import other peoples' bookmark files so that you can use their bookmarks. In addition, this command can be used to convert any HTML document's hyperlinks into bookmarks.

- **Menu Adds After**   Specifies the bookmark submenu to which you want to add new items. If the box is blank, Netscape adds new bookmark items to the top level of the Bookmarks menu.

- **Menu Starts With**   Specifies the bookmark submenu to display in the lower portion of the Bookmarks menu.

- **More Options/Fewer Options**   Controls how many options appear in the Bookmark List dialog box.

- **New Bookmark**   Creates a new, blank bookmark item. The item is inserted below the currently selected bookmark.

- **New Divider**   Creates a new divider bar for the Bookmarks menu. The divider is inserted below the currently selected bookmark.

- **New Header**   Creates a new header or subheader for the Bookmarks menu. The header is inserted below the currently selected bookmark. You use this command to create bookmark submenus

- **Remove Item**   Removes the currently selected bookmark item. *Warning:* This command does not ask for confirmation before performing the deletion.

- **Up Arrow**   Moves the currently selected bookmark up in the bookmark list.

- **View Bookmarks**   Places the current bookmarks in an HTML document and displays it on-screen.

Additional Items on the Bookmarks Menu

If you have added bookmarks, you will see the names of documents. You can also add dividers and submenu (header) names, as shown in Figure 8.6.

OPTIONS MENU

The Options menu (Figure A.6) enables you to choose options for Netscape's operation, as well as to specify program configuration settings, the location of helper programs, and much more. A few options appear on

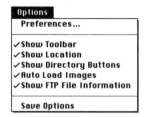

Figure A.6   Options menu

the menu itself, but the blockbuster is the Preferences option, which displays a dialog box with eight pages of options.

Preferences

Displays the Preferences dialog box, which has the following eight pages:

- **Window and Link Styles**   Displays options for window and hyperlink styles. In the Show Toolbar As area, the options control the display of the toolbar (pictures, text, or both). In the Start With area, the Blank Page option starts Netscape with a blank page, while the Home Page Location starts Netscape with a default home page (you must specify the location in the text box). In the Link Styles area, the Underline Links checkbox specifies whether links are underlined (if you deselect this option, links are shown in color only). In the Followed Links area, the Never Expire option keeps a permanent record of all the links you have visited and displays them in distinctive colors, while the Expire After box enables you to choose an expiration period. The Expire Now button causes all visited links to expire immediately.

- **Fonts and Colors**   Specifies options for on-screen fonts and colors. In the Fonts/Encodings area, the For the Encoding list box enables you to specify which character encoding scheme (Latin or Japanese) you are choosing fonts for (the default is Latin1). The Default Encoding list box enables you to choose the default encoding system. Next to Use the Proportional Font and Use the Fixed Font, you see the current font setting. To change this setting, click the list box's down arrow, and choose a new font. In the same way, choose a default font size. In the Colors area, the Colors options specify whether the document overrides your color choices (Let Document Override); to preserve your choices, click Always Use Mine. The color boxes show the current settings for links, followed links, and text. To change these options, click the check box next to the option you want to change, and choose a color from the dialog box that appears. In the Background area, the Default option uses the background colors associated with the document you are displaying; the Custom button enables you to override this choice with a color you specify. Similarly, the File option enables you to choose the background pattern that you want to appear in every document you display.

- **Mail and News**   Specifies information needed to send mail and access USENET. In the Mail area, the Mail (SMPT) Server area specifies the Internet domain name of your service provider's mail server; if you're not sure what to type, contact your service provider. The following three text boxes enable you to specify your name, e-mail addres, and organization. In the Signature File area, specify the location of the text file that contains your signature (a four-line bio to be appended to the mail and USENET postings you send). In the News area, specify the News Server that you want to use (contact your service provider for the domain name of your NNTP server). The News RC directory specifies the location of the configuration file Netscape uses to display USENET newsgroups. In the Show box, you specify the number of articles that Netscape displays at one time.

- **Cache and Network**   Specifies settings for Netscape's cache usage and network connections. In the Cache area, you specify disk cache options and sizes—and, in general, the larger the better (if a document is present in the cache, Netscape retrieves it from the cache rather than the network, speeding operation considerably. The Cache Size area specifies the amount of disk space to be set aside to store copies of recently retrieved Netscape documents, while the Browse button enables you to change the cache's location. Increase the size of the cache if you have plenty of disk space. The Clear Disk Cache Now button enables you to clear the cache, which forces Netscape to retrieve all documents from the network; this is slower, but you're certain you're seeing the latest versions of the documents.

In the Check Documents area, you can choose how often Netscape goes to the network to find out whether a cached document has changed; you can choose Once per Session, Every Time, or Never. In the Network area, the Buffer Size box enables you to specify how much memory should be set aside to store network information temporarily, while the Connections box enables you to specify how many Netscape windows you can open.

- **Images and Security** Specifies options for image display and security alerts. In the Images area, the Colors option controls how Netscape displays colors; the Dither to Color Cube option uses optical tricks to try to simulate the color of the original graphics, while the Use Closest Color in Color Cube option uses the default colors (choose this option for fastest processing). In the Security Alerts area, you can choose which warnings you want Netscape to display in situations involving secure transactions.

- **Applications and Directories** Specifies the locations of Telnet and text helper applications as well as the locations of temporary directories. When you configured Netscape (Chapter 5), you should have indicated the locations of the Telnet and 3270 helper applications. In the View Source area, you can optionally specify a text editor to display HTML documents when you choose Source from the View menu—but Netscape can display these documents in a non-editable window. In the Directories area, the Temporary Directory box enables you to specify a directory to use for downloaded files (this directory isn't really "temporary," since Netscape does not erase these files after they have been downloaded). The Bookmark File box specifies the default bookmark file.

- **Proxies** This page enables you to specify the location of proxy servers, which are required to access the Internet if your network is protected by a firewall (a device that protects a network from unauthorized access). You can ignore these options if your computer is not positioned behind a firewall. If your network is protected by a firewall, contact your network administrator for the locations of the proxy servers, if any.

- **Helper Applications** Specifies the helper applications that Netscape uses by default. For information on using this page of the Preferences menu, see Chapter 5.

Show Toolbar

Hides or displays the Toolbar.

Show Location

Hides or displays the Location box.

Show Directory Buttons

Hides or displays the Directory buttons.

Auto Load Images

Disables or enables the automatic decoding of in-line graphics. If this option is switched off, you can view a single graphic by pointing to it, holding down the mouse button, and choosing View This Image from the pop-up menu. Alternatively, you can choose Load Images from the View menu to view all the images in the current document.

Show FTP File Information

Hides or displays the icons used to identify the items in an FTP directory.

Save Options

Saves the current preferences and options, including window sizes. Netscape saves options automatically when you quit using the Quit command (File menu).

DIRECTORY MENU

The Directory menu (Figure A.7) provides menu equivalents (and then some) for the Directory buttons.

Directory
Netscape's Home
What's New?
What's Cool?

Go to Newsgroups

Netscape Galleria
Internet Directory
Internet Search
Internet White Pages
About the Internet

Figure A.7   Directory menu

Netscape's Home

Displays Netscape Communications Corporation's home page, which is the default home page for Netscape (unless you've changed the setting in the Styles page of the Preferences menu).

What's New?

Displays Netscape Communications Corporation's "What's New" page, which lists new Web sites of unusual interest. Same as clicking the What's New? button.

What's Cool?

Displays a selection of unusual, interesting, or pioneering Web pages; well worth a look. Same as clicking the What's Cool? button.

Go to Newsgroups

Accesses USENET, but only if you've specified a News (NNTP) Server in the Mail and News page of the Preferences menu. Same as clicking the Newsgroups button.

Netscape Galleria

Displays a list of Web servers that offer secure transactions using Netscape's Secure Socket Layer (SSL) technology.

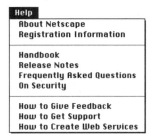

Figure A.8   Help menu

Internet Directory

Displays a document that enables you to access Yahoo and other subject trees. Same as clicking Net Directory.

Internet Search

Displays a document that enables you to access search engines such as Lycos and WebCrawler. Same as clicking Net Search.

Internet White Pages

Displays a page that enables you to search for people on the Internet, using services such as Netfind.

About the Internet

Displays a page that enables you to access information about the Internet.

HELP MENU

The Help menu (Figure A.8) accesses documents stored on Netscape Communications Corporation's server. It's loaded with interesting and helpful information, including an on-line Netscape handbook.

About Netscape

Displays a dialog box indicating which version of Netscape you're using.

Registration Information

Displays information on how to register your copy of Netscape if you are not eligible for free trial use.

Handbook

Accesses Netscape Communication Corporation's on-line help manual for Netscape Navigator.

Release Notes

Displays a page of notes about the version of Netscape you are using.

Frequently Asked Questions

Displays a page of frequently asked questions (and answers) about Netscape Navigator.

On Security

Displays information about Internet security and Netscape's Secure Sockets Layer (SSL) security technology.

How to Give Feedback

Displays a page providing instructions about submitting bug reports and providing feedback on Netscape Navigator.

How to Get Support

Displays a page providing instructions for obtaining technical support for registered users.

How to Create Web Services

Displays a page about creating World Wide Web sites. Tons of links to Internet-based information.

Appendix

B

Installing the CD-ROM Software

P ackaged with this book is a CD-ROM disc containing a full suite of helper applications, which unlock your Mac's multimedia potential. This Appendix describes two ways to use these helper applications: You can run them from the CD-ROM disc, saving space on your hard disk, or you can copy them to your hard disk.

WHAT'S INCLUDED

Here's what you'll find on the enclosed disk:

    Adobe Acrobat   This program enables you to view richly formatted documents created with Adobe's Acrobat software.

Fetch	This excellent FTP program comes in very handy for obtaining Netscape, as described in Chapter 4.
MPEG/CD	This helper application is designed to play stereo MPEG sound files. Internet Underground Music Archive, here I come!
NCSA Telnet	This Telnet helper application enables you to access resources stored on VT-100 comptaible computer systems, including mainframes, bulletin board systems, and freenets. See Chapter 19 for details.
SoundApp	This helper application plays just about every type of sound you can throw at it, except stereo MPEG.
Sparkle	This helper application plays QuickTime and MPEG videos.
StuffIt Expander	This program enables you to decompress all that wonderful Macintosh software you're going to download from the Internet.
TN3270	This Telnet helper application enables you to access resources stored on computers that require IBM 3270 terminal emulation. See Chapter 19.

INSTALLING THE SOFTWARE

If you're short on disk space, you can run the helper applications from the CD-ROM disc. For faster operation, you can copy them to your hard drive. To do so, just select the folders you want to copy, and drag them to your hard drive's icon.

Whether you run the helper applications from the CD-ROM disc or your hard drive, be sure to tell Netscape where they're located. For information, see Chapter 5.

Index

A

About Netscape command, 300
About the Internet command, 299
absolute links, 165
Add Bookmark command, 29, 94–95, 291
Add Bookmarks for this Link command, 94
Adobe Acrobat Reader, 56–57, 61, 177–182, 301
  Bookmarks and Page mode, 178
  changing modes, 178
  copying text and graphics, 181
  finding text in documents, 180
  full-screen mode documents, 180
  Page Only mode, 178
  paging through document, 178–179
  printing documents, 181
  saving documents, 181
  sizing document on-screen, 179–180
  Thumbnails and Page mode, 178
  viewing documents, 177–182
  Zoom To dialog box, 179
AIFF (Apple IFF) files, 62
ALIWEB search engine, 149–150
alternative newsgroups, 236
anchors. *See* hyperlinks
AND operator, 133
anonymous FTP, 213–214

Apple menu, 19
Application menu, 12
application workspace, 10
Archie, 216–218
ArchiePlex gateway, 217–218
articles
    button bars, 244–247
    displaying all, 245
    header, 245
    marking as read, 244
    message body, 245
    navigation, 247
    posting, 244
    printing, 247
    reading, 243–247
    threads, 243–244
AU (Sun/NeXT) files, 63
Auto Load Images command, 86, 88,
    190, 297
Awesome List personal home page, 77,
    120–121

B

Back button, 8, 11, 23, 84
    disk caches, 169
Back command, 24, 290
background
    color, 187
    patterns, 188
base fonts
    fixed (monospace), 185–187
    proportionally spaced, 185–186
Best of the Web pages, 117, 126–127
BinHex, 56
Black Hole, 194
Bookmark List dialog box, 97–101,
    104–105, 109–111, 113
    adding bookmarks, 97
    additional options, 98
    expanded, 99–100, 104
    finding bookmarks, 98
    going directly to bookmark, 97–98
    moving up or down list, 98
    options, 291–293
bookmark.html file, 111
bookmarks, 28, 93–102
    adding, 94–95, 97
    choosing, 96–97

choosing menu to display, 109
deleting, 99–100
editing, 99
exporting, 110–111
finding, 98, 100–102
headers for submenus, 105–108
importing, 111–113
indenting, 105
menu, 99
redisplaying entire list, 109
reorganizing, 102–108
setting, 29
submenus, 105, 109–110
Bookmarks menu, 7, 29, 93–97, 101,
    104, 109–111, 113, 291–293
    adding documents to, 29
    dividers, 107–108
    header, 102–104
    plan for organizing, 104
    submenus, 102–103, 105–106
borders and in-line graphics, 23
browsers
    default home page, 71
    hotlist, 71, 94
button bar, 244

C

Cache and Network dialog box,
    170
cache, 24, 92, 168–169
    flushing, 170–171
    increasing size, 170
    resizing defaults, 170
    security, 171–172
Capital One, 272
CERN (European Center for Particle
    Physics), 117–118
ciphertext message, 265
circuit-switching networks, 40
Clear command, 288
clickable maps, 26
Close command, 91, 287
color
    background, 187
    default, 187–189
    hyperlinks, 187
    text, 187
    visited hyperlinks, 187

commands
  About Netscape, 300
  About the Internet, 299
  Add Bookmark, 29, 94–95, 291
  Add Bookmarks for this Link, 94
  Auto Load Images, 86, 88, 190, 297
  Back, 24, 290
  Clear, 288
  Close, 91, 287
  Control Panels, 19
  Copy, 288
  Cut, 288
  Directory Buttons, 190
  Document Information, 287
  Find, 289
  Find Again, 163, 289
  Forward, 290
  Frequently Asked Questions, 300
  Go to Newsgroups, 240, 298
  Handbook, 300
  Hide Netscape, 12
  Home, 291
  How to Create Web Services, 300
  How to Get Support, 300
  How to Give Feedback, 300
  Internet Directory, 299
  Internet Search, 299
  Internet White Pages, 299
  Load Images, 88, 289–290
  Load This Image, 87, 166
  Location, 190
  Mail Document, 251, 287
  Netscape Galleria, 298
  Netscape's Home, 298
  New Window, 90, 286
  New Window with This Link, 90
  On Security, 300
  Open File, 76, 111, 164, 286
  Open Location, 18, 64, 286
  Paste, 288
  Preferences, 59, 75, 170–171, 186–187, 239, 294
  Print, 163, 167, 287
  Quit, 12, 257–258, 287
  Quote Document, 251
  Release Notes, 300
  Reload, 92, 289
  Save As, 164–165, 286
  Save Options, 5, 190, 297
  Save This Image As, 167
  Save This Link As, 175
  Select All, 289
  Show Directory Buttons, 297
  Show FTP File Information, 190, 297
  Show Location, 297
  Show Toolbar, 297
  Source, 290
  Stop Loading, 84, 291
  toggle, 86
  Toolbar, 190
  Undo, 288
  View Bookmarks, 97, 99, 101, 104, 109–111, 113, 291
  View History, 89, 291
  View This Image, 87
  What's Cool!, 298
  What's New!, 298
commercial sites, 271
  Capital One, 272
  DAMARK, 280–281
  Internet Shopping Network (ISN), 275–276
  marketplaceMCI, 278–280
  software.net, 273–274
  Virtual Vineyards, 277–278
communications programs, 41
Configure MIME Type dialog box, 60
Connection Refused message, 198
connectionless network, 40
contiguous strings, 133
Control Panels command, 19
Cool Links pages, 117, 127
Copy command, 288
Courier, 184–185
credit card information, 268–269
customizing Netscape, 183, 190–192
  color, 187–189
  fonts, 184–187
  Options menu, 190
  Preferences dialog box, 191–192
Cut command, 288

D

DA-CLOD search engine, 150–151
DAMARK, 280–281
decryption, 265

default home page, 4, 70–71
    changing to HOME.HTML home
        page, 75–76
    redisplaying, 8
dialup access, 41
Directory buttons, 9
Directory Buttons command, 190
Directory menu, 7, 240, 297–299
disk cache, 169
    Back button, 169
    flushing, 170–171
    increasing size, 170
    visiting hyperlink, 169
distributed subject tree, 139
dividers, 107–108
DNS lookup has failed message, 195–
    196
Document Information command, 287
documents
    adding to Bookmarks menu, 29
    downloading, 8, 10–11
    finding, 8
    finding text in, 162–163
    going back to, 23–24
    HTML (HyperText Markup Lan-
        guage), 164–166, 177
    in-line graphics, 166–167
    internal navigation buttons, 24–26
    managing, 161–171
    next, 24
    plain text, 163–164
    PostScript, 177
    previous, 8, 11, 23–24
    printing, 8, 167–168
    related, 24
    reloading, 92
    retrieval status, 10
    saving, 163
    starting points, 30
    uploading, 11
    URL (Uniform Resource Locator) of
        viewed, 8
    viewing, 10
doorkey icon, 10
download directory, 64
downloading
    documents, 10–11
    in-line graphics, 23

speeding up, 86
stopping, 84–85
turning off automatic in-line image
    download, 86

E

e-mail, replying to newsgroup messages,
    251
Edit menu, 6, 7, 163, 287–289
EINet Galaxy
    Gopher Jewels, 158
    Hytelnet, 158
    searching, 157–159
    subject classifications, 155–157
    World Wide Web, 159
encryption, 265–266
ERIC Digests, 226
Error 404 message, 20
exporting bookmarks, 110–111

F

false drops, 147–148
FAQs (Frequently Asked Questions), 9,
    235, 252–253
Fetch, 47, 302
    downloading Netscape, 48–50
    Open Connection dialog box, 49–50
    quitting, 50
    uploading files to FTP directory, 48
file decompression software, 56, 61
file extensions, 58
File menu, 6, 12, 18, 64, 76, 90–91,
    164–165, 167, 251, 257–258,
    285–287
file viewing software, 56
    Adobe Acrobat Reader, 56
    configuring, 61
files
    bookmark.html, 111
    editing, 6
    local, 6
    Netscape1.1N.hqx, 50
Filo, David, 31, 134
Find Again command, 163, 289

Find Backwards button, 162
Find button, 8, 162
Find command, 289
Find dialog box, 162
fixed (monospace) base font, 184–187
   changing, 186–187
FLI (Autodesk) video files, 63
fonts
   changing, 186–187
   Courier, 184–185
   fixed (monospace) base, 184–187
   proportionally spaced base, 184–186
Forbidden message, 196–197
Forward button, 8, 24
Forward command, 290
404 Not Found message, 196
freeware, 214
Frequently Asked Questions command,
   300
FTP (File Transfer Protocol), 47, 213–
   216
   anonymous, 213–214
   Archie, 216–218
   file icons, 216
   finding resources, 216–218
   navigating directories, 215–216
   Virtual Shareware Library (VSL),
      218–223

G

Galleria page, 271
GhostScript, 177
Go menu, 7, 24, 84, 88–89, 290–291
Go to Newsgroups command, 240, 298
Gopher, 203–211
   accessing sites, 204
   directly typing URL (Uniform
      Resource Locator), 204
   Gopher Jewels, 206–207
   hyperlinks, 204
   icons, 205–206
   Jughead, 206–207
   menus, 205–206
   searching, 206–211
   Veronica, 206–211
Gopher Jewels, 158, 206–207

H

Handbook button, 9
Handbook command, 300
header, 39, 102–104
   deleting, 108
   expanding and collapsing, 106–107
Help menu, 7, 299–300
helper applications, 27–28, 55–60, 173
   Adobe Acrobat Reader, 57, 61, 177–
      182
   configuring, 59–62
   enclosed CD-ROM, 56–57
   file decompression software, 56, 61
   file viewing software, 56, 61
   MIME type, 58
   MPEG/CD, 57, 64–65, 175
   NCSA Telnet, 57, 61
   QuickTime, 57
   running from CD-ROM, 302
   sound players, 55, 60
   SoundApp, 27–28, 57, 174–175
   Sparkle, 57, 176
   StuffIt Expander, 57, 61
   Telnet viewer software, 56, 61–62
   testing, 64
   TN3270, 57, 61, 255, 258–259
   video players, 56, 61
   when to launch, 60
   will not start, 64
Helper Applications page, 59
Hide Netscape command, 12
hiding windows, 12
History dialog box, 89
history list, 88–89
Home button, 8, 26
Home command, 291
home pages, 71–78
   automatically displaying, 90
   customizing, 69–70
   default, 70–71
   HOME.HTML, 70, 72–76
   personal, 71–72, 77–79, 122
   Planet Earth Home Page, 118–
      119
   trailblazer pages as, 79–81
   Web-accessible personal, 72

HOME.HTML home page, 70, 72–73, 116
  changing default home page to, 75–76
  hyperlinks, 74
  Lycos search engine, 72
  obtaining without CD-ROM drive, 75
hotlist, 71, 94
hotlist item, 94
HOTLIST.HTML file, 112–113
How to Create Web Services command, 300
How to Get Support command, 300
How to Give Feedback command, 300
HTML (HyperText Markup Language), 71, 161
  backgrounds, 165, 167
  documents, 56, 177
  in-line graphics and, 165
  saving documents with, 164–166
  when to save documents, 164
hyperlinks, 10–11, 22–23
  activating, 22–23
  adding bookmarks, 94
  color, 187
  finding sites by clicking, 18
  formatting, 22
  Gopher, 204
  hidden in clickable maps, 26
  HOME.HTML home page, 74
  in-line graphics, 23
  nothing happened when clicked, 194
  opening in new window, 90
  stopping download, 84–85
  visible, 22
  visited, 11
  Yahoo, 31, 136
hypermedia, 173–175
  Adobe Acrobat documents, 177–182
  animations, 176
  sound, 174–175
  videos, 176
Hytelnet, 158, 260

I

icons, doorkey, 10
IFF (Amiga) files, 62

Images button, 8
importing bookmarks, 111–113
in-line graphics, 20
  borders, 23
  decoding multi-part files, 253
  downloading, 23, 86
  HTML documents and, 165
  hyperlinks, 23
  navigation buttons, 24–25
  selectively loading, 87–88
  viewing and saving, 166–167
internal navigation buttons, 24–26
  Yahoo, 31–32
Internet, 37–44
  direct connection to, 37, 41
  IP (Internet Protocol) address, 40
  local area network (LAN) access, 42
  network access, 42
  network connections, 41
  operation of, 38–40
  PPP (Point-to-Point Protocol), 41–43
  service provider, 44
  SLIP (Single Line Internet Protocol), 41–43
Internet Directory command, 299
Internet Points of Interest page, 122
Internet Search command, 299
Internet Shopping Network (ISN), 275–276
Internet White Pages command, 299
InterRamp, 44
IP (Internet Protocol) address, 40

J

John's Monster Hotlist page, 121
Jughead, 206–207

K

keyboard shortcuts
  Command + B (View Bookmarks), 97, 99, 101, 104, 109–111, 113
  Command + C (Copy), 76, 81, 99
  Command + D (Add Bookmark), 29, 95

Command + F (Find), 162–163
Command + H (View History), 89
Command + I (Load Images), 88
Command + L (Open Location), 18
Command + N (New Window), 90
Command + P (Print), 167
Command + period (.) (Cancel), 84
Command + Q (Quit), 12, 257–258
Command + R (Reload), 92
Command + S (Save As), 164–165
Command + V (Paste), 76, 81, 99
Command + W (Close Window), 91
Command + [(Back), 24
Command +] (Forward), 24
key-word search, 133–134, 225
kill files, 253
Krol, Ed, 143

L

links. *See also* hyperlinks
    absolute and relative, 165
Load Images command, 88, 289–290
Load This Image command, 87, 166
local area network (LAN), 42
Location command, 190
Lycos search engine, 72, 151–152

M

MacTCP, 37, 41–42
Mail Document command, 251, 287
managing documents, 161–171
marketplaceMCI, 278–280
McLaughlin, Margaret L., 21
memory, 19, 175
menu bar, 6–7
messages
    404 Not Found, 196
    about what program is doing, 10
    Cannot start Helper program, 175
    Connection Refused, 198
    DNS lookup has failed, 195–196
    Enter a PERL regular expression, 142
    Error 404, 20
    Forbidden, 196–197
    No application has been configured
        for this file, 28
    Search String not found, 101
    Server timed out, 218
    The Information You Have Submit-
        ted Is Not Secure, 199–200
    This Site Has Moved, 198
    Too many connections—Try again
        soon, 208
MIME (Multipurpose Internet Multime-
    dia Extensions) types, 58–60
mirror sites, 50
modems, 43
Most Popular Links pages, 117, 126
moving windows, 12
MPEG (Motion Picture Expert's Group)
    format, 56, 63, 65
MPEG/CD, 57, 64–65, 302
    playing stored sound, 175
mpg (MPEG) audio file, 63
multiple windows, 91

N

navigation, 83–91
    articles, 247
    buttons, 24–26
    FTP directories, 215–216
    history list, 88–89
    reloading documents, 92
    in-line images, 86–88
    stopping download, 84–85
    windows, 90–91
NCSA (National Center for Supercom-
    puter Applications), 117
    starting points page, 118
NCSA Telnet, 56–57, 61, 302
Net Directory button, 9
Net Search button, 9
netiquette, 236, 248–249
Netscape Navigator
    configuring to access USENET, 238–
        240
    customizing, 183–192
    direct Internet connection and, 41
    domain name of NNTP server,
        239

Netscape Navigator (*con't.*)
   FAQs (Frequently Asked Questions),
      9
   Installer program, 51–52
   latest version, 47–50
   navigation, 83–92
   not enough memory to launch, 19
   quick reference, 285–300
   quitting, 12
   returning to Welcome page, 26
   starting, 4–17
Netscape Galleria command, 298
Netscape's Home command, 298
Netscape1.1N.hqx file, 50
Netsite box, 8
network connections, 41
networks, 39–41
New Window command, 90, 286
New Window with This Link command,
   90
newsgroups, 9
   alternative, 236
   articles, 237
   automatic subscription to, 248
   crossposting, 248
   downloading list of, 240
   FAQs (Frequently Asked Questions),
      235
   follow-up messages, 252, 237–238
   hierarchical organization, 236–
      237
   moderated, 234
   navigating list, 242
   netiquette, 248–249
   original messages, 244, 249–250
   posting messages, 235–237, 248–
      252
   reading articles, 243–247
   replying by e-mail, 251
   signature, 248–249
   standard, 236
   subscribing, 241–242, 245
   threaded, 238
Newsgroups button, 9
newsreaders, 234
   levels, 238
   threaded, 238
NNTP server domain name, 239

O

On Security command, 300
Open button, 8
Open File command, 76, 111, 164, 286
Open Location command, 18, 64, 286
Open Location dialog box, 19
Options menu, 5, 7, 59, 75, 86, 170–171,
   186–187, 239, 293–297
   options, 190
OR operator, 133

P

packet-switching networks, 39–40
packets, 39
passwords, 264–265
Paste command, 76, 81, 99, 288
PERL (Practical Extraction and Report
   Language), 142–143
   search tricks, 144
personal home pages, 71–72, 77–79, 122
Pick a Color dialog box, 187
plain text documents, 163–164
plaintext message, 265
Planet Earth Home Page, 118–119
Post Reply button, 252
PostScript documents, 177
PPP (Point-to-Point Protocol), 42–43
Preferences command, 59, 75, 170–
   171, 186–187, 239, 294
Preferences dialog box, 75
   capturing and adding URLs, 81
   customizing Netscape options, 191–
      192
   options, 294–296
Preferences menu, 64
Print button, 8, 167
Print command, 163, 167, 287
Print dialog box, 168
printing
   Adobe Acrobat documents, 181
   articles, 247
   documents, 8, 167–168
problems, 193
   404 Not Found, 196
   Connection Refused message, 198

DNS lookup has failed, 195–196
Forbidden message, 196–197
information not secure, 199–200
nothing happened when hyperlink
was clicked, 194
passwords, 199
This Site Has Moved message, 198
progress bar, 10
proportionally spaced base font, 184–
186
protocols, 42–43
proxy servers, 192
public key cryptography, 266
publicly accessible file archives, 213–
214

Q

QuickTime, 56, 57, 63
Quit command, 12, 257–287
quitting Netscape, 12
Quote Document command, 251

R

Recipes database, 226
relative links, 165
Release Notes command, 300
Reload button, 8, 84, 92
Reload command, 92, 289
reloading documents, 92
resizing windows, 12
ROT-13, 266
routers, 39

S

S-HTTP protocol, 267
Save As command, 164–165, 286
Save As dialog box, 164–165, 167
Save Options command, 5, 190, 297
Save This Image As command, 167
Save This Link As command, 175
saving documents, 163

screen, 6–11
application workspace, 10
default home page, 4
Directory buttons, 9
doorkey icon, 10
hyperlinks, 10–11
menu bar, 6–7
Netsite box, 8
progress bar, 10
status bar, 10
status indicator, 11
title bar, 7
toolbar, 7–8
welcome page, 4–5
search engines, 30, 132
ALIWEB, 149–150
DA-CLOD, 150–151
false drops, 147–148
HOME.HTML home page, 74
key-word searches, 133–134
listing, 9
Lycos, 151–152
search techniques, 133–134
spiders, 30, 132, 147–148
WebCrawler, 153–154
worms, 30, 147
search string, 101
search techniques, 133–134
secure messages, 199–200
secure server, 9–10, 200, 268
Secure Socket Layer (SSL) protocol,
266–267
security, 263
accessing secure server, 268
authentication, 264–265
caches, 171–172
confidentiality, 265
credit card information, 268–269
encryption, 265–266
integrity, 265
passwords, 264–265
S-HTTP protocol, 267
Secure Socket Layer (SSL) protocol,
266–267
standards, 267
Select All command, 289

Selected Newsgroup button, 242
Server timed out message, 218
servers
    busy, 50, 198
    secure, 9–10, 200
service providers, 37, 44
shareware, 214
    library, 218–223
Show Directory Buttons command,
    297
Show FTP File Information command,
    190, 297
Show Location command, 297
Show Toolbar command, 297
signature, 248–249
sites
    busy, 194
    clickable maps, 26
    directly typing URL (Uniform
        Resource Locator), 17–20
    following hyperlinks to, 18
    mirror, 50
    moved, 198
    no longer on Web, 20
    previously accessed, 88–89
    registering, 199
    web, 24
SLIP (Serial Line Internet Protocol), 42–
    43
SLIP/PPP connection, 41
SND (Sounder/Soundtools) file, 63
software.net, 273–274
sound, 55
    adjusting volume, 174–175
    decoding multi-part files, 253
    playing, 174–175
    saving, 175
sound formats, 62–65, 174
sound players, 55, 174
    configuring, 60
SoundApp, 27–28, 57, 302
    adjusting volume, 174–175
    playing stored sound, 175
Source command, 290
Sparkle, 56–57, 176, 302
spiders, 30, 132, 147–148
standard newsgroups, 236

starting points pages, 30, 72, 74, 117–124
    Awesome List, 120–121
    Internet Points of Interest, 122
    John's Monster Hotlist, 121
    NCSA (National Center for Super-
        computer Applications), 118
    personal home pages, 122–124
    Planet Earth Home Page, 118–119
    World Wide Web home Page, 118
status bar, 10
status indicator, 11
Stop button, 8, 84
Stop Loading command, 84, 291
strings, 101
    contiguous, 133
StuffIt, 56
StuffIt Expander, 57, 61, 302
subject trees, 9, 30–32, 131–132
    distributed, 139
    searches, 133–134
    Virtual Library, 139–143
    Whole Internet Catalog, The, 143–147
    Yahoo, 30–32, 134–139
submenus, 29, 102–103, 105–106
    adding bookmarks, 109–110
    choosing menu to display, 109
    headers, 105–106
    limits, 106
Subscribe to Selected Newsgroups but-
    ton, 242
substrings, 134
surfing the Web, 15–32
System 7.5
    hiding windows temporarily, 12
    MacTCP, 37, 42

T

Telnet, 56, 255. *See also* NCSA Telnet
    accessing, 256–258
    searching for resources, 260
    VIRGO, 257
Telnet viewer software
    configuring, 61–62
    NCSA Telnet, 56
Temporary folder, 64

text
    color, 187
    finding in documents, 162–163
3270 Telnet sessions, 258–259
title bar, 7
TN3270, 57, 61, 255, 258–259, 302
toggle command, 86
toolbar, 7–8
Toolbar command, 190
trailblazer pages, 72, 115, 117, 147
    Best of the Web, 117, 126–127
    Cool Links, 117, 127
    as home page, 79–81
    Most Popular Links, 117, 126
    starting points, 116–124
    Weird Links, 117, 128
    What's New, 117, 129
    Worst of the Web, 117, 127–128

U

Undo command, 288
uploading documents, 11
URLs (Uniform Resource Locator), 18
    capturing and adding to Preferences
        dialog box, 81
    case-sensitivity, 20
    copying, 76, 81, 99
    directly typing, 8, 17–20
    displaying, 10
    erasing existing, 19
    mistakes in, 20
    parts, 8–9
    pasting, 99
    PDF Samples, 181
    pertaining to particular subject, 79–81
    record of visited, 88–89
    saving, 93–96
    subject-oriented catalog, 30
    that no longer exist, 40
    viewed document, 8
    Virtual Library, 21
USENET, 235
    accessing, 9
    configuring Netscape to access, 238–
        240

FAQs (Frequently-Asked Questions),
    252–253
history, 234
netiquette, 236
newsgroups, 233–238
newsreader, 234
Search Today's USENET News,
    252
searching recent postings, 252
site, 233

V

V.32bis standard, 43
V.42bis standard, 43
V.FC (Fast Class) standard, 43
Veronica, 206–208
    search tips, 210–211
    Simplified Veronica Search, 209
video, 53, 56, 61, 63, 176
View All Newsgroups button, 240,
    242
View Bookmarks command, 97, 99,
    101, 104, 109–111, 113, 291
View History command, 89, 291
View menu, 7, 88, 92, 289–290
View This Image command, 87
VIRGO, 257
Virtual Library, 73, 139
    accessing, 140
    Category Subtree hyperlink, 140
    Index hyperlink, 141
    Library of Congress hyperlink,
        140
    on-line art page, 21
    searching, 141–143
    table of contents, 81
    trailblazer pages, 79–81, 126
    URL, 21
virtual memory, 19
Virtual Shareware Library (VSL), 218–
    223
Virtual Vineyards, 277–278
visited hyperlinks, 11
    color, 187
VOC (SoundBlaster) files, 63

W

WAIS (Wide Area Information Server)
   advanced searches, 231–232
   database description page,
      229
   directory of servers, 227
   document matching, 230–231
   ERIC Digests, 226
   listing databases, 227–228
   Recipes database, 226
   searching databases, 225–231
   Speeches of Bill Clinton database,
      226
   U.S. Congressional Record database,
      226
   WAISGATE directory of servers, 228
WAIS gateways, 226
WAISGATE, 228–229
WAV (Windows) files, 63
weather map, 73
web, 24, 71
   welcome page, 71
Web. *See* World Wide Web
Web sites, 71
   Black Hole, 194
   busy, 20–21, 194
   erotic, 196–197
   listing new and interesting, 9
   Mozilla favorites, 9
   no longer available, 20
   really dumb, 16
Web-accessible personal home page, 72
WebCrawler search engine, 153–154
Weird Links pages, 117
Welcome page, 4–5, 71
What's Cool button, 9
What's Cool page, 127
What's Cool command, 298
What's New button, 9
What's New pages, 117, 129
What's New command, 298
Who's Who on the Internet (WWOTI),
   77
Whole Internet Catalog, The, 143–144
   INDEX tags, 147
   subject classifications, 145–147

whole-word searches, 134
windows
   close box, 91
   hiding, 12
   limitations, 91
   managing, 11–12
   moving, 12
   multiple, 91
   opening hyperlink in new, 90
   opening new, 90–91
   resizing, 12
   Restore box, 12
   size box, 12
   switching between, 91
World Wide Web (WWW or Web), 24
   disorganization, 29–30
   getting lost on, 26
   home page, 118
   navigation, 23–26
   problems, 193–200
   surfing, 15–32
   Useless Pages Site, 16
   Virtual Library, 73
worms, 30, 147
Worst of the Web pages, 117, 127–128

Y

Yahoo (Yet Another Hierarchically Officious Oracle), 30–32, 134
   accessing, 31
   asterisk next to document name, 32
   exploring, 31, 136–137
   help, 32
   hyperlinks, 31, 136
   internal navigation buttons, 31–32
   key-word searches, 32, 138–139
   Search page, 138–139
   service provider directory, 44
   subject classifications, 135
   subject tree, 9
   toolbar options, 137
   top-level headings, 31
   up one level in headings, 31
Yang, Jerry Chih-Yuan, 31, 134

About the CD-ROM

The CD-ROM packaged with this book contains all the helper applications you need to realize Netscape's hypermedia potential. Included are the Adobe Acrobat Reader (for reading richly formatted documents), Fetch (an FTP program that you can use to obtain Netscape), MPEG/CD (a sound player that plays stereo MPEG files with CD-like quality), NCSA Telnet (a helper application that enables Netscape to access resources on mainframe computers), SoundApp (a sound player that can handle just about everything you can throw at it), Sparkle (a movie player that can play QuickTime and MPEG videos), StuffIt Expander (a decompression program that enables you to use software that you obtain on the Internet), and TN3270 (a helper program that enables Netscape to access data on IBM 3270 mainframe computers).

System Requirements

Macintosh (with at least a 68020 processor) or Power Macintosh wtih 4 MB of RAM (8 MB is preferred) and at least 10 MB of free disk space (2 MB for Netscape and 8 MB for the helper applications included on the CD-ROM).